Allende's Chile

Allende's Chile

Edited by Kenneth Medhurst

St. Martin's Press   New York

Published in association with
Government and Opposition,
A Journal of Comparative Politics

AFFILIATED PUBLISHERS: Macmillan Limited, London
—also at Bombay, Calcutta, Madras and Melbourne

Contents

Contributors

K. Medhurst is Lecturer in Government at the University of Manchester

Joan Garcés is Professor at the Latin American School of Political Science (FLACSO) Santiago, and adviser to President Allende

J. Biehl del Río formerly Director of the Institute de Ciencias Politicas in the Catholic University, Santiago, at present Visiting Lecturer in the Centre for Latin American Studies at the University of Liverpool

H. Zemelman is a member of the Department of Sociology in the University of Chile, Santiago

H. E. Bicheno formerly a member of the Department of Political Science in the Catholic University, Santiago, at present studying in Cambridge

G. Martner is Minister of Economic Planning in President Allende's Government

L. Quiros Varela is Professor of Political Science at the Catholic University, Santiago

Kenneth Medhurst

1 Why Chile?

THE ELECTION OF SALVADOR ALLENDE AS PRESIDENT OF CHILE IN
1970 awoke world-wide interest. He obtained executive power at
the head of an electoral coalition whose chief members were the
Chilean Socialist and Communist Parties and he entered upon his
term of office dedicated to finding a 'Chilean Way to Socialism'
that would entail a continuing observance of Chile's well established constitutional traditions.

The peaceful election of a government led by a self-styled
'Marxist-Leninist' and containing two strong avowedly Marxist
parties was in itself the cause of comment. Still more interest was
aroused by the government's declared intention of conducting a
revolution within the framework of a 'liberal-constitutional'
system of government.

Credibility was given to this approach by Allende's personal
position. On past form it seemed that he was committed to 'the
peaceful road' rather than pursuing the path of violent revolution.
He in fact entered politics with a desire for radical change but
probably without any well thought out philosophical position.
His 'Marxism-Leninism' may have provided him with a *post hoc*
rationale for his activities rather than with a particularly coherent
guide to action. His career had been marked by a significant
degree of pragmatism in which one of the consistent threads had
been adherence to Chile's constitutional traditions.

His experiment seemed to be important for it not only appeared
to offer Latin America the possibility of a new way forward but
was also regarded as a pointer to the possible development of
Socialist and Communist Parties in the quite distinct context of
Western Europe. Above all the performance of Allende's 'Unidad
Popular' (UP) was regarded by some as a crucial test case for those
European Communist Parties, notably the Italian and the French,
who claimed to have dedicated themselves to obtaining a share in

power through the ballot box and who now claim to be following the 'peaceful road' to socialism. Some feel that a spectacular failure on the part of the UP would cast doubt on the viability of the 'parliamentary or peaceful road to socialism'. Equally, there is a feeling that failure followed by a refusal to hand power over to a successful opposition candidate for the presidency would neces-sarily cast doubt upon the good faith of European Marxist parties who are committed to observing the present 'rules of the game' and who maintain that they would only change those rules by constitutional means. Undoubtedly the Communist Parties of Italy and France are viewing the Chilean experiment with much interest and some concern, for its fate could have some, albeit limited, repercussions within their own polities.

Chilean authors drawn from supporters and opponents of the UP have been invited to debate in these pages some of the salient issues and problems posed by the current situation. Within the scope of a volume of this size the discussion is inevitably less than comprehensive. Moreover, any one contribution must necessarily present a partial view of the situation. Complete academic detachment, which may in any case be an illusory goal, is un-likely to be found in the midst of Chile's present political dilemmas. It was felt, however, that a useful purpose could be served by assembling contributions from distinguished Chilean academics and participants, at different levels, in Chile's political processes. The clash of views and interpretations sometimes apparent in succeeding pages itself constitutes an interesting comment upon tensions within Chile at this time and the politicized state of the Chilean intellectual community.

THE POLITICAL PARTIES

In assessing the UP's likely development certain features can be singled out as relevant factors. Firstly, it is apparent that though now in alliance the Communist and Socialist Parties have long histories of rivalry for leadership of the left and that latent tensions still exist. Secondly, these tensions could emerge more openly if the UP ran into difficulty. Faced with serious reverses or possible electoral defeat a strong element within the Socialist Party might be attracted by a violent revolutionary solution whilst, on past form, the Communist Party would probably favour adherence to constitutional procedures, if only to prove its good faith and so make another subsequent step on the 'peaceful road to socialism' more likely. The well disciplined, highly bureaucratized Communist Party is less disposed than many socialists to put itself at risk in an attempt at violent revolution. Thirdly, it is apparent that in recent years a radicalization process has been going on to the left of the political spectrum and that some communists and considerable numbers of socialists have been attracted to movements which are suspicious of or hostile to the 'peaceful road to socialism'.

This raises the question of the extra-parliamentary left-wing forces in Chile which today enjoy unprecedented strength and which must be examined for they exert considerable pressure upon the UP and are in a position to cause it considerable embarrassment.

Extra-parliamentary groups on the far left are several in number. There are some small sects of little obvious importance but two do warrant special attention. They, both in their different ways, present the UP with serious dilemmas and they each represent significant political currents. The first is the Revolutionary Communist Party. This group, which broke away from the traditional Communist Party, takes its inspiration from China and almost entirely rejects the desirability or feasibility of 'the peaceful road to socialism'. It has been prepared to contest congressional elections as a way of advertising its cause and of infiltrating members into influential positions, but it wholly rejected the UP's fight for executive power. In its view acceptance of 'the rules of the game' necessarily involves a betrayal of the revolution for the existing constitutional system is by definition a bourgeois instrument that inevitably protects the interests of the 'ruling class'. The possibility of reform is admitted but it is argued that reforms realized through parliamentary channels are simply a particularly sophisticated device on the part of Chile's socio-economic elites for undermining fundamental challenges to their interests. Thus the UP may, for example, greatly extend the public ownership of industry but this will amount to the creation of 'state capitalism' that, at bottom, preserves or even reinforces the established order. This group's solution is the violent overthrow of the existing system and the declaration of a 'dictatorship of the proletariat' based mainly upon working-class support.

This view had evidently got some middle-class intellectual and some working-class support. It commands less support, however, than the *Movimiento de Izquierda Revolucionaria* (MIR) which, at present, undoubtedly constitutes the most potent left-wing 'extra-parliamentary' force in Chile. Formed in 1966 from a variety of left-wing factions, notably Trotskyites and dissident socialists, it too repudiates the feasibility of a 'peaceful road to socialism'. It has, however, been less intransigent than the Revolutionary Communists for it has accepted that the UP could be a useful, albeit limited, step on the road to socialism and that changes initiated by the UP could smooth the way for a subsequent revolutionary thrust. Thus, prior to 1970 the movement advertised itself partly through urban guerrilla operations (designed also, of course, to provide itself with funds) but during the election campaign it gave the UP conditional support. Since the election the MIR has kept up pressure upon the government with a view to radicalizing its activities whilst continuing to build up its own support. At the same time, it has sought to avoid the provocation of violent right-wing responses with which, as yet, it feels unable to cope. Its final goal is a radical break with the past but in the meantime it is seeking to create a mass movement and a heightened political awareness amongst its actual or potential followers.

Though the exact size of its following cannot be precisely measured it is clearly considerable. It comes from three main sources. Firstly, much of its leadership comes from radical student circles. Indeed, the movement's initial impetus came from that quarter. Secondly, both before and, still more, since the 1970 elections it has been making inroads into the 'shanty towns' surrounding Santiago and the other major urban centres. Some in fact see an attempt to encircle the big cities by a well organized and potentially revolutionary mass. Certainly, there are areas where MIR appears to be the effective local governing force. Equally, it is plain that amongst the rootless *lumpen-proletariat*, composed often of new under or unemployed arrivals from the countryside, MIR's revolutionary appeal has made a significant impact. It is in rural areas, however, that MIR probably sees its most important task. Though seeking urban support they look to rural based guerrilla warfare as the chief means of undermining and discrediting the existing order. Thus they are seeking to radicalize peasant groups, presumably with a view to the time when open warfare may seem necessary. Particularly in Southern Chile they have been organizing land invasions in advance of official ex-propriation measures. In some cases, this has inevitably produced sharp reactions from landowners which place the government in a difficult position. To countenance illegal action tends to solidify the opposition and to drive moderate opponents (Christian Democrats, for example) into the arms of more intransigent elements, but to insist on strict legality creates the risk of strengthening radical opposition and so of being outflanked on the left. In many cases the government's dilemma has been eased because MIR has focused its efforts upon estates where the owners have been threatening to destroy assets rather than handing them over peacefully to the state. In the long run, however, such situations may serve to build up MIR's support and greatly to embarrass the UP.

THE ARMY AND THE CHURCH

MIR appreciates that ultimately all its efforts could be fruitless if it cannot count on at least some military support. Because of this it is apparently seeking to make contacts in the army's lower ranks and so to divide that institution. This raises perhaps the most important imponderable of all in the present situation; the likely response of the army to possible future developments. In practice accurate information on this subject is hard to come by and views conflict. Joan Garcés sees no incompatibility between the UP's aims and the likely position of the military. The army's traditions certainly indicate that the provocation would have to be extreme before successful military intervention becomes likely. Observance of constitutional forms has generally characterized army behaviour. By the same token, however, it seems conceivable that a radical break with Chilean traditions could provoke a radical response; a response that revolutionary forces are probably not yet equipped to counter. Indeed, Allende's assiduous courting of the army and the continuance of established military commitment, noted in the concluding chapter, are perhaps signs of nervousness on the government's part and a measure of the army's current bargaining power. As Mr Bicheno indicates the army cannot be dismissed as an entirely 'apolitical' force.

Though ultimately less significant than the army the Church is another 'extra-political' force with which the UP may have to contend should it ever have to choose between the abandonment of its revolutionary aims and the creation of a dictatorial system. It is therefore with a brief examination of this body that this chapter concludes.

Traditionally the Chilean Church, in common with the Roman Catholic Church throughout Latin America, was a bulwark of the established social order and closely allied to traditional elites. This alliance took its most peculiar form in the partnership of the Conservative Party and the Church, but it lost some of its importance once the clerical issue in Chilean politics had been resolved and the Church was finally disestablished. Nevertheless, large proportions of the clergy and most bishops for long remained associated with the traditional right wing and exercized a generally conservative influence in politics.

On the other hand, influential minorities in the Chilean Church were already, from the 1920s, ahead of most of their counterparts elsewhere in Latin America in expressing some practical concern for the under-privileged and in attempting to implement Catholic social encyclicals. It was socially conscious Jesuits, in close touch with Europe, who influenced that group of Catholic intellectuals which broke away from the Conservative Party to found the 'Falange Nacional'. Equally, Catholic unions, and above all, Catholic peasant organizations, during the 1950s, mobilized much of what was to become Christian Democratic support.

Until 1958, most of the hierarchy's political sympathies lay with the traditional right but Allende's near victory in that year finally persuaded many of them to throw their weight behind the Christian Democrats. From the outset that body has claimed to be non-confessional and the fact that one of its chief ideologues is not a Christian lends weight to this view, but Church support must be counted amongst the important factors paving the way for Frei in 1964. Pastoral letters and popular Catholic organizations were used to influence voters and to build up a popular base. Moreover, the international contacts of 'progressive' elements in the Church secured substantial financial help from Europe for the Christian Democrats, both before and after their electoral success.

This switch of loyalties was in part a defensive reaction designed to head off a left-wing electoral victory. It has also to be seen, however, in the context of a general change of climate within the Roman Catholic Church in general and the Latin American Church in particular. Prior to Vatican II shifts in attitude were perceptible in portions of the Latin American Church, not least in Chile, and the Vatican Council gave new impetus and respectability to such changes. Groups emerged within the Church with stronger commitments to social change and with some belief in the Church's responsibility for promoting reform. In Chile there was initially, in the wake of these developments, a fair degree of unity about the appropriate Church response. Most shades of clerical and much lay opinion could unite in support of the Christian Democrats. The realities of power, however, led eventually to a greater fragmentation of the Catholic community. Radical Catholics, impatient with the slowness of change and emboldened by changes in the Church's official ideology, sought dialogue with Marxists and eventually committed themselves to support for the UP. Traditionalists, however, were worried by the possible advent of a left-wing government and by the identification of the Church with a Christian Democratic Party that was likely to suffer defeat. The latter, therefore, tended, in 1970, to look to Alessandri as their standard-bearer.

At the moment it is possible, at the risk of some over-simplification, to see three main tendencies in the Church. Firstly, there is a small very conservative wing, associated with right-wing political elements, who remain opposed to change within the Church and society at large. Secondly, there is another but perhaps growing minority, especially amongst younger Catholics (both lay and clerical), who are not orthodox Marxists but who are prepared to view political problems in terms of Marxist categories and who would certainly support 'the Chilean Way to Socialism'; some of them might even accept the need for violence. Finally, there is another group, accounting perhaps for a large majority (including many bishops) who are committed to fairly drastic but gradual and peaceful change. They have generally been prepared to adopt a 'wait and see' attitude towards the UP though threats to ecclesiastical interests and the prospect of violent revolution would bring them into sharp opposition to the government. Efforts by Allende to remain on good terms with Church leaders suggest that he does not wholly discount Church influence in Chilean society. That influence may have been weakened, both by long-term secularization processes and by shorter term divisions within the Church itself, but it remains a factor conditioning and probably limiting the UP's freedom for manoeuvre. The Chilean Church's political influence cannot perhaps be equated with the Italian Church's influence but, especially in some rural areas, it could act as something of a brake upon the UP's activities.

Throughout the rest of the following discussion developments, past present and future, within the Chilean polity will be examined more closely with a view to seeing more clearly how the UP emerged, what its precise significance may be, and what are its chances of success. At the end there will be a discussion of the comparative significance of the problems described in the essays contained in this issue.

Kenneth Medhurst

2   The Chilean Background

THE EMERGENCE OF THE UP CANNOT BE SEEN SIMPLY AS AN
isolated and more or less accidental phenomenon, but has to be
set against the background of long term developments within
the Chilean polity and long-standing problems within the Chilean
economy and Chilean society. Similarly, any analysis of the UP's
present dilemmas cannot be undertaken without some reference
to the problems it has inherited and the environment within which
it must operate. By isolating the factors which have gone into the
shaping of contemporary Chilean political problems and forces it
may become easier to see whether or not 'the Chilean road to
socialism' is viable and whether Chile can stand as an example to
other polities or must be regarded as wholly *sui generis*.

   To even the most casual observer the stability of Chile's political
institutions must appear as a salient feature of its development.
By marked contrast with most of its Latin American neighbours
Chile, throughout the bulk of the post-independence period, has
enjoyed relative tranquillity. With limited exceptions Chilean
political life has not been plagued by large-scale violence. As
H. Bicheno's article indicates, it is possible to underestimate the
significance of violence, or the threat of violence, as a factor in
Chilean political history but it is also true that the country's
political system has generally shown a fairly high capacity for the
peaceful resolution of conflict. By the same token acceptance of
established political institutions and practices has apparently been
widespread. Existing institutions have quite widely been regarded
as legitimate and the political system has operated on the basis of a
considerable degree of consensus among elite groups in the
society. The country lived with one constitution from 1833 until
1925 and the new constitution, enacted in 1925, remains in being.
A corollary to this has been the relative absence of overt military
intervention in the political arena. As H. Bicheno further shows,

there is a well-established tradition of conspiracy in some military circles and groups of officers have quite frequently put themselves at the service of the 'extra-parliamentary opposition' but up to the present such activity has infrequently resulted in the seizure of power.

Whilst there have always been groups within the army possessing political ambitions, the majority of their colleagues have normally appeared to be most reluctant to become involved in the government of the country. On the contrary, most officers, in so far as they have been politicized, have tended to regard themselves as the defenders of established political institutions. They have otherwise remained content with their role as a pressure group, bargaining behind the scenes over such matters of professional interest as improved salaries and military equipment.

In part the military's attitudes can be explained by its high degree of professionalism. On the other hand, the Chilean military's attitudes towards politics are also partly explicable in terms of the military's relationships with the rest of society and the role which, in the past, circumstances have permitted the army to play in domestic political controversies. Without a fairly high degree of social cohesion and in the absence of political institutions widely regarded as legitimate among the major participants in Chilean public life a vacuum might have been created into which Chile's army, in common with many other Latin American armies, might well have frequently stepped. The army might then have emerged more clearly as the principal arbiter of the nation's political life. But, as already noted, the conditions making for such a vacuum have generally not developed within the Chilean polity.

THE STRUCTURE OF SOCIETY

To understand this situation one must understand the structure of Chilean society, as it developed in the post-independence period, and the values of Chile's socially dominant groups. On its emergence from the colonial era Chile possessed a relatively simple, quasi-feudal social structure. On the one hand was a relatively small elite whose wealth, prestige and political power stemmed principally from the ownership of land. On the other hand was a mass of poor peasants, farmers and landless labourers who were economically and socially dependent upon the land-owning groups. The former, in co-operation with the Roman Catholic Church, were the sole participants in the nation's political life.

A form of constitutional government was forged but it was operated solely by and in the interests of the traditional elites. They could be divided into competing factions struggling hard over the spoils of office and the exact nature of public policy, but they had a broad community of interest in the maintenance of the established social order and the constitutional arrangements which emerged as an expression and guarantee of that order.

At least two other factors also encouraged cohesion among the nation's ruling groups and promoted support for its political institutions. Firstly, the country found in Diego Portales (the President responsible for the 1833 constitutional settlement) an outstanding president who gained wide acceptance for a system of strong executive rule – a system which did not finally break down until 1891 and which guided Chile through the early stages of its development. Secondly, Portales and his successors were assisted in their task of 'nation-building' by the facts of geography. Much of Chile's northerly and rich mineral bearing territories were not part of the national territory until the War of the Pacific (1879–83). Moreover, large parts of what is now Southern territory were inhospitable and not effectively under the Chilean state's control. The vast majority of Chileans therefore were concentrated, and are still concentrated, in the central or 'Mediterranean' region of Chile which provides much of the cultivable land and in which Chile's three main cities (Santiago, Valparaiso and Concepción) are situated. Similarly, Chile had a much smaller Indian population than many Latin American countries and had to absorb fewer late arrivals from Europe than did a country like Argentine. Thus Chile developed as a relatively homogeneous, close-knit society, less plagued than its neighbours by centrifugal regional forces. Furthermore, the long Pacific coastline provided Chile with unusually good communications that not only promoted trade but also enabled the government to deal quickly with such regionally based revolts as did develop. In Chile, by contrast with most other emerging Latin American nations, 19th-century rebels could not repair to impenetrable areas totally outside of the central government's control.

As H. Bicheno clearly shows, 19th-century economic developments led to the emergence of new social groups which complicated but did not fundamentally alter the traditional pattern of social relationships. The chief 19th-century impetus to economic development came, in the wake of the War of the Pacific, with the enlargement of Chile's territory and the opening up of new mineral deposits. Above all, at that stage, the mining of nitrate became a major economic undertaking. Its sale abroad made it Chile's chief single source of foreign exchange. In the short run this led to an overall growth in national economic activity. In the long run, however, it contributed to the increase of problems which, in essence, still confront Chilean society. On the one hand there was the growth of serious and chronic inflationary pressures which, given the existence of important structural obstacles to sustained economic growth, have proved uncontrollable. On the other hand Chile's integration into the international economy as a primary producer, largely dependent for its foreign exchange earnings upon the sale of minerals, has left the country's economy vulnerable to shifts in the terms of international trade – terms which have generally favoured Chile's European and, more recently, North American trading partners and not Chile itself. Moreover, the dominant role of foreign companies and foreign capital in the exploitation of mineral resources left immediate control over Chile's principal exports to a large extent in the hands of outside interests. Outside interests who were free to withdraw their profits from the country and whose investment policies were not bound to serve Chile's own economic interests.

THE POLITICAL PARTIES

On the political front the growing complexity of Chilean society was reflected in the emergence of new groupings. The principal division was initially between the Liberal and Conservative Parties. The former tended to be urban based, anti-clerical and to represent the interests of commercial groups. The latter tended to be identified with landowning and pro-clerical interests. There were not, however, completely clear cut distinctions between the constituencies of these two bodies. Similarly, policy differences tended to represent differences of emphasis rather than basic conflicts of interest. The Liberal Party tended to give priority to the promotion of commercial and industrial interests whilst the Conservative Party was more likely to give priority to the defence of agrarian interests. Both parties were, however, wholly dominated by established socio-economic elite groups and had a stake in the existing hierarchically structured order of society. The clerical issue was perhaps the one obviously important bone of contention between the two groups. Whilst the Conservative Party was committed to a close alliance between Church and state and official buttressing of the Church's social influence, the liberals sought to curtail clerical intervention and influence in public life. By as early as 1873, however, reformist pressures had proved sufficient to produce legislative changes that took a good deal of the sting out of this particular controversy. The official separation of Church and state had to wait until the new constitution of 1925, and even then the Church's role in such fields as education remained a potential source of conflict, but by the turn of the century debates over this issue had already become somewhat muted. With this reduction of tension the traditional distinction between liberals and conservatives, though to remain until the 1960s, lost much of its *raison d'être*. Throughout much of this century the two parties have co-operated (usually in alliance with other and smaller groups) in resisting pressures for social and economic change or, at the least, channelling such pressures in acceptable directions.

During the later part of the 19th century other factions, describing themselves as political parties, formed and reformed but most proved to be transient phenomena. One group emerged, however, which was to be of long-term importance. This was the Radical Party. It first appeared in the 1860s as a break-away from the most 'progressive' wing of the Liberal Party. It was 'upper class' in leadership but reformist in its ethos. Subsequently, the party emerged as a potentially powerful coalition of interests, in some measure cutting across class lines. It contained some provincial landowners and spokesmen for new mining interests. It also came to speak for significant portions of new urban middle-class groups who emerged in the wake of economic development. Finally, it attracted some support from the developing industrial working class. Such a coalition naturally tended to pull the Radical Party in different directions. One wing of the party espoused a fairly far-reaching reform programme. Another wing, however, had more defensive attitudes towards demands for radical social reforms. Nevertheless, the growth of the party quite clearly indicated that Chilean politics could no longer be regarded as the exclusive domain of the traditional elites and that other groups were beginning to press for some share in the running of the state.

Despite such warning signals it was not until 1920 that the traditional pattern of Chilean politics was first seriously disturbed. Prior to that the most important new development was a first breakdown, in 1891, of the long-established tradition of strong presidential government, and the inauguration of an era during which constantly changing coalition governments found themselves at the mercy of an irresponsible and faction-ridden Congress. This change, however, in no way signified a reduction in the political power of established elites. On the contrary, Congress, in this new situation, was dominated by 'upper-class' groups who manipulated the governmental and electoral machinery, sometimes in a corrupt fashion, to secure private advantages and to underwrite their dominant position in Chilean society.

This situation bred mounting dissatisfaction among those sections of society which had begun to articulate their own distinctive political demands but which still found themselves excluded from policy-making. Such dissatisfaction was further aggravated by economic recession caused partly by the development of synthetic nitrates. Ultimately opposition to the *status quo* found expression through the election to the presidency, in 1920, of Arturo Alessandri. The latter, though himself associated with the 'upper class', won the presidency as a populist 'anti-oligarchic' candidate. His victory did not even remotely signify the destruction of Chile's traditional ruling classes but it did demonstrate that 'the passive obedience of the masses of the people to the old oligarchy had ceased to exist'. Because of this, Alessandri's election has been labelled 'the revolt of the electorate' and is regarded as the first of a series of major turning points in 20th-century Chilean political history.

Alessandri's administration is the subject of comment by H. Bicheno and it will not be discussed at length here. It should, however, be noted that this period witnessed overt military intervention in Chilean politics on a scale unknown since 1891 and that, with military backing, Alessandri was able in 1925 to introduce a new constitution, with which the country still lives.

Alessandri's constitutionally elected successor was pushed aside by the former's defence minister, Ibáñez, another key figure in Chilean political history about whom Bicheno has much to say. This dictatorial regime ultimately came to an end when Chile began to feel the effects of the world depression and a crisis of confidence was triggered off. Following Ibáñez's departure there was a period of confusion that included a very shortlived 'Socialist Republic' under the auspices of an air force officer, Colonel Marmaduke Grove. Eventually the military put power back into civilian hands and Alessandri was elected for a second presidential term that terminated in 1938. That government turned out to be the prelude to another significant turning-point in modern

Chilean political history, the creation of a 'Popular Front' government. This administration was led by a member of the Radical Party (the first radical to hold the office) and it was this party. which provided the new government with its most substantial support and which benefited most from the new situation. By capturing executive power the party was able to break the stranglehold that traditional elites had possessed over the spoils of office and ushered in a period, lasting until 1952, during which it held the centre of the stage.

It has been argued that the election of the 'Popular Front' government signified a breakthrough on the part of emergent middle-class groups who then first obtained a major share in the running of the Chilean polity. Post-1938 developments can perhaps be seen as signifying an irreversible eruption into the political arena of social groups, particularly professional and managerial elements, who had previously been largely confined to the sidelines. This new departure, though pioneered under Radical Party leadership, required the support of other groups. Help was forthcoming, above all, from the Chilean Socialist and Communist Parties. Because of the particular importance of these two entities for the entire discussion they will receive special attention below. Here it is sufficient to note the emergence of these two left-wing parties and that, as early as 1938, they were substantial enough to help the Radical Party to secure power and, for a time, to run the government.

As Biehl and Fernandez explain, the 'Popular Front' collapsed by 1941 but it was succeeded by other centre-left coalitions, each under the leadership of a member of the Radical Party (by that time the largest single Chilean party). In 1946 one such coalition came to power with the curiously mixed support of radicals, communists and liberals and its leader, President González Videla, ruled for five months with the aid of some communist ministers; a development without precedent prior to 1970.

This short period in office represented a culminating point in the Communist Party's development. Since 1938 its policy had been to give merely conditional support to incumbent governments. This had paid dividends, for it was able to claim credit for popular measures and disclaim responsibility for unpopular actions. Subsequent advances in its popular support aided it in struggles with the socialists for control over organized labour. Repeated splits in socialist ranks further smoothed the path for their much better disciplined rivals. Moreover, once in office,

the communists were able to use their official positions for prose-
cuting their feuds and González Videla, for a time, was prepared
to use the communists to counter socialist influence in the labour
movement.

Eventually, the communists made such headway that the Liberal
Party left the governing coalition and González Videla, particularly disturbed by communist inroads into portions of the Radical
Party's following, dismissed their representatives in his administration. Perhaps taking advantage of fears engendered by the
'Cold War,' he also gained congressional approval for a 'Law for
the Permanent Defence of Democracy' which outlawed the
Communist Party. Though the latter continued to operate *sub
rosa* the new measure dealt the party a serious blow. Moreover,
experience of 'internment' left a deep impression on a whole
generation of Communist Party leaders. It left them determined
not to repeat the experience and hence cautious in many of their
future political dealings.

The outlawing of the Communist Party sowed dissension
among socialists just when they had begun to resolve former
differences. One faction, including Senator Allende, opposed
González Videla's action whilst others favoured support. Divisions like this contributed to the creation of a very confused
political situation. It was a situation that helps to explain a
remarkable resurgence of support for Ibáñez. His come-back
indicated the continuing importance of *personalismo* in Chilean
politics and it served notice to established parties that there was
mounting popular dissatisfaction with the performance of recent
coalition governments.

In part this dissatisfaction with conventional political activity
arose from the disappointing of popular expectations and the
apparent inability of established parties to deal decisively with the
problems of national development. The advent of the 'Popular
Front', and its successors, may have led many underprivileged
Chileans to look for fundamental socio-economic reforms but
these did not materialize. This is not to suggest that post-1938
governments had no significant achievements to their credit.
It was during this era, for example, that the Chilean Development
Corporation was established as part of a state-directed economic
development programme, a programme which enmeshed the
Chilean state in the process of industrialization and so gave 'the
public sector' a high degree of legitimacy. But such developments
did not get to the root of the country's most pressing problems.

Efforts to promote economic expansion ultimately ran into difficulties because the structure of the industrial sector (characterized
by a high concentration of ownership, on the one hand, and by a
large number of small inefficient enterprises, on the other) put
obstacles in the way of speedy sustained growth and ensured that
the fruits of growth were channelled, to a disproportionate extent,
into the hands of upper- and middle-class groups. This, set against
the background of rapid population growth and accelerating
urbanization, constituted a recipe for continuing inflation that, as
always, hit hardest at the least prosperous social groups. Such
inflationary pressures were further and very seriously aggravated
by a stagnating agricultural sector, characterized by under-
cultivated estates, in the hands of traditional elites, and highly
fragmented and totally inefficient farming units.

The failure to address themselves to this vital agrarian problem
was the clearest sign given by the post-1938 governments that
they had no intention of drastically tampering with the existing
structure of Chilean society. The unwillingness or inability of
even the 'Popular Front' government to generate an agrarian
reform programme indicated, as Quiros Varela shows, that the
processes of change were expected to work within the framework of the traditional social order and that there was no intention of removing from Chile's traditional elites the sources of
their economic and political power.

The explanation of this situation lay partly in the nature of the
then dominant Radical Party. As already noted it was a relatively
broad coalition of interests which tended, as a consequence, to
be pulled in differing directions. Thus relatively bold reformist
measures, adopted with the aid of left-wing allies, frequently
appeared to be followed by periods when the party recoiled from
the results of its actions and went into alliance with more conservative elements. Moreover, Radical Party leaders and sym-
pathizers, once they became entrenched in the bureaucracy or became prominent in the business world, often lost their reforming
drive and sometimes associated themselves with traditional elites.

Lack of sustained reforming drive within the Radical Party was
compounded by continued resistance to change from the traditional Chilean elites. Not only did these groups continue to
dominate much of the economy but they also could often exercise
a veto power through their congressional spokesmen in the Liberal
and Conservative Parties. Control in the countryside, unchallenged
by the government, enabled these two groups to return a

substantial number of representatives to the legislature. On the other hand, it has to be borne in mind that these years also saw some potentially significant shifts in attitudes on the Chilean right. Though the advent of the 'Popular Front' naturally caused alarm it was only a minority who reacted in an extreme way and identified themselves with extra-parliamentary opposition of a radical right-wing variety (including a Chilean Nazi Party). The majority adjusted to the new situation and showed themselves prepared to bargain with spokesmen for other interests in the society. Though determined to defend their still powerful position they did so whilst observing 'the rules of the game' and whilst implicitly acknowledging that they could never again occupy a monopolistic position within the Chilean polity.

The growing gap between popular expectation and performance culminated, in 1952, with the election to the presidency of Ibáñez. Standing as a candidate 'above party' he mobilized an *ad hoc* electoral coalition that cut across normal party lines. It was a remarkable personal triumph which registered, above all, a massive reaction against the failure of successive governments to curb inflation. Disillusionment provoked many to look for a 'strong man' who would break through the log-jam in Chilean politics.

The election of 1952 was noteworthy in two other ways. Firstly, it indicated that the processes of social change were beginning to disrupt the traditional pattern of life in rural Chile. Large numbers of rural workers and tenant farmers for the first time defied their landlords by voting for Ibáñez rather than the traditional right-wing parties. Secondly, the election saw Allende standing for the first time for the presidency and, what was still more important, he stood with the support of the Chilean Communist Party and in opposition to a large part of his own Socialist Party. Whilst a majority of socialists were attracted by Ibáñez and the prospect of a brand of authoritarian rule similar to that of Perón in Argentina, the Communist Party, following its recent experiences, was determined to demonstrate its loyalty to constitutional government. Allende provided them with a useful ally in this undertaking. At the time this seemed to be a quixotic gesture on Allende's part for he came in a poor fourth, in a field of four candidates. In the long run, however, it helped to make his reputation as a truly substantial left-wing leader.

The chief reason for this was that, before long, Ibáñez was discredited and those who had swum against the pro-Ibáñez tide were therefore vindicated. In office the ex-dictator wholly failed to fulfil the promise of his demagogic electoral campaign. Contrary to expectations he did not seize dictatorial powers but played the traditional political game, ruling through rapidly changing parliamentary coalitions that were unable to pursue decisive or coherent policies. Likewise, he did nothing to translate his initial popularity into solid institutionalized support. Thus he produced none of the major structural reforms many of his 1952 allies had hoped for. Ibáñez served out his presidential term but by the end, in 1958, he had lost the political initiative whilst his opponents among the established parties had had a long period in which to put their houses in order.

Among Ibáñez's most consistent opponents was the Communist Party. It was understandable therefore that, under the impact of disillusionment with the ex-dictator, the socialists should move into an alliance with the latter body. Having first repaired their own internal divisions the socialists joined with the communists (and some smaller left-wing groups) to form a *Frente de Acción Popular* (FRAP), which, under Allende's leadership contested the 1958 presidential election. Indeed, but for the intervention of an obscure defrocked priest who some believe was put up by the right-wing elements as a decoy to capture left-wing votes, Allende would have won. As it was, Jorge Alessandri (son of the former president) won by a narrow margin in a field that also contained a radical and Frei standing for the first time on behalf of the very recently constituted Christian Democratic Party (PDC).

Alessandri enjoyed considerable personal popularity but his administration could not cope adequately with Chile's chronic developmental problems nor contain mounting demands for radical change. Ultimately unsuccessful attempts were made to check inflation with the aid of orthodox fiscal policies that laid heavy burdens upon wage earners and left much of the country's industrial capacity under-used. As Quiros Varela indicates in his article, some efforts were also made to tackle agrarian problems but the traditional right-wing parties obviously could not be expected to promote profound structural changes in the rural sector.

It was against this background that the electorate, taken as a whole, experienced a move to the left. Electoral reforms, enacted in 1958 and 1962, removed obstacles which had previously stood in the way of potential voters seeking to register themselves. Chile continued to possess, as it always had, a literacy test for voters but the numbers of those registering and voting increased as a result of these changes. Similarly, a stop was effectively put to the appearance of 'fly-by-night' parties which had previously led to a blurring of divisions within the polity. The net effect of these changes was twofold. Firstly, the party system became better organized and defined. Six major parties were left, each representing fairly well defined socio-economic interests. Secondly, parties of the left and the new reformist Christian Democratic Party experienced some enlarging of their potential constituencies. In particular, left-wing and Christian Democratic elements began to make significant inroads into rural areas and to mobilize peasant support. Changes in peasant voting patterns, hinted at in 1952, heralded a perhaps more substantial and enduring erosion of traditional right-wing rural bastions.

THE CHRISTIAN DEMOCRATIC PARTY

Though FRAP made headway during Alessandri's period in office the most spectacular advances were made by the Christian Democrats. Because of this it is necessary briefly to examine this new phenomenon.

The party can trace its origins back to a group of young Catholic students (including Frei and Radomiro Tomic) who, in 1938, broke away from the traditional Conservative Party. The new breakaway group took the name *Falange Nacional* which was in some respects misleading for, though influenced by contemporary European corporativist thinking, it was never truly fascist in nature. Moreover, under the impact of changes on the international scene and of changes within the group's own leadership it moved considerably to the left.

Ideologically the Christian Democrats (as they later became) combined a belief in social pluralism and political democracy. Though largely inspired by Catholic social teaching they had no intention of seeking after ideological hegemony and remained non-confessional. Similarly, they repudiated *laissez-faire* capitalism and accepted the need for large scale state intervention but were firmly wedded to constitutional government. A limited form of class struggle was generally accepted as a necessary pre-condition of significant change but their ultimate goal was not the triumph of one class over another but the harmonization of diverging interests within the context of a 'communitarian society'. The latter was perhaps a vague concept but it was one which led many to see the possibility of a viable non-Marxist alternative to capitalism and to the traditional Chilean social order. It offered the prospect of gradual peaceful changes that would not so much destroy Chile's established social and econo- mic institutions as make them operate more efficiently and compel them to serve the interests of the mass of Chileans. Thus it was proposed to foster greater popular participation in policy-making, rather than leaving the bulk of Chileans as the largely passive objects of government decisions. Similarly, it was proposed to conduct a radical agrarian reform and to make the country's copper industry serve the purposes of the state rather than the interests of private and, above all, foreign investors. In the domain of foreign affairs a rather more independent policy was advocated in the place of the close co-operation with the United States which had become the salient feature of Chile's external relations. There was an appeal to that Latin American nationalism which has anti-Americanism as one of its principal features though, in this instance, the anti-Americanism aimed at partner- ship with (as opposed to subordination to) the United States and was not militant or doctrinaire in nature. Latin American inte- gration was advocated as a means of placing Chile, and other countries, on terms of greater equality with the developed world.

Particularly after 1957 a substantial and broadly based electoral coalition was mobilized in support of this approach to Chile's problems. Though the party, by then under Frei's leadership, did not succeed in its original aim of drawing away the working classes from the Marxist left it did attract substantial urban working-class support. As already noted, it also made inroads in the countryside. Above all it won much middle-class support. In part this was a question of disaffection from the Conservative Party and in part the recruitment of young reformist elements who had not previously been politically involved. The latter included not only socially conscious Catholics but also pragmatic middle-class technicians and professional people who were attrac- ted by the prospect of bringing reforming zeal and modern techniques into the business of government. Not least, the party, thanks presumably to the Catholic influence, also attracted a disproportionate share of the female vote.

Prior to 1964 it was widely presumed that it would not be the Christian Democrats but FRAP which would be the heirs of Alessandri. Starting from an already firm base FRAP was con- tinuing to gather strength and outwardly, at least, appeared very

well organized. Confirmation of this view came in an important
by-election when, in a normally conservative area, a FRAP
candidate gained a handsome victory. To the pro-government
coalition which had been formed to contest the next presidential
elections this came as a severe jolt. The Radical Party withdrew
from the coalition and as they were due to supply the right-wing's
standard bearer this left the candidates of FRAP (Allende) and of
the Christian Democrats (Frei) as the only serious contenders. In
these circumstances the Conservative and Liberal Parties rallied
behind Frei. They opted for him as the lesser of the available evils.

Thanks partly to right-wing support Frei won with well over
half of the popular vote. In 1965, moreover, the Christian Democrats won enough congressional support to put through their
programme without help from other parties. Frei's own victory
may have been due to right-wing help but this triumph was won
in the face of a disenchanted right wing who had been alienated
by the government's proposed reforms and had used their position in Congress to block them. The right-wing's set-back on this
occasion was in fact so severe that it led immediately to the
conservatives and liberals joining to form one National Party.

Such a position of strength, combined with a radical reform
programme entailed a massive raising of popular expectations.
They were expectations that were almost bound to be disappointed.
Though Frei's administration had many solid achievements to its
credit the problems it had to face were probably too intractable
for wholly adequate solutions to be forthcoming. In 1970 the
electorate recorded its verdict on this situation.

On the positive side Frei initiated the 'Chileanization' of copper.
After a rather tentative start the government successfully exerted
pressure upon the large American owned Anaconda company
and so obtained 51% shareholding on terms that even some left-
wing opponents found hard to criticize. In addition, large investments were made in the copper mining industry, investments
which in some cases began to pay off following the Christian
Democrats' departure from office. As Quiros Varela indicates,
lasting changes were also made in the countryside. A start was
made on the expropriation of large estates and, after a law of
1967, there was a spectacular growth in the organization of rural
labour. In the process the balance of political power in Chile was
probably shifted significantly to the left.

In the realm of social policy official policies demonstrated
considerable concern for the underprivileged. They fostered some

redistribution of income and of tax burdens. They also produced a reduction of illiteracy and the building of about a quarter of a million new houses.

The obverse side of this coin was an inability to cope with the related problems of inflation and economic growth; a short-coming which was eventually to prove the government's un-doing. Initially it was possible to make use of under-used indus-trial capacity and so have some growth without serious inflation. But the growth in national income was small and by 1967 there was a resumption of inflationary pressures that drove the govern-ment to retrench and led government departments to scramble so strongly for scarce resources that economic planning broke down. Such difficulties were compounded by a failure drastically to boost agricultural productivity and to reduce Chile's foreign debts to more manageable proportions.

It is apparent from this that despite significant reforms structural obstacles to sustained growth were still present. The quick re-moval of these obstacles was probably incompatible with what was considered politically feasible and desirable. Though Frei started from a position of strength he had to face serious divisions within his own party over the nature and speed of change. On the left wing of the party were elements who regarded Frei as too conservative and on the right significant numbers were alienated by the scope of his reforms. Particularly serious, in electoral terms, was the withdrawal of right-wing support to what it saw as the safer sanctuary of the National Party. In other words, when faced by the realities of office, latent conflicts of interest within Frei's winning electoral coalition came to the surface and so reduced freedom for manoeuvre.

It was in this situation that, in 1970, Allende was elected presi-dent. The preceding election campaign is analyzed at length by Biehl and Fernandez and will not be discussed here. What is appropriate, however, is to look closely at the evolution of the Chilean left for this not only explains the emergence of the Unidad Popular but may also provide clues as to its future development.

THE EVOLUTION OF THE CHILEAN LEFT

The Chilean Communist Party was founded in 1921 and for a decade enjoyed a virtual monopoly on the left of Chilean politics and in the realm of organized labour. From the outset it regarded itself as a loyal ally of the Soviet Communist Party and looked to the latter for its inspiration. When it was first created there was still a belief in orthodox international communist circles that the Russian revolution could be the prelude to fairly rapid world-wide revolution. Thus, for ten years, the Chilean Party operated on this assumption although, in fact, the assumption bore little relation to the local reality. The party's conspiratorial efforts, moreover, were limited in scope and ineffectual in nature. The net effect was to leave the party stranded as a not very successful sect.

It was in reaction against this situation that the Socialist Party was created. Whilst European Communist Parties generally developed as breakaways from socialist movements the Chilean socialists came into being as a protest against the ineffectiveness of communist leadership. The party quickly established itself as a substantial political force and during the 1930s was more signifi-cant than its communist rival.

Four factors about this situation are worth bearing in mind, for they have an enduring importance. Firstly, the catalyst that sparked off the creation of the Socialist Party was Grove's 'Socialist Republic' and Grove was one of the movement's founding fathers. From the start, therefore, the party had an anti-parliamentary wing and was, as a whole, not unequivocally committed to consti-tutional government. Secondly, taking its cue from men like Grove, the party tended from its inception to be nationalist in its tone and to resent external interference from any quarter. Thirdly, because the party owed no loyalty to an outside movement it lacked the ideological conformity and organizational cohesiveness that was imposed on the Communist Party. Thus, throughout its history, the socialist movement has been peculiarly prone to factionalism. Unlike the Communist Party it is possible for out-standing leaders, notably intellectuals, to rise rapidly within the party without following a painstaking career inside a party bureaucracy. Equally, the Socialist Party has been much more receptive to new ideas, to such an extent that some have regarded it as a chameleon pursuing a course of conduct in which little consistency is perceptible. The price for such openness, however, has been constant internal conflict from which, in the long run, the communists have benefited. On the other hand (and this is the final point worth noting), the Socialist Party has never been the communist's junior partner to the same extent as some Euro-pean Socialist Parties. Having been founded as a protest against communist leadership of the left it has never become dependent on funds from communist controlled labour movements nor infiltrated, to a significant degree, by Communist Party members.

The formation of the 'Popular Front' proved to be a turning point for the Chilean communists. They co-operated in the experiment more willingly than the socialists partly because this fitted in with the Soviet Union's current policy and partly because it gave them the chance to establish their respectability in the eyes of the Chilean electorate. The socialists, who were less pragmatic in their approach, were from the start unhappy about 'selling out' to the 'bourgeoisie' and soon withdrew their co-operation. They continued, moreover, to be deeply divided about the whole question of participating in government. The communists, however, as noted earlier, profited from these circumstances to extend their influence and build up their organization. When for a time they were outlawed this simply confirmed them in their caution and in their determination to work within the established political framework. Thus, apart from their early relatively unsuccessful years, the communists have always been cautious and insisted on observing Chile's constitutional traditions. They have insisted that the final revolution would only be feasible and desirable when the objective conditions were wholly right. In other words, they can be said to have practised 'the peaceful road to socialism' long before it became the orthodox teaching of pro-Soviet parties. Remote from the Soviet Union and the possibility of Soviet protection for a local communist regime they had strong incentives to adjust firmly to local domestic circumstances.

The advent of Ibáñez in 1952, underlined the difference between communists and socialists. Whilst the communists (and a minority of socialists) opposed what was regarded as a threat to constitutional government most socialists welcomed the new president. The latter, then currently influenced by Perón, saw in Ibáñez the possibility of enforcing drastic socio-economic changes. Only when they were disillusioned with Ibáñez did they form an electoral alliance with the communists; an alliance led, significantly enough, by the one major socialist leader whom the Communist Party trusted.

Standing with a relatively moderate programme Allende, in 1958, almost won the presidency. This induced the Socialist Party to push Allende forward again, in 1964, at the head of a left-wing alliance. This time, however, the left-wing programme was more radical. Under the impact of the Cuban revolution the alliance, chiefly due to socialist pressure, espoused a more obviously socialist programme. Nationalization of 'the commanding heights

of the economy' and constitutional changes designed to reduce
the obstructive capacity of conservative forces were among
FRAP's proposals. The Communist Party would probably have
preferred to return to a more broadly based alliance with more
modest objectives but the Socialist Party's initiative and the
success of the Cuban experiment cut the ground from under its
feet. In private, however, communist leaders were apparently
more cautious than many socialists about the relevance of the
Cuban experience for Chile and they remained firmly committed
to the one 'peaceful road' to socialism. Whilst one vocal wing of
the Socialist Party believed that the fighting of elections should be
accompanied by preparations for violent revolution the Communist Party insisted that, for the foreseeable future, the 'parliamentary road' was the only appropriate one. The communists, in other
words, resisted the radicalization process observable on the
Socialist Party's left wing.

Prior to the 1970 election the Socialist Party had difficulty in
falling in behind Allende once again. It was worried about his
political moderation and twice tried to recruit more militant
candidates. Indeed, some maintain that Allende was effectively
chosen by the Communist Party to lead the Unidad Popular.
Certainly, it was only on the second ballot that Allende was
adopted by the central committee of his own party and that body
recorded thirteen votes for him as against eleven abstentions. As
on previous occasions, Allende entered the lists at the head of a
divided party and dependent for his best organized support upon
a potential rival of that party. On the other hand, no other socialist, and probably no other left-wing politician, would have been
capable of commanding the loyalty of all the UP's constituent
groups. Successive electoral campaigns had given him a nation-
wide reputation and an electoral following that others could not
claim. Moreover, long political experience reaching back to
ministerial office in the 'Popular Front' had developed in him, to
an unusual degree, the tactical skills necessary for holding together diverging groups.

Joan E. Garcés

3 Chile 1971: A Revolutionary Government within a Welfare State*

THE CHILEAN REVOLUTIONARY EXPERIENCE HAS MORE THAN enough characteristics to arouse admiration amongst those who support it and astonishment or scepticism among everyone else. A rapid glance backwards is enough to establish that their *non-institutional legitimation* is a factor common to practically all revolutions, ancient or modern. To such a point that political theory has devised the category of *revolutionary* legitimation in order to compare it with other (religious, dynastic, historical, democratic etc.) categories. Revolutionary movements have always sought justification of their *raison d'être* in the causes or goals which have motivated them. Usually these goals have been in conflict with those forming the bases of the pre-existing system of political institutions. Hence revolution seems to be associated with conflict against institutionalism, and the triumph of the revolution seems to have involved the institutional collapse of the former regime.

Essentially, the Chilean process is no different from the general norm. An authentic revolution presupposes the transformation of socio-economic structures. And faced with a change of this scope, no politico-institutional regime can avoid being transformed in its turn. Hence the establishment of new political institutions is one of the fundamental points in the programme set out in the Programa Básico de la Unidad Popular. It has found its first important concrete embodiment in the Project for Constitutional Reform (Proyecto de reforma constitucional) presented in November 1971, which seeks to replace the bicameral structure of the legislative power, to grant the executive the power to dissolve

* Written in Santiago, 12 December 1971.

Congress, and to renew the personal composition of the Supreme
Court.

What is specific to the Chilean case relates to something
different: to the gestation of the new revolutionary political
power *through* the traditional institutional mechanisms. Normally
the revolutionary forces have had to break the institutional
political regime to attain the government of the country. Revolutionary action disabled it simply because it was the institutional
political regime. Generally, revolutionary action, coupled with
physical violence, has served as an instrument for bringing about
change. And 'legal' violence has usually been associated with
physical violence; the revolutionary flood has pulled down the
political institutional mechanisms as well as the legal norms which
inspired them. In systems possessing a written constitution the
latter has been purely and simply ignored, when not actually
replaced by another, following the abrupt interruption in its
operation; and, of course, without observing the formal and legal
procedures established for its modification – as explained by the
constitutionalist, Karl Schmitt, in a counter-revolutionary context,
when he affirmed that no constitution has foreseen its own death.

On the other hand, in Chile, the revolutionary process is
developing by the association of the two legitimations which have
always seemed opposed: the revolutionary legitimation and the
institutional. The first is defined by the nature and content of the
Popular government. But the second has allowed it to establish
itself and to begin to carry out its programme of structural transformations. This simultaneous presence of both forms of legitimation is of fundamental importance for an understanding of the
meaning of the Chilean revolutionary process.

THE CONSTITUTION AND LEGALITY

The characteristics peculiar to the Chilean political system have
made it possible for anti-system social forces to develop within a
framework of behaviour which did not conflict with the constitutional and legal norms. Without breach of continuity, the
evolution of the social struggle has led these social forces to take
over the government within a state which we could qualify as
developed in terms of its administrative and economic capacities
and its coercive control of the country. Whatever the indicators
we might choose, to measure these capacities, their application
would give clearly positive results. Moreover, it is a state which is

characterized by the total hegemony – both formally and materially – of the executive. This implies two consequences:

(1) In the apparatus of the Chilean state, every power of economic intervention, administrative direction and management, political definition and use of the forces of coercion, responds to the dynamics and orientation of the executive. Control of the Presidency of the Republic not only allows a government to be formed which is autonomous as regards parliament; it allows the government to use to its own advantage all these powers.

(2) The exercise of political power is subject to norms, procedures and forms. The level of institutionalization of the Chilean state is sufficiently high and the para- and extra-state controls sufficiently strong to force the executive to act in accordance with the normal prevailing order. Should it not do so, it might bring about the collapse of the existing political system.

A government such as that which was installed in La Moneda on 3 November 1970, could count on using the mechanisms of the state according to the criteria of its programme, assisted by the very strength of the constitutional mechanisms let alone their existence. But there was one fundamental pre-requisite: that the government would not act beyond the co-ordinates allowed it by the constitution and the law. The reason for this is simple. Within the apparatus of the state, at all instances and levels, the Popular government has to coexist with social institutions and forces which oppose it, to a greater or lesser degree, and which do not fully share either its ideological outlook or the aims of its programme. The Chilean state which the Unidad Popular is now directing is a state with a predominantly liberal-bourgeois structure. If these state institutions – from parliament to bureaucracy, by way of judicial magistracy – tolerate and recognize the authority of the Popular government it is precisely – and only – because of the *institutional* legality of the latter. They not only fail to accept its *revolutionary* legitimacy but even question it or contest it.

The bond, then, which links the bourgeois elements of the state to the Popular government is none other than the constitutional origin and behaviour of the Popular government – a bond which can be either tenuous or firm. It depends on the strength of the government outside the apparatus of the state. That is, on the political, social and economic force which, in an organized and coherent way, the movements and institutions which make up or support the Unidad Popular accumulate. But, whatever the allegiance of the popular forces, it is different in kind from the bond subordinating the state apparatus to Allende's government. This bond could be broken in many ways, one of them being, without doubt, that the Popular government should fail to respect the constitution or the laws.

The prime example of this point is that of the coercive forces of the state. Created and developed in a spirit of deep respect for their constitutional role – and the first requisite for the institutionalization of a state is that its armed forces should respect and become integral parts of the institutionality – they have consciously exercised the role of armed support of the state. The direction and orientation of the state is determined by means of politico-electoral mechanisms in which the armed forces have no business to interfere. In logical terms, while the mechanisms by which the leadership in the state is chosen function normally, the liberal-democratic political system in power requires that the armed forces should restrict themselves to carrying out the specific functions which belong to them. Nevertheless, although this is correct in politico-institutional terms, it is not enough by itself. One must consider, also, the social class content of the state apparatus.

It is evidently difficult to conceive of armed forces which identify themselves socially with the aristocracy or the high bourgeoisie, supporting a government with an anti-capitalist orientation, however institutionalized the state might be. The contradiction can only be resolved by means of the elimination of one or the other of the opposing terms. Of the anti-capitalist government – when the counter revolution wins; of the conservative armed forces – when the revolution wins. Armed forces and a government with antagonistic class characteristics cannot co-exist in the same state, without contradicting the essential logical demands of a state.

And this historical feature – needless to say – is also found in Chile. Its political evolution shows that the period of political predominance of the middle sectors, allied now to the right, now to the left, and which began in the 1920s, coincides with a social composition predominantly linked to the middle sectors in the armed forces. The successive governments of the last forty years fall within a political spectrum ranging from the centre-right to the centre-left. But the middle sectors always participated in a decisive way.

The Chilean armed forces have shown only too clearly, except to those who do not wish to see, that they no longer feel involved in the defence of the economic interests of the *latifundistas* and industrial-financial high bourgeoisie. In the case of the *latifundistas* one need only remember that their social elimination began under the Frei government, against the most energetic resistance by the proprietors affected and their representatives. The Popular government has only pursued at a more rapid pace, an anti-*latifundista* process already begun. In the case of the financial/industrial bourgeoisie, the achievements of the first year of the Popular government which have removed the principal centres of bourgeois economic power from private control, speak for themselves.

Anyone who faces the Chile of today with realism must have the courage to recognize that there is no social or class antagonism between the government of Allende and the coercive forces of the state. This affirmation may appear rash in this dawn of the revolutionary process. There is no antagonism for a fundamental reason: President Allende's government is committed to the fulfilment of the programme of the Unidad Popular. And this Programme, in an explicit and coherent way, proposes to end the economic power of the high bourgeoisie and of the *latifundistas* – of the economically dominant class. But it respects the middle sectors. It desires neither conflicts nor confrontations with them. Every economic and legislative policy of the government has sought to give them security, and to prevent them being drawn into violent opposition in the service of the dominant class.

It is in relation to these elements that Salvador Allende's frequently repeated affirmation, namely that *my greatest strength lies in legality* acquires its full connotation. It is only by observing the constitution and laws that the Popular government can utilize for its purposes the enormous resources of a modern bourgeois state. All this potential, its very inertia, which now predominantly favours the government – and the balance-sheet of the first twelve months of government speaks for itself – would turn against it if the government should be the first to act beyond the bounds of legality.

Of course, the extent of the transformations allowed by the present legality is a different matter. The structural transformations underway are producing an ever greater maladjustment with a legal and institutional regime devised to regulate a very different social reality. This implies a contradiction which will only be solved by modifying and developing the prevailing normative reality. But these are changes which do not imply, in themselves, the unavoidable necessity of disregarding legality – and its institutional sources – if what President Allende put forward in his First Message to Congress takes place:

> The flexibility of our institutional system allows us to hope that it will not be a rigid barrier of contention. And that together with our legal system it will adapt itself to the new demands in order to generate, through constitutional channels, the new institutionality demanded by the victory over capitalism.[1]

PUBLIC ORDER

The state, power organized in the service of the interests of those social sectors which, at any given moment, have achieved hegemony, assumes, as a secondary form, the function of maintaining order. When revolutionary political forces are marginal to the governing of the state one of their tactical procedures is to question and challenge the conservative state in order to increase the tensions between the demands of the class which makes use of it on the one hand, and those of the class which suffers it, on the other. Public disorder, the pressures against the order of the state – of the social class which directs it – are the external manifestations of the social struggle, which at its point of greatest intensity reaches open and total insurrection.

The Unidad Popular has succeeded in controlling the dynamic and directing centre of the Chilean state without having to seize it by means of a violent insurrection. Instead, it has made use of the normal mechanisms provided by the state to designate the representatives of the general will in the management of the state apparatus. Here again, the observations made with regard to legality are relevant. The Popular government is within the state and can make use of the ample powers institutionally recognized as belonging to the executive. But this requires, undeniably, that it should not violate rules which govern the operations and functioning of the state, and that it should fulfil the essential tasks inherent in governing the state. Among them is that of regulating the social process, including the maintenance of public order.

We are here, apparently, faced with a dilemma. Public order and social revolution have always been in opposition, have excluded

---

[1] 'Primer mensaje al Congreso' in Salvador Allende: *Nuestro Camino al Socialismo, La Via Chilena*, Buenos Aires, Ed. Papiro, 1971, p. 36.

each other in the capitalist system. In the name of the first the external manifestations of revolutionary tensions have been attacked. For some people it remains paradoxical that the Popular government should wish to carry out a socially revolutionary policy while maintaining public order.

But there is no such paradox. On the contrary, both assumptions complement one another at this moment, overlapping to such a degree that if one of them ceased to exist the tactical line of Allende's government could not be maintained and would give way to violent confrontation between Chileans, eventually to civil war. If those changes which are revolutionary in content were conceived and carried out more slowly than the process demands and allows, the government would find itself hindered and harassed by those who, being opposed to it, have the power to obstruct its economic and political management. And this in turn would create conditions such as to prevent the government from containing the attempts at violence on the part of the most extremely radicalized revolutionary sectors. Probably both phenomena would complement one another, in a dialectical relationship.

On the other hand, government action which allowed a state of affairs in which public order was ignored to a degree considered significant in the present circumstances would give the opposition the best pretext to deny the effective existence of governmental authority. This would entail the rejection of the government's legitimate right to use the state mechanisms of order and coercion, and open the way to active civil disobedience. In such circumstances the Popular government can resort to two means of defence, one institutional, the other extra-institutional. The first is the armed forces. The second is the mobilization of the masses and organized workers for the struggle. In realist terms, going beyond formal principles, a situation of such general disorder would place the armed forces in an ambiguous and dubious position to say the least. Not only because the opposition would call on them to intervene to re-establish order (i.e. to alter the course of the revolution), but, above all other considerations, because of the weakness of the government's own situation. Indeed, one must admit that the government's authority in this situation, would be rejected by the conservative sectors. But its authority would also be disputed or unrecognized by the radicalized revolutionary sectors. On what basis then, would the government's authority rest? On a very weak one which institutionally could be described as a 'minority' one. And it is reasonable to suppose that the Popular government can, in principle, count on the support of the armed forces in direct proportion to the amount of popular support it receives, and vice versa. Therefore, a government without real ascendency over the great popular masses and openly attacked by the conservative sectors cannot really expect the armed forces to side unanimously with it.

On 8 June 1970, events took place which served to prove this contention. The assassination of the ex-minister, D. C. Eduardo Pérez Zujovic, provoked the most serious crisis the Popular government has experienced to date. The whole of the opposition united to denounce the indirect responsibility of the government for this crime. For three days the political scene was dominated by calls for military intervention on the one hand, and the fear that such intervention might take place on the other. Since the government had *no part whatsoever* in the action of a completely isolated group of paranoiac activists, it overcame the situation without more serious consequences. And the armed forces remained integrally, from beginning to end, in the position which is institutionally theirs. The government, scarcely two months after the manifestation of popular support it received in the municipal elections of 4 April, found enough strength in this political support and in its internal cohesion to withstand the surge of the furious opposition.

There are thus two major factors which the Popular government must balance day by day: public order and social revolution. Maladjustment between the two can have serious results for the continuity of the process. The government must find a political line the development of which will not drive them apart, since mutual balance is one of the pre-requisites for the progress of revolution in a political way. Lack of balance would lead, by a concatenation of perfectly foreseeable events, to counter-revolution or to armed confrontation.

Nevertheless, there are revolutionary leaders who do not sufficiently perceive all the modifications implied by the move from opposition to government. Opposition imposes on the working-class movement in particular resorting to pressure – in any of its forms – to manifest and eventually to enforce many of the claims which it could not otherwise achieve. But the manipulation of the institutional mechanisms at the disposal of the government permits, in general, and particularly in the present structure and social context of the Chilean state, a range of action which is infinitely greater, more effective and deeper than what can be achieved by any type of pressure. The transformations carried out by the Unidad Popular in its first months of government prove this conclusively. Without one shot being fired, without a single worker being exposed to death, it has achieved more than many armed revolutions in the same period of time – even after these had been installed in power.

This does not, however, exclude the thought of resorting to social pressure – from the bottom – in specific cases or for very concrete objectives. And this has indeed happened on many occasions in the last few months, but in a secondary form and subordinate to government action. It is therefore the opposite of political realism and a deformed vision of the political process to affirm: 'We suggest to the Unidad Popular and to the Government that to rely on the *real protagonists* of the social process under-way would have been more serious and more courageous on their part: between February and October of this year 345,000 industrial workers, peasants, settlers and students have participated in strikes and illegal take-overs who, along with their families amount to more than 1,700,000 people in the country.'[2]

This tactical position, necessary in a violent revolutionary process, carries with it – as an innate and normal characteristic – the need to resort to authoritarian government to further the revolutionary process. In the terms of its prospective programme this is not desired by Allende's government.

The maintenance of public order, is not only a requirement of every government; it always favours whoever controls the government. In the Chilean situation, a revolutionary who supports the present process with regard to public order, must previously accept two assumptions: (a) that the present govern-ment is carrying out a policy of revolutionary orientation, (b) that the institutional apparatus on which the government relies allows it to proceed on its revolutionary path. If a revolutionary denies either of these, logically, he will not accept the kind of social revolution which requires public order in a state with bourgeois roots. But if he shares both assumptions he must be consistent in his reasoning and understand the need for the government to carry forward its programme, while maintaining public order. This is not the moment to enumerate the reasons which give full revolutionary meaning to the work of the Popular government.

[2] Declaration by the National Secretariat of the Movement of the Revolu-tionary Left, Santiago, 8 November 1971.

But the flexibility of the institutional system in terms of clearing
the way for the revolutionary process is another matter which
would require detailed analysis. That those responsible for the
direction of the government believe it possible is proved by the
direction of its evolution in fact and, in its intentions, by the declarations of the governmental parties, particularly that of the President
of the Republic: 'We indeed wish that there should be a very clear
understanding of the fact that public order is one thing and a new
social order quite another. Public order obeys juridical formulae,
legal formulae. Social order implies material things, class positions,
confrontations of interests. The government over which I preside
is the product of an effort made by the popular sectors. We have
maintained public order because that is our duty. We shall bring
about transformations to change the social structures, because for
this purpose we were elected. But we are doing this and shall do
this within a legal and juridical framework. The political constitution of Chile opens the way to the framing of a new up-to-
date constitution and this is a road we shall also take.'[3]

This statement summarizes the fundamental stand of the government on this point. In the first place, while respecting the legal
and institutional order, it is proceeding with the social transformation. This is a necessary prerequisite if the *will* to maintain
public order is to have any real possibility of being put into
practice. Secondly, it regards as inevitable the modification of the
institutional and legal system to adapt it to the new social reality
which is in the process of developing. Here again a maladjustment
between the two processes would threaten a breakdown for the
political road at present being followed.

The Popular government must make a constant effort to
continue with a policy of economic and social transformation,
with revolutionary depth and with all the speed permitted by the
human and technical resources now available. At the same time,
however, it must very carefully calculate beforehand its plan of
concrete achievements, their order and their manifest and latent
effects so that they may develop in step with the increasing power
of control of the popular movements and, particularly, of the
government. This power of control would thus be capable
of absorbing or neutralizing the tensions produced by the
changes, both in those social sectors whose privileges are being
openly attacked, and in the sectors which are assuming greater

[3] Salvador Allende, *Nuestro Camino al Socialismo, op. cit.*, pp. 87–8, Inaugural
speech at the eighth International Fair at Talca, 6 March 1971.

responsibilities and seeing new prospects opening before them.

If in any revolutionary process the unity and cohesion of the popular forces is of the greatest relevance, in the Chilean case it is a prerequisite *sine qua non*. When a revolutionary government disposes of the monopoly of coercive force, subordinate to its own political criteria, it can consider using it to preserve the future of its policy in the face of those who threaten it within the left itself. This has happened, at one time or another, in all socialist experiments, with positive or negative results according to cases and circumstances. But in Chile now, when the apparatus of the state inspires and legitimizes its functioning according to pre-dominantly bourgeois criteria, when the capitalist class not only retains an important part of its economic power but also has complete freedom to act as a political opposition – even to act demagogically, when – at the state level – the Chilean revolutionary process meets with little support among its immediate neighbours, when the Popular government bases itself entirely on freely given popular support, to fragment the conscious identification of the popular sectors with the government will quite simply lead to the erosion or undermining of its political base. And the situation becomes much more serious if not only indifference or passivity but active hostility towards the Popular government develops in the public sector. To maintain public order against abnormal pressures from the popular sectors would mean that the government would have to confront itself, with all the negative consequences that this implies.

For this very reason the opposition has, from the first, tried to breach the unity of the popular sectors which support the government, using all the resources available to a political opposition which can speak – and offer inducements – without responsibility. They misrepresent the meaning of the achievements which correspond to the logic of development towards a socialist socio-economic organization. For example, they suggest that the social ownership of a company would signify for its employees only the replacement of the private manager by the state-manager, even if the workers themselves assume the fullest responsibility in the running of their company. Or the opposition contrasts the revolutionary achievements with demagogic chimaera which, put into practice, would mean the rapid dissolution of the social body amidst the greatest chaos. For example, it proposes that the management of nationalized monopolist companies – including the banks – and their surplus, should be left to the free decision of their workers, in the midst of a capitalist economic system and in accordance with its internal logic.

In a systematic and very concrete way, throughout the whole of 1971, the opposition has in fact been fostering scepticism, a split in the workers' movement, confrontation amongst workers and even chaos. In itself, this weakens the government. Moreover it places the government in a dilemma: either it must try to maintain public order – which brings it into conflict with the workers – or it shows itself incapable of maintaining public order – which opens the door to authoritarian solutions of 'pacification'. In the one case as in the other, the counter-revolution synchronizes the complete utilization of its capacity to cause disorder with the tensions between workers and the Popular government, in order completely to destroy the latter and afterwards to repress the former. This is the sad lesson of the Second Spanish Republic.

Day after day, from the very date on which Salvador Allende assumed the presidency, the front pages of all opposition newspapers have collected and magnified any incident which could be interpreted as abnormal or disorderly, from the relevant to the insignificant, whether its cause is to be found in a conscious political action or in circumstances totally outside the dynamics of the Popular government. The objective is obvious: to create the image of bad government or chaos. Thus it matters little that the number of agricultural properties *occupied* by peasants is no more than 0·5% of the total for the country. The situation is portrayed as *anarchy and violence in the countryside*. Thus the opposition has made intelligent use of biased news and has been the more successful, because, one must admit, of the technical incapacity of the mass-media of the left, their failure to devise an information service with modern, effective criteria, even to provide counter-information to the campaigns of the opposition.

There is a reverse side to the coin: that public disorder should be provoked by conservative movements, groups or people. If the coherent popular movement keeps solidly behind the government, the government in turn can rely on the use of the institutional coercive force to make the state's function of maintaining order a real one. Perhaps the best – if negative – proof of this has been the extreme care which the opposition – including the fascist opposition – has taken to avoid creating such a situation in 1971. When on 18 November the opposition was carried away by passion, lost their grip, and forced an entrance into the Palacio de la Moneda, they presented the government with the possibility of dealing with fifteen opposition deputies under the law of internal security of the state (Seguridad Interior del Estado) – a dispute in which the Corps of Carabineros itself also took part.

As long as the Popular government can depend on the organized and disciplined support of the majority any disturbance of public order by the conservative sectors is bound to bring them into conflict with the repressive logic of the liberal state itself. This is no paradox, though it may seem one, in a state whose government is entrusted, institutionally, to the representatives of the majority, of Rousseau's *volonté générale*. The apparent paradox is but the result of the one essential fact that the very mechanisms of the liberal political system have been successfully used by the socialist movements to take over the state. In this way the socialist movement has started to change the class significance of the state, since it is not so much the institutions which give a state apparatus its bourgeois nature but rather the social forces which animate and use it.

THE ECONOMIC ORDER

Socialism seeks to create the material and cultural conditions which make man a free being in all the manifestations of human life. The growth of revolutionary social forces and anti-capitalist political values is the result, in the first place of economic exploitation, social subordination and poverty to which the capitalist economic system condemns the great popular masses. In every country, anti-system movements reach a greater or lesser degree of power, in absolute terms, depending on the expansion of its internal potential which each particular economic structure has achieved. But exploitation, subordination and poverty, speaking in relative terms, differentiates some social classes from others, in any capitalist country. It is in the revolt against this situation that one finds the cause and the legitimation of the modern revolutions.

Political awareness about a given socio-economic regime is not always concrete and precise, more particularly so among the social sectors of lower cultural level. In a contemporary capitalist society the direct or indirect control exercised by the institutions of capital over the nerve centres of the social process is so great and can be so effective with present-day technological and scientific methods, that the accumulation of very exceptional circumstances is required for the great masses to succeed in escaping from it, and to formulate clearly and explicitly their own anti-capitalist values, beliefs and sentiments. Much time, and great perseverence is necessary.

It would be useless to think that only when the new political values favourable to socialism have become concrete and specific among the majority of the population, could a revolutionary political movement expect to receive its support. It has never happened thus, and there is no reason why it should. In the first place, not all the public sectors – however exploited and dis-criminated against – combine the economic and socio-cultural con-ditions necessary to generate a revolutionary socialist political conscience. If it has always been said that the proletariat would assume the leadership in the struggle against the capitalist regime, it is because the proletariat – more than any other social sector – possesses these conditions. But in a modern industrial society the so-called proletariat has never constituted more than one third of the economically active population, and not so much in economic systems of less industrial development. It has had to ally itself with other exploited social sectors, both in the struggle for power, and in the transition to socialism, once power has been won.

Secondly, in the real political world, it is not necessary for political values to become explicit and concrete in order to influence the political process. Even in a latent state they can contribute in a functional sense to the development of the social movement around which they revolve.

This explains why, of the 36·3 per cent of the electorate who voted in September 1970 for the government programme of the Unidad Popular, and of the 50 per cent who, in the following April, supported the government of Salvador Allende, only a limited percentage – the size of which would be too complicated to study here – consciously voted in favour of a socialist concep-tion of economic, political and social order. The rest acted rather by deliberately rejecting the negative manifestations with which the economic regime in power oppressed their personal or group lives: poverty and starvation, redundancy, disguised unemploy-ment, very high rates of chronic inflation, shortage of housing, all of them resulting from a profoundly unbalanced static economic structure, of which the development is subjected to internal and external limitations.

A revolutionary government like President Allende's, the

formal origin and real authority of which lies in the freely expressed support of the neglected masses, faces the fearful challenge which is implicit in having to satisfy – *simultaneously* – some of the material needs most painfully felt by the workers, peasants, employees and the rest of the neglected masses on the one hand; and at the same time, to carry through the great socio-economic transformations which the revolutionary process demands.

In all previous socialist revolutions this problem has been tackled in many different ways. But they have all had one common feature: the suppression of free demand in accordance with the norms of the capitalist market. The state has controlled not only the *supply* of goods and services but also the *demand* for them. When, for some reason or another, it was impossible to supply certain goods, the state disposed of adequate economic mechanisms to control the situation, ranging from the total suppression of the sale of the product to rationing in any form. The state has also possessed the requisite administrative and political apparatus to convince the citizens of the reasons for such shortages. In the last resort, the state's control of information and of the mass-media enables it to prevent any building up of the sense of the existence of shortages by controlling the expression of demand.

All this implies that the economic system functions on totally different bases from those of capitalism. It is not the great companies which direct production and consumption, through their vast and sophisticated machines, seeking the incessant increase in consumption in accordance with the rules of maximum profit; it is the state to which the economic production of socialized companies – at least the basic ones – is subordinate and which seeks to satisfy general needs, in accordance with more rational criteria of social and human priority, guided by its own norms. Demand must therefore be controlled, in order to adjust it to the general process of production.

The power of the socialist state must thus rest on very different bases from those which shape the activity of the liberal-democratic state. At a stage of economic development when needs of all kinds, both individual and collective, are much greater than the capacity to satisfy them, the control of the free expression of economic demand leads on to another requirement: the limitation, if not the suppression of the free manifestation of the political opposition. The latter always exploits unsatisfied demands – economic as well as political – to its own advantage. Any opposition tends to underline existent expectations and to create new ones.

This seems to be a vicious circle. In order to proceed with economic, social and political transformations, a revolutionary government must limit or suppress the capitalist market rules, which control demand. And this can lead it, willy-nilly, to limit the free expression – and even the existence – of the political opposition. Is it not then possible to transform a capitalist economic system, while accepting the existence of the political opposition? From the theoretical point of view, the transition towards socialism does not necessarily imply the suppression of the liberty to oppose the revolutionary government. Everything depends on the circumstances in which the process develops, and, fundamentally, on the correlation of forces between the revolutionary movement and the non-revolutionary opposition, not only inside the country but also in the countries surrounding it, and even in the rest of the world. In the last third of the 20th century, bearing in mind the degree of global integration and interdependence, no national process can develop independently of the concrete situation in the rest of the world; nor, in the struggle between socialism and capitalism, can the state of the capitalist and socialist blocks nor the relations between them be left out of account.

When violent confrontation between revolutionary and anti-revolutionary forces takes place in circumstances of reciprocal exclusion and of the precarious superiority of one over the other, the preponderance of the latter has led to a blood-bath for the workers and to reactionary authoritarian dictatorship. The predominance of the revolutionary forces has led to their affirmation and consolidation by means of the forced submission of the anti-revolutionaries. In both cases, the negation of the opposition has appeared as a requisite for survival. The harsh reality of facts imposes itself on more tolerant wishes.

Nevertheless, it is possible to conceive of the development of the revolution towards socialism in a regime of respect for the free opposition. In the first place, the revolutionary movement must have succeeded in creating the social, economic and political factors which would enable it to consider itself as objectively superior to the organized, opposing – national and foreign – capitalist forces. Secondly, the political system must have reached a high level of democratic institutionalization, which might permit it to absorb the activities of the opposition without permanent danger of institutional collapse. To the extent that the government of President Allende is increasing its popular base, developing the organization of the parties and unions which support it, and proceeding with the transformation of the political values of the masses, one can reasonably assume that it is securing for itself the strength sufficient to continue the revolution, while recognizing the political opposition. Counting on the majority support of the country, the new institutionality can be progressively constructed – without the violent rupture of the inherited institutionality.

To be victorious in this great challenge the Popular government must overcome enormous difficulties which accumulate or closely follow one another. In the strictly economic field it seems clear that the government has a great capacity for controlling supply by means of the mechanisms for intervention acquired by the Chilean state over a long period. Not so in the case of demand, in which it must make use of the traditional mechanisms of prices and wages, deeply corroded and vitiated by the chronic inflation which has dragged on for decades. The Chilean consumer has been guided by criteria of the freedom of demand, and to change this factor would run counter to the context of complete political freedom, in all its aspects, for the opposition. The government does not control information, still less, propaganda. Scarcely 50 per cent of radio-stations and of the press follows its political line. Its economic policy is at the service of the poorest among the masses. It must satisfy their most imperative needs at a rapid, if not lightning, pace. Otherwise the sectors with the least developed political consciousness might be won over by the demagogic promises of the opposition. Allende's government must demonstrate something very unusual, that revolution means immediate, and not only future, material improvements. It must increase the consumer capacity of the masses, in the context of a market economy ruled by the classic norm, i.e. that subjective needs increase with the available material resources, and in which, therefore, the greater purchasing power exacts the existence of the goods sought. Recourse to rationing some of these is presented by the opposition as a failure by the government, and considered as such by the majority of consumers. This, inevitably, is reflected in electoral behaviour.

The Popular government needs uninterrupted and rapid economic expansion to ensure a greater capacity to satisfy the consumer. Hence the emphasis, throughout 1971 on mobilization for the battle for production. Only a spectacular increase in production can prevent generalized scarcity or the rationing of goods.

This is a simple, partial manifestation of a more general hypothesis. The political power of the Popular government is indissolubly linked with its short term economic success. Those socialist revolutions which have been consolidated have been able to survive great economic crises because their power rested on totally different foundations from those of Allende's government. The road followed by the Chilean government requires economic effectiveness as a *sine qua non*.

Again the question: Is it possible to transform the socio-economic structures without damaging economic growth? There is still no definite answer. As in the case of public order, Allende's government has the institutional duty – and the revolutionary need – to achieve good economic order. It can achieve it to the extent to which it controls the strategic, internal economic factors, and uses them adequately. It also requires that the economic factors external to Chile, the control of which is beyond it, should not be too adverse, and this, in accordance with a time sequence which implies neither delays nor foolish haste.

We can be sure of this: the advance along such a narrow path will serve to prove that the Chilean anti-capitalist forces are objectively more powerful than the capitalist ones, within the country, and that capitalism, in the countries surrounding Chile, cannot now easily destroy a budding revolution.

RELATIONS AMONG THE POWERS OF THE STATE

The present structure of the Chilean state is that of the equilibrium/autonomy of powers, one of the most rigid autonomies established in modern constitutions. The judicial power is more independent of the executive in Chile than in the United States. In Washington the judges of the Supreme Court are appointed by the Head of State with the approval of the upper Chamber of Congress. In Santiago the Supreme Court itself puts forward the names from among which the Head of State nominates the new minister of the highest court of justice. The Chilean executive cannot dissolve Congress and only after 1969 was allowed to resort to the referendum in order to overcome the opposition of parliament. But it can only use this method for amendments to the text of the constitution, and then only after a long and complicated process, in the course of which parliament can profoundly alter the initiative of the executive, in such a way that the text finally submitted to popular consultation can be totally different from the one initially proposed by the executive.

A government like that of the Unidad Popular, with a minority in parliament can, therefore, face obstruction and institutional blockade. All the more because parliament can accuse, judge and condemn ministers for failure to observe the constitution. This applies even to the President of the Republic himself. One of the essential bases on which the present Chilean process rests is the absence of confrontation between Popular government and constitutional regime. But such confrontation can hypothetically be provoked by the parliamentary opposition without the executive having the adequate legal mechanisms at its disposal to overcome it. Such a project was publicly launched as a programme for action by a right-wing senator of the Radical Democratic Party on 13 January 1971.[4]

The Popular government has tried hard to avoid creating a situation of confrontation with the other independent powers of the state. It has respected the decisions of the law courts, although it has vigorously denounced the class spirit which inspires some of its sentences (e.g. the rejection by the Supreme Court, at the beginning of 1971, of the charges against Senator Morales Adriasola; he had been accused of conspiring against the security of the state to prevent Salvador Allende assuming the presidency). In 1971, however, no matter of vital importance for government policy did in fact go before the courts. There has thus not been any real occasion for a possible confrontation between the executive and the judiciary. Only when such a situation should arise can its implications be considered. But for the time being, this has not been a source of conflict for the government.

On the other hand, the matters with which the Contraloría General of the Republic has had to deal have been of the utmost importance. Inevitably the Popular government, making use of its administrative power to carry out its wide-ranging transforming and innovating policies, has been unable to avoid conflict with the traditional practices and criteria of the Contraloría. This has occurred particularly when companies in private ownership were placed under the direct control of the state and the workers. Had there been an appeal against the decisions of the Contraloría the

[4] Speech by R. Morales Adriasola in the Audax Club, 13 January 1971.

conflict between it and the government would have been insoluble. Confrontation would have ended in crisis. But this has not been the case. On several occasions the government has exercised its ordinary powers under the 'Decreto de Insistencia', which allows it to overcome the opposition of the Contraloría. In turn, the Contraloría, by appealing to parliament, as occasion arose, has given the opportunity to the legislative power to examine and sanction government decisions.

Here we reach the centre of gravity of the institutional opposition to the Popular government, i.e. the parliament. When drawing up the balance sheet of the first year of the Popular government in its relations with parliament, one might well refer to the frequently repeated declaration of President Allende: 'No President of the Republic has reproached Parliament less than I have.' Why? In the first place, because the government has avoided confrontation with the legislative power. But this is a secondary effect rather than a cause. The fundamental, and complementary, reasons are two:

(1) Because the executive has, institutionally, at its disposal a most comprehensive complex of statutory or discretional powers to carry through its political programme in all aspects, without the intervention of parliament.

(2) Because the Christian Democrat Party which holds the balance in parliament has not wished to appear openly to reject the social changes promoted by the Unidad Popular.

Behind these two political reasons are others of a social nature which make them possible. In the first place, the Popular government relies on wide popular support both highly conscious and organized, and which was manifested in the municipal elections of 4 April 1971. Secondly, what some people have called an 'electoral draw' between government and opposition at national level is something very different from a 'political draw'. The first was a reality in 1971, the second was not. The political draw became impossible from the moment when an important sector of the principal opposition party, the Christian Democrats, began to share many of the aims of the Unidad Popular – even if many did not accept the means or the ultimate goals. For whereas the government coalition block has a homogeneous programme, within the opposition there is an important sector which is identified with an anti-capitalist and anti-imperialist rather than a pro-imperialist and anti-socialist policy.

The fact that there is no political 'draw' in Chile, but rather a social disequilibrium in favour of revolutionary transformations, leads to most important consequences.

(1) *The Nationalization of Copper*. The opposition majority which controls both chambers of Congress unanimously approved the nationalization of the large copper mines, in conformity with the fundamental criteria proposed by the government on 11 July 1971. It also legalized President Allende's decision to reduce the indemnity by 774 million dollars, because of the swollen capitalization of the North American companies between 1955 and 1969, by decree of 28 September 1971. Thus, in fact Allende's government has carried through the most important measure of confrontation with North American capital, paying practically no indemnity, but with the explicit institutional and political backing of the *whole* of Chile. This is a great and unprecedented national victory.

The nationalization of copper could be carried out in this way because the government chose to incorporate it in the text of the constitution. This opened the way for the use of the referendum should Congress oppose the measure. Great political pressure was brought to bear on the opposition parties. But any other policy would have given the government an easy electoral victory, in which Allende would have assumed the national position, and the opposition that of defenders of North American interests – at heavy political cost for them.

(2) *Constitutional Legitimation of the Government's Policy*. We have alluded above to the hegemony of the executive in the prevailing structure of the Chilean state, and to the broad legal powers accumulated by successive governments in a political system characterized historically by the intervention and strong control of the economic process through the apparatus of the bourgeois state. Both factors were indispensable for the Popular government to be able to begin to apply its programme while respecting legal norms. But there is no doubt that, in the last extreme, what we have here is a neo-liberal state apparatus used by an essentially anti-capitalist government. It was inevitable that contradictions should appear, however the government might act, in certain fundamental measures such as the transference of private monopolies to the socialized area, when legality is pushed to its limits.

Parliament has examined those contradictions and these extreme legal actions in many excited debates, and also by means of constitutional interpellations of various ministers. The National Party has successively accused the Ministers of Justice, Labour and Economy of violating the constitution and legal norms.[5] But their accusations proved fruitless and indeed counterproductive precisely because there was no political-social 'draw' in the country. The Christian Democrat Party refused to give parliamentary support to these accusations, which was necessary for them to succeed.

The government has evaded confrontation with parliament and the Christian Democrat Party has evaded confrontation with the Popular government. This is the main political feature of President Allende's first year. But this has naturally not prevented the Christian Democrat Party from flatly rejecting legislative measures of the executive, e.g. the creation of Neighbourhood Courts, the replacement of the bicameral system by a unicameral system. An *impasse* has been avoided because the government has ceased to regard these projects as urgent and has withdrawn them from parliamentary debate. In the same way the Christian Democrats have not refrained from proposing amendments to legislation submitted by the executive, and have used their decisive weight to try to impose their own criteria on the government. This occurred in the fundamental case of the draft law establishing the three areas of the economy, which legalized the nationalization of strategic companies and the mechanisms of workers' participation in their management, which had until then been put into effect by 'administrative' means.[6] The parliamentary debate goes on at the time of writing but the Christian Democrats have almost completely amended the government's original draft.

To sum up, the tactical assumptions which have enabled the Popular government to carry out its policy during 1971 without a parliamentary crisis are: (a) the availability of a wide margin of action reserved for decisions belonging to the administrative and mandatory power of the executive; (b) the deliberate desire to avoid conflict with the middle sectors and their representative institutions – social, economic and political; (c) the decision of the government to operate within the institutional framework.

On its part, the Christian Democrat Party has modelled its policies in 1971 in accordance with principles natural to an opposition which desires to operate within the democratic frame-

[5] The National Party constitutionally impeached the Minister of Justice in January 1971; the Minister of Labour on 10 March; the Minister of Economy, on 7 September.

[6] The draft law of the Three Areas and workers' participation was signed by President Allende, 19 October 1971.

work of the Chilean system, seeking such objectives as: (a) to discredit the government's image, by presenting itself as an alternative better equipped to ensure 'social evolution in liberty'; (b) to erode the popular base of the government by stressing factors which could make the workers enter into conflict with the government (increase in salaries, immediate satisfaction of social needs, private ownership of expropriated lands, 'enterprises to the workers' etc); (c) to maintain the present relationship of forces in parliament which places it at the centre of the balance. And to ensure the continuation in office of those who at present direct the judiciary, which they have achieved by rejecting the project of constitutional reform of the executive, of 10 November 1971, proposing a renewal of the corporation of the Supreme Court, and a time limit on their exercise of judicial power.

As for the Right – the National Party and the Radical Democratic Party – their relative isolation has reduced them simply to supporting the Christian Democrats when the question of opposing the government arises. They have thus submitted themselves to pursue only those possibilities which Christian Democrat parliamentary policy permitted them.

But the revolutionary process has progressed considerably during 1971, and the starting positions have been changed to that extent. What in November 1970 was 'a wide range' of statutory power at the disposal of the executive, has now mostly been used up. Transformations in the institutional structure of the state to adjust it to the new socio-economic reality and to its dynamics, have become more and more imperative. On the other hand the initial differences with the Christian Democrat Party have increased in conformity with the logical development of the contradictions between the Programme of the Unidad Popular and that of the Christian Democrats. The fact that on 3 December 1971 the leadership of the Christian Democrat Party decided, by 10 votes to 8, to impeach the Minister of the Interior is clear evidence and prefigures the party's hardening against the government, and the internal crisis it will thus provoke.

The next electoral consultation will take place in March 1973 to elect all the members of the Chamber of Deputies and half the membership of the Senate. The whole of 1972 lies ahead, a difficult but decisive year. For in 1972 a definitive electoral confrontation might take place should the project for constitutional reform, presented in November, lead to a referendum.

The Chilean revolution demands institutional transformations in order to proceed on the way it has planned. The key to these is to be found in parliament, the socio-political composition of which depends on the will of the electorate. It is the electorate which must decide the content and future means by which the capitalist regime in Chile will be overthrown. The will of the electorate will depend on the fortune which will have attended the developments outlined above.

J. Biehl del Río and Gonzalo Fernández R.

4   The Political Pre-requisites for a Chilean Way

WE PROPOSE TO ANALYSE HERE SOME OF THE BASIC PROBLEMS POSED
by the attempt to pursue 'the Chilean road to socialism', and in
particular to assess the possibilities of successfully following this
path within the political and constitutional framework in being
when Allende became president, always bearing in mind that he
came to power with the support of 36·3% (or little more than one
third) of the popular vote. It is necessary first to discuss the
constitutional system, the background to the 1970 election and the
election campaign. This will serve to place Allende and his
coalition in proper perspective. Subsequently we will attempt to
analyse the legal and political resources at Allende's disposal after
his election in order to see if the powers these gave him were
sufficient for the Unidad Popular to honour its commitments and
the alternative strategies he could have pursued when and if these
resources proved insufficient. Finally, there will be some discussion of the present state of the Unidad Popular, and its future
prospects.

CONSTITUTIONAL BACKGROUND

The constitution under which Chile is at present governed dates
from 1925. This document declared Chile to be a unitary state
with a republican representative form of government. The legal
basis of the governmental system is the classic separation of
executive, legislative and judicial power with the executive clearly
predominant over the other two.

The executive power. Article 60 of the constitution states that 'a
citizen with the title of President of the Republic of Chile adminis-
ters the state and is supreme head of the nation'. This president is
elected for one six-year term and he may not immediately succeed

himself. The election, which is initially by direct popular vote,[1] has to be held sixty days before the day on which the incumbent president's term of office expires. The procedure after the popular vote has taken place is established in Article 64. It lays down that both houses of Congress, in a public session convened within fifty days of the election, shall proclaim as president the candidate who has obtained over half the validly cast votes. Thus it is usual for Congress to follow the alternative course of action foreseen in the constitution which is (again in a session of both houses) to choose the president from amongst the two candidates who have been most successful in the popular ballot.

Once elected the president is free to appoint and remove his ministers. The latter cannot be members of Congress but they have the right to participate, without a vote, in its debates. There is no question of collective or cabinet responsibility to Congress but individual ministers can be held responsible for failing properly to fulfil their ministerial functions. In reality the spirit of the constitution is, at this point, frequently not observed for the procedure is often used to make atttacks of a political nature upon ministers.

Despite this, the executive power plays a decisive role in the legislative process. Laws may not only originate within the Chamber of Deputies or in the Senate but also (and most frequently) in messages sent by the president. Furthermore some very important types of law are bound to stem from the president. Thus, article 46 states that . . . 'supplementary financial measures on the general budgetary law may only be introduced by the President of the Republic. The President shall also have exclusive power to initiate legislation involving the political or administrative division of the country, the creation of new public services or temporary positions, and the granting or increase of salaries and gratuities to the personnel of the Civil Service and the nationalized and semi-independent corporations. The national Congress may only accept, reduce or reject the services, positions, emoluments or increases which are proposed . . .'[2] Such prerogatives, moreover, have been further extended by constitutional reforms approved during Frei's administration.

[1] All literate Chileans over 21 had the duty to vote in elections. Towards the end of the Frei administration a constitutional reform lowered the age to 18, and extended the vote to illiterates.

[2] Cf. Paul Sigmund, *Models of Political Change in Latin America*, Praeger Inc., New York, 1970.

The president is also empowered to speed up the legislative process. Thus article 46 indicates that when the president declares the dispatch of a bill to be a matter of urgency, the respective Chamber has thirty days in which to come to a decision. Later on it is the president who promulgates laws. If, however, he disapproves of a Bill which may be sent to him . . . 'he shall return it to the Chamber of origin with suitable suggestions within 30 days' (Article 53). To override such a 'veto' requires the vote of two thirds of those present.

Another important presidential prerogative is the rule or ordinance-making power (*Potestad Reglamentaria*) through which the state apparatus is administered. Administrative decrees, issued in the use of this power are of considerable importance for often, when implementing laws, the executive enjoys great discretion on points of interpretation and so may be enabled to pursue its own policy objectives.

In the past there have been two other types of decree. Decree Laws (Decretos–Leyes) and decrees having the force of law (Decretos con fuerza de ley). The latter are presidential decrees issued by virtue of a delegation of powers from Congress to deal with specific matters stated in the act of delegation. The constitutionality of this device is doubtful but many properly constituted governments have made use of it.

The Decree Law has been the characteristic legal instrument of *de facto* governments who have usurped congressional authority. Its unconstitutionality is apparent but some laws instituted in this way have been sanctioned through usage and are still in being.

Further proof of the executive's leading role exists in the realm of foreign policy making which is almost entirely in its hands, subject to Congressional approval for such important matters as the declaration of war, the signature of treaties and the nomination of ambassadors.

Finally, under this heading, mention should be made of a constitutional reform approved during Frei's presidency. It applies to situations in which the president and Congress are deadlocked over the question of constitutional reform. The president, in such circumstances, can call a national plebiscite which, if it approves his position, will lead to the dissolution of Congress and the calling of fresh elections. The president can, however, only use this prerogative once during his term of office.

The Legislature. The Congress is bi-cameral, consisting of a Chamber of Deputies with 150 members and a Senate with 50

members. Deputies are elected for four-year periods, by Departments (sub-divisions of Provinces) on the basis of one for every
30,000 inhabitants or a fraction of 30,000 if it is not less than
15,000. The calculations have been made, however, with reference
to a census taken in 1931 when the population was half its present
level. Subsequent censuses have not been officially approved
precisely because this would lead to an increase in the size of the
chamber. The Senators are elected by ten provincial groupings
(*agrupaciones*) with five Senators for each grouping. Their term of
office lasts for eight years, with half their number being subject to
re-election every four years, at the same time as elections to the
lower house.

The constitution grants specific powers to each chamber and to
both acting in conjunction. These cannot be examined here in
detail but one may say, in general terms, that the lower house acts
as a check upon all senior members of the administration and the
Senate must share responsibility with the president for decisions
considered vital for the nation, such as declarations of war and
international treaties. Both houses are fully involved in the
legislative process but, as already noted, it takes a two-thirds
majority to override a presidential veto.

Two special points about this situation require underlining.
Firstly, congressional elections (and local government elections)
are conducted upon the basis of the Victor D'Hont system of
proportional representation. This is designed to allow for the
representation of the maximum number of political tendencies
and, in practice, has probably done something to encourage the
fragmentation of parties and has aggravated the problem of
constructing viable coalitions capable of electing presidents and of
providing them with continuing support. Secondly, it must be
noted that presidential and congressional elections occur at
different times which, given fluctuations in the state of public
opinion, can lead to the election of presidents and Congresses
hostile to one another and therefore incapable of cooperating in
the resolution of pressing national problems.

The Judiciary. The judiciary is characterized by its formal
independence and, in practice, by a long established tradition of
attachment to the present constitutional order. Members of the
judiciary are only responsible to their superiors. The Supreme
Court, the ultimate judicial authority, has thirteen members.
They are appointed by the President of the Republic but he can
only choose from a list of five candidates presented to him by

the Supreme Court itself. Once nominated they remain in office until they choose to retire unless they are subjected to disciplinary measures.

The Supreme Court's main function is to see that all lower courts interpret the law in a uniform fashion and to pronounce upon the constitutionality of laws. Legally it can only veto the application of a law in a particular case and must leave the law on the books. Nevertheless, the Supreme Court can in reality render a particular law useless by consistently obstructing its implementation. Moreover, such powers, in practice, have tended to be used to obstruct legislation harmful to the interests of the wealthier sectors of the society.

Contraloría General de la Republica. This institution is sometimes considered as the fourth power of the state. Its head, the Contralor, is independent of the other three powers. He is appointed with the Senate's agreement and can only be removed with the latter's approval. The institution's main function is to ensure that all decrees emanating from the executive conform to the law. If a given decree is held to be illegal it is returned to the president. He has to amend the decree in question or else insist on pushing it through, in which case he must obtain the signatures of all his cabinet who may be subsequently held to account for their action by the legislature.

POLITICAL BACKGROUND TO THE 1970 ELECTION

United Fronts embracing Marxist parties bent on coming to power by legal means are not a new phenomenon in Chile.

During the 1930s, when Europe was faced with the growth of Nazism and Fascism, Chile self-consciously followed the European example and witnessed the advent of a 'Popular Front'. Thus the call of the 7th Congress of the International Communist movement (held in Moscow in 1935) to form broadly based anti-fascist alliances, led, in Chile, to the formation of a *Frente Popular*. This alliance, containing the Radical Party, the socialists, the communists and two other parties, won the 1938 presidential election under the leadership of a Radical Party member, Pedro Aguirre Cerda. From the start, however, the strength of the new government was sapped by internal dissension. Radicals and socialists fought over the distribution of patronage whilst socialists and communists feuded about the implications of the second world war and struggled for control over organized labour.

Moreover, the Communist Party merely gave conditional congressional support to the government and the socialists were uneasy about participation. The latter, in fact, eventually split over the whole question of participation. Thus, on the president's death in 1941, the front collapsed.

Nevertheless, the Popular Front was succeeded by other centre-left coalitions. In 1942 another radical, Juan A. Ríos, won the presidency at the head of a 'Democratic Alliance' composed of communists, socialists and his own party. Like its predecessor the impact of Ríos's government was limited because of continuous friction between the coalition's constituent groups and between the president and his followers. Also like its predecessor the administration ended with the president's death and, in 1946, fresh presidential elections had to be convened. In these elections the Marxist left for the last time backed a radical candidate, Gonzalez Videla, who came to power, thanks to an unlikely alliance including not only the communists, but also the Liberal Party.

For five months after his election Gonzalez Videla ruled with the aid of three communist members. But, he eventually turned on his erstwhile allies and obtained congressional approval for a 'Law for the Defence of Democracy' that eliminated all known communists from the electoral registers and confined them to remote areas.[3] This marked an end to the long partnership of the Marxist left and the Radical Party; a partnership that was only revived (in very different circumstances) prior to the 1970 elections. As recently as 1968 the Socialist Party declared '. . . Likewise we cannot accept alliances with the Radical Party, for this would merely re-establish another version of the now discredited policy of conciliation and compromise, which has created the present crisis in Chile. We know that because of its social composition, its ideological history, its political habits and the interests and aspirations of its members, as well as its links with imperialism, the Radical Party could not form an alliance with the revolutionary social and political forces.'[4]

Between 1948 and 1970 the Marxist left three times entered presidential elections under the leadership of Allende, namely in 1952, 1958 and 1964. In 1958, Allende, with support from the

[3] See H. Bicheno, below, p. 382.
[4] Declaration of the Executive Committee of the Socialist Party published in No. 46 of *Punto Final*, Santiago, 16 January 1968. Translated by P. Sigmund, *op. cit.*

Communist and Socialist Parties, came very close to victory. The other candidates were Jorge Alessandri leading the traditional right-wing parties, Eduardo Frei leading the Christian Democratic Party, Luis Bossay for the Radical Party and an obscure defrocked priest, Antonio Zamorano. The latter, who had some localized support, took away enough votes from Allende to deny him victory. The results of this election were:

Alessandri	389,909 votes
Allende	356,493 votes
Frei	255,769 votes
Bossay	190,077 votes
Zamorano	41,304 votes

In the ensuing congressional election Alessandri was elected but it is important to note that members of Allende's coalition continued to give their votes to the candidate who had come in second in the popular ballot.

Allende's near success in 1958 is probably the main reason why this coalition remained together and also entered the 1964 elections with the same candidate. This time, however, the circumstances were different for the right wing, following a by-election defeat, threw their support behind Frei who consequently got 55·7% of the popular vote against Allende's 38·6%.

Frei's administration acting under the slogan of 'revolution in freedom' was for a while regarded as an alternative model for Latin America to Castro's regime. It failed, however, to fulfil many of the expectations it had aroused. Particularly in the case of land reform, policies were implemented that affected powerful interests, thus creating bitter right-wing opposition. On the other hand, a more radical Christian Democratic group became increasingly impatient with Frei's policies, particularly with what they regarded as an unwillingness to depart radically from the existing capitalist system. This group finally left the party in 1969 and formed the MAPU, which was involved from the beginning in building the 'Unidad Popular'. Their departure, however, did not end the Christian Democratic Party's internal divisions and it became apparent that there were two main tendencies represented by Frei on the one hand and Tomic on the other. In this situation and confronted by an impressive decline in popular support for the Christian Democrats, from 42% in the congressional elections of 1965 to 29% in those of 1969, Tomic, as his party's presidential candidate, decided upon an opening to the left. He had the clear intention of avoiding the 'structural engagements' that prevented Frei from going further and also of producing a coalition strong enough to overcome the right which, by the end of Frei's administration, had experienced an impressive revival.

Tomic put his proposals to the Marxists parties but they were sharply rejected in terms that can best be summarized in the picturesque words of the Communist Party, 'with Tomic not even to Church'. After this rejection it was clear that Tomic had to face the presidential campaign with his own party and a very small group, *Padena*, that represented only 1·9% of the votes. Tomic could not and would not consider the alternative possibility of a right-wing coalition and was in fact preoccupied with his original idea of an opening to the left all through the campaign. This situation led the right wing to coin the slogan, with reference to Tomic and Allende 'They are the same – give your vote to somebody else'.

The right was led by ex-President Alessandri, a name and a personality with immense support in the country. He gave the right great confidence, particularly after the early opinion polls which showed him clearly ahead of the other candidates. The amount of middle- and working-class support this candidate managed to enlist was going to prove fatal for Tomic and almost fatal for Allende. In fact the support Alessandri got is one of the most striking features of this election.

The third candidate was Allende, backed by four political parties and two political movements, his principal political support coming from the Communist, Socialist and Radical Parties. In theory this coalition had the best electoral prospects, as long as the field was restricted to three candidates, for in 1964 it won 38·6% of the votes without Radical Party support.

Before electing their candidate this left-wing coalition decided on a joint programme for their future government, a programme which in fact constitutes the *vía chilena* (the Chilean way). This programme was agreed upon with remarkably little friction but the same did not apply to the choice of a candidate. Allende was finally nominated, having once been rejected by his own party. The decisive influence in his favour was that of the Communist Party.

The campaign and the election. It is important to consider campaign strategy even if briefly, because it helps to explain post-election developments.

Alessandri levelled his attacks equally against Allende and

Tomic and based his own claims to office purely upon his own personal qualities. His personality was described during the campaign as holding the solution to every problem. This helps to explain why 'Alessandrismo' disappeared as a political force as soon as the election was over, and why post-election attempts to capitalize upon his vote were unsuccessful. By the same token this perhaps explains the maintenance of Chile's democratic traditions for it is very difficult to envisage a Marxist president with a well-organized right effectively controlling 34·9% of the votes.

Unidad Popular tried a balanced strategy to keep both their opponents in the race. This was their best guarantee of success. In their presidential programme they stated that 'the campaign should be directed as much against the demagogy of the ultra-reactionary and conservative candidacy of Alessandri as against the reformist and "continuist" candidacy of Tomic'.[5] Tomic, as already stated, focused his attacks on the right and insisted consistently upon his opening to the left. Thus he frequently appeared to the general public as a more radical candidate than Allende.

It was against this background that Allende won the election. But between the popular vote and the election of the president by Congress, a dangerous atmosphere began to develop throughout the country. On top of a financial crisis, caused by panic in right-wing circles, there was a feeling that a *coup d'état* would be a most natural development. There was a sense that someone should fulfil his 'duty' in an 'unexpected crisis' like this. Here we can only briefly note this atmosphere without entering into details, or considering the damage which was caused to the country's economy.

Two main issues during this period probably contributed decisively to a reduction of tension. One was the decision of the Christian Democratic Party to vote in Congress for Allende, on the basis of some constitutional reforms under the heading of 'Statute of Democratic Guarantees'. They comprised a number of provisions aimed at strengthening individual liberties, indepen-dence of the universities, and freedom of the mass media.

The other decisive 'issue' was the assassination of the army's Commander-in-Chief by an extreme right-wing group during the course of an abortive kidnapping attempt aimed at provoking military intervention. This general had held the army back from

[5] *Programa básico de gobierno de la Unidad Popular*, Ed. Horizonte, Santiago, 1969, p. 45.

intervention and his death focused popular attention upon the dangerous situation into which the country might be drifting.

ALLENDE'S POWER POSITION WITHIN THE POLITICAL FRAMEWORK

The amount of power Allende won. Following Allende's election it becomes important to understand the power position of his coalition within the political framework just described, in terms of the commitment to pursue 'the Chilean road to socialism'. For it is probably only then that one can understand the task he faced when elected and what he has done to accomplish it. In other words one must ask if he had secured the power needed to carry out his programme of transforming Chile into a socialist society.

The executive power. By winning the presidential election Allende won for his coalition control over the executive branch of government which is certainly the most important of the three branches described earlier. The victory, however, is placed in its proper perspective when one remembers the narrowness of his majority over Alessandri. The result was in fact as follows:

Radomiro Tomic (CDP)	821,801 votes	27·8%
Jorge Alessandri (National Party and other right wing support)	1,030,159 votes	34·9%
Salvador Allende (UP)	1,070,339 votes	36·3%

What this election in fact did for Allende was to strengthen his bargaining hand in the ensuing election by Congress in which supporters of his coalition were in a minority. Constitutionally Congress could have elected Alessandri but Allende's strength was that, in practice, Congress had never used its prerogative to select the runner-up in the popular vote. On this occasion Alessandri went to the length of declaring that if he was elected president he would immediately resign[6] thus leading to another presidential election in which Frei would have been free to run and which the latter might well have won. He was, in other words, virtually offering the Christian Democrat Party a second term in office in exchange for their votes in Congress. The Christian Democrats and Frei declined this offer and after extracting the

[6] *El Mercurio*, 13 September 1970.

'constitutional guarantees' mentioned above they supported Allende's election as president. This result can only be understood within the context of Chilean political tradition and helps one to grasp how Allende won control of the executive power in a weak political position and through a coalition that could well be described as a 'minimum winning coalition'.

The legislative power. When Allende became the head of the Chilean state he had to face a Congress that had been partially elected in 1965[7] and partially elected in 1969. The Congress's term was due to expire in 1973 and therefore if Allende thought that his programme needed a congressional majority, he had to think in terms of working with this legislature, for his first two years in office, unless he was prepared to make use of a plebiscite to force a general parliamentary election before that time.

In the 1965 election 20 senators were elected for an eight-year term. The senators elected by different political parties were:

Radical Party	3
Christian Democrat Party	11
Socialist Party	3
Communist Party	2
Padena	1

In the elections of 1969 the Chamber of Deputies, consisting of 150 members, was entirely renewed and 30 more senators were elected for an eight-year period. The results of this election were:[8]

(a) DEPUTIES

Political Parties	Votes	%
Communists	383,049	15·9
Popular Socialist Union	51,904	2·2
Radicals	313,559	13·0
Socialists	294,448	12·2
Social Democrats of Chile	20,560	0·9
Total Potential UP	1,042,960	44·2
Christian Democrats	716,547	29·8
National Party	480,523	20·0
National Democratic Party	44,818	1·9
Independents	2,104	0·1
Void	98,617	4·0
Total	2,406,129	100·0

[7] At the beginning of Frei's 'revolution in freedom'.
[8] *Dirección del Registro electoral*, oficina de información del Senado, Boletín de información general No. 67, 30 June 1970.

(b) FOR SENATORS IN 6 AGRUPACIONES

Political Party	Votes	%
Communists	181,628	17·3
Socialist Union	24,427	2·3
Radicals	161,014	15·4
Socialists	120,641	11·5
Total Potential UP	487,707	46·5
Christian Democrat Party	375,403	32·9
National Party	173,424	16·6
Void	42,195	4·0
Total	1,048,729	100·0

This election completed the Congress Allende would have to work with until March 1973. Before the 1970 presidential election two minor re-alignments took place. A faction of the Radical Party which was not prepared to support Allende left the party, led by two senators and three deputies. On the other hand a faction led by two senators and one deputy left the Christian Democrats to support Allende. The first group constituted the Radical Democratic Party and became an opposition party when Allende became president. The second group called MAPU (*Movimiento de Acción Popular Unitaria*) carried with them a large proportion of the Christian Democratic youth and a number of technicians, especially those linked with Frei's agrarian reform team.

The net effect of their re-alignments still left the Unidad Popular in a minority in both chambers. The composition of Congress when Allende came to power was thus:

SENATE

Unidad Popular		Opposition	
Party	*Seats*	*Party*	*Seats*
Socialists	6	Christian Democrats	20
Communists	5	National Party	5
Radicals	7	Democratic Radical Party	2
Independent Popular Action	1	Total Opposition	27
Popular Socialist Union	1		
Social Democrats	1		
MAPU	2		
Total UP	23		

The president of the Senate is the Christian Democratic Senator Patricio Alwyn.

HOUSE OF DEPUTIES

Unidad Popular		Opposition	
Party	*Seats*	*Party*	*Seats*
Socialists	15	Christian Democrats	55
Communists	21	National Party	34
Radicals	20	Democratic Radical Party	4
MAPU	1	Total Opposition	92
Total UP	57		

Out of 200 members of Congress Allende, when elected president, could count on the support of 80, or 40 per cent, formed by the followers of four political parties and two 'movements'. This figure of 40 per cent is higher than the proportion of the popular vote Allende captured in the presidential election.

At this point, and before considering how the UP faced up to this balance of forces, it is important to note that the three opposition parties had very different attitudes towards Allende's government. While no help could be expected from the National or Radical Democratic Parties the Christian Democrats, as suggested during the presidential campaign, showed themselves willing to discuss an eventual collaboration. Thus Allende started with a good chance, if he wanted it, of gaining additional support from the Christian Democrat Party.

THE SECOND WAY TO SOCIALISM OR THE CHILEAN ROAD

Ever since Marx declared at The Hague Conference of the First International that 'I do not deny that there are nations like England and America and if I know your institutions at all, Holland, where the working class could achieve their ends by peaceful means' there has undoubtedly been a division in the Marxist camp between those advocating evolution and those urging revolution.

In recent years the CPSU has strongly advocated the peaceful way to achieve power and there has been no mystery about the Chilean Communist Party's loyalty to the Russian Party (for example, far from protesting against the invasion of Czecho-slovakia it defended it). Thus the Chilean Party has resolutely opposed Maoist groups and it has regarded the Cuban model as inappropriate in the Chilean situation. In short, the Chilean Communist Party can be described as an evolutionary Marxist party which has played a decisive role in keeping the bulk of the traditional left within the framework of legality.

Allende, as has been described, has a long standing tradition of support for legality. Nevertheless, he has had a continuous struggle within his own party where the 'legal way' has by no means been unanimously accepted. In fact the Socialist Party has always been prone to cleavages over the use of legality or violence. In the past this has produced frequent divisions. Today this division still certainly remains in the Socialist Party and there is every reason to believe that a significant group within it has only accepted the present strategy in the belief that through the use of power they will improve their position in the final violent confrontation with the bourgeoisie. The party's present General Secretary, Carlos Altamirano, is an outstanding representative of the sector that believes only in the 'first way to socialism'. Allende finds his freedom for manoeuvre on behalf of 'the second way to socialism' similarly reduced by pressure from outside his party exerted by the MIR. This body advocates armed revolution and purports to play the role of 'guardian angel' of the revolution. Though not openly against the government it develops its own tactics in the belief that it is speeding up the revolutionary process and preventing the government from compromising its programme. This group, significantly enough, has many contacts within the left of the Socialist Party.

When the Unidad Popular was created, the Radical Party, in accordance with its long democratic tradition, favoured the peaceful route to power. Its weight within the coalition was precisely due to this fact, for it could give a credibility to the Unidad Popular's claims that, in the minds of many people, the socialists or communists could not give.

In Allende's first message to Congress he stated his belief that in Chile it was possible to work for a socialist society within the existing constitutional framework. He said on that occasion, 'the flexibility of our institutional system permits us to expect that it will not be a serious bone of contention and also that our legal system will adapt itself to the new demands placed upon it in order to generate, through constitutional channels, the new institutional system needed to supersede capitalism'.

In the quotation the way in which the Unidad Popular envisages its policy is clearly stated. The present constitutional order does permit the creation of a new order while respecting its rules. But it becomes immediately clear that an indispensable requisite of such an attempt is to have a *majority within the institutions of the present system*. This will be seen more clearly when we describe the Unidad Popular's commitment to the creation of a new order.

The possibility of building socialism in this way is contained in Engels's words: 'One can conceive that the old society may evolve peacefully toward the new society in the countries where the popular representatives have all power in their hands and where, according to the constitution, one can do what one wishes from the moment one has the backing of a majority of the nation.'

This raises the question of whether or not the Unidad Popular
has the power necessary to fulfil its commitment, and the nature
of those commitments.

The Unidad Popular's commitments. We can summarize the commitments of Unidad Popular by following their basic governmental programme.

The creation of a new institutional order of 'El Estado Popular'
(Popular State). This will require a new constitution whose central
features are described as follows: 'A new political constitution
will institutionalize the massive incorporation of the people into
state power. A single state organization will be established at
the national, regional and local levels which will have an Assembly
of the People as its principal organ of power. The popular
assembly will consist of one chamber which will express popular
sovereignty on a nation wide scale. The diverse currents of
opinion will come together in it.'[9] The transformation of the
judiciary is also envisaged in this constitutional reform.

The construction of a new economy. The Unidad Popular's aim is
to build a new economy based upon state control (or the existence
of a 'social area') but also allowing for a significant sector to
remain in private hands and for a third, or 'mixed sector', which
will be jointly developed by the state and private investors.

This aim was stated in the programme as follows: 'The
United Popular forces seek as a central policy objective to replace
the existing economic structure, doing away with the power of
national and international monopoly capital, and of the latifundia
in order to initiate the construction of socialism.' 'The process of
transforming our economy will begin with a policy designed to
create a dominant state sector.'[10] The state sector should control:

(1) The large copper, nitrate, saltpetre, iron and steel mines.

(2) The country's financial system especially private banks and
insurance.

(3) External trade.

(4) Large scale distributive enterprises and monopolies.

(5) Strategic industrial monopolies.

(6) In general, those activities which condition the country's
economic and social development such as the production and
distribution of electric power; rail, air and sea transport;

[9] *Programa básico de Unidad Popular*, p. 15.
[10] Quoted in J. Garcés, *La pugna política por la presidencia en Chile*, Editorial
Universitaria, Santiago, 1971.

communications; the production, refining and distribution of petroleum and its derivatives including liquid gas; steel; cement; petrochemicals; heavy chemicals; cellulose and paper.

All these will be expropriated with full respect for the interests of the small shareholder.[11]

Land reform is specifically considered in the Unidad Popular's economic policy but their policy is fundamentally based upon Frei's agrarian reform. The idea is to speed up the process and to introduce 'qualitative' changes in relation mainly to the ownership of land.

One must underline the fact that in this attempt to build a state sector the Unidad Popular is far from having to start from scratch. In fact there is a significant tradition of state intervention in the Chilean economy. President Allende said when referring to this matter 'The importance of the public sector is traditional in our country. Approximately 40 per cent of expenditure is public and 70 per cent of investment originates with the state. The public sector was created by the national bourgeoisie to favour private accumulation, and to consolidate the productive structures concentrated according to technological and patrimonial requirements. Our government seeks to make it quantitatively still more important but also to make it qualitatively different.'[12]

Social, Cultural and Educational Tasks. Under this heading the Unidad Popular describes its commitment to better social security, education and health services and to better policies for wages and housing.

In the context of Chile's traditions these pledges are not likely to arouse any bitter opposition and though most of the Unidad Popular's proposals in this field would require legislation they involve reforms that all parties are generally inclined to support. However, two policies are contemplated under this heading which, because of their importance, may arouse strong opposition and would require support of the sort necessary for carrying through Congress the major (and most controversial) part of Allende's programme. These are developments concerning the educational system and the nature and control of the mass media.

Foreign Policy. In this field the main objectives were stated as 'To affirm the full political and economic independence of Chile.

[11] *Programa básico de Unidad Popular*, pp. 19–20.
[12] G. Martner, ed., *El pensamiento político del gobiernode Allende*, Editorial Universitaria, Santiago, 1971, pp. 32–3.

Relationships will be maintained with all countries in the world, irrespective of their ideological and political positions, on the basis of respect for the self-determination and the interests of the Chilean people.' 'A strong Latin American anti-imperialist sentiment will be promoted through an international policy of peoples rather than chancelleries.' The programme also advocates Latin American integration and the revision of all treaties that could affect Chilean independence.

In short one could say that Allende's government was committed to carrying out its programme through the existing constitutional and legal procedures or to reform these while continuing to accept the established rules of the game. In fact, as we have seen, these rules do not allow for the system itself to be affected unless there is agreement between the executive power and a congressional majority. Allende does not control such a constitutional majority. Keeping this in mind we shall now examine the alternatives and ways in which the Unidad Popular could, and might still, achieve this institutional majority.

THE ALTERNATIVES AVAILABLE TO GAIN THE POWER NECESSARY FOR PURSUING THE CHILEAN WAY

It is clear that the governing coalition, from the very beginning of their period in office, lacked the power needed to enforce their own policies within the framework of the existing constitutional system. Although it was possible to think in terms of beginning to enforce their programme by making the best possible use of the executive power, the limitations on this approach are obvious. For the profound changes envisaged a congressional majority is essential.

We believe that the first option open to the government, the option which can be described as consensus amongst the social and political forces prepared to work for substantial changes in the political and economic system, was to attract the Christian Democratic Party into the governing coalition. If it had been possible it would have been the quickest way to initiate the constitutional and legal changes needed to establish a new political framework. On the side of the Christian Democratic Party there appear to be substantial reasons for believing that this would have been possible. The first and most important reason was perhaps Tomic's electoral platform. There was a remarkable similarity in many respects between the presidential programmes of Tomic and Allende. In addition one must recall that it was the CDP in Congress that secured the presidency for Allende. Moreover the party's hierarchy seemed bent on forcing through the opening to the left advocated by Tomic during and after the election campaign. The Christian Democrats were at this point officially committed to the programme presented for the election and the more moderate sections of the party were not in a strong position to obstruct such a policy.

On the government's side the position remained very confused; no official strategy was devised to consolidate a majority by these means. Indeed, one may see here the first signs of divergencies over strategy within the government coalition. Had the government wished to take up the approaches of the Christian Democrats, had such a line been agreed upon, it is difficult to understand why for example, it then decided to contest the senatorial seat vacated by Allende when he became president. It was a safe seat for the government. But when the possibility appeared of not contesting the election, and supporting instead Bosco Parra, a well known left-wing Christian Democrat (later a member of the government coalition), Unidad Popular failed to appreciate the political importance of the issue. Not only did it contest the seat, but it put up a socialist, Adonis Sepúlveda, well known for his support of methods more revolutionary than those of the Unidad Popular. A good opportunity of achieving a political *rapprochement* with the Christian Democrats was thus lost.

At the same time the mass media controlled by government supporters embarked upon a systematic campaign of personal attacks upon prominent Christian Democrats. The government did nothing to stop the campaign, presumably because opinion within the coalition was divided.

From the many political opportunities which occurred, one may single out a second very important one which arose after the municipal elections of April 1971. Following an initiative of the Christian Democrats, there was an opportunity for Unidad Popular and the Christian Democrats to elect jointly almost all the mayors in the country. The importance of this possible political development for a *rapprochement* with the Christian Democrats is self-evident. President Allende is said to have favoured it, but failed to obtain the agreement of the coalition.

A third opportunity, along the same lines, came with a by-election in Valparaiso, following the death of a Christian Democrat deputy. There was a possibility of Unidad Popular support for the candidacy of Luis Badilla, a left-wing Christian Democrat (later a member of the government coalition) but again it did not materialize despite presidential backing. After the by-election, in which the government candidate was defeated by the Christian Democrat (who was supported by the right-wing parties), it became clear that the government no longer had the possibility of pursuing a 'consensus strategy'. The lack of well-defined strategy on its part explains why Allende never went further in his approaches to the Christian Democrat Party than vague references to a search for collaboration – references that never materialized in any more solid form.

A second option open to the government as an alternative to approaches to the official Christian Democratic Party, was what we may describe as 'the polarization option'. This would have entailed trying, early on, to capitalize on the sympathy that every new government enjoys, and which Allende certainly had. He could then have sought to press ahead with the aid of a plebiscite. It is possible that the government had a plebiscite in mind when it introduced a project for constitutional reform providing for the nationalization of the copper mines. But it seems more likely that the government never had enough confidence to devise a strategy of this sort. It would have been moreover, politically naive to select an issue such as this one to force a plebiscite since Congress could not have been expected to come to the defence of foreign companies. In fact the project was unanimously approved.

After the municipal elections of April 1971, when the Unidad Popular received 49·73 per cent of the popular vote, the government lost an important psychological advantage. Though satisfactory in itself, such a result, if applied to congressional elections would not have provided a majority in Congress for the government. The chances of using the weapon of the plebiscite to good effect deteriorated still further after the government's defeat in the Valparaiso by-election. Ultimately, when in November 1971, the government did bring its proposals for a new constitution forward as a matter of urgency, and were then forced to withdraw them, it became clear to all that a plebiscite offered no chance of success.

A third option open to the government in the search for an enlarged coalition was to look for a significant split within the Christian Democrat Party. As we have seen, this was not unlikely, in view of the known determination of a group within this party

to work with Allende in building a socialist society. This development, which the government, and in particular the government-
controlled mass media encouraged, finally occurred after the
Valparaiso by-election in July 1971. Eight deputies then left the
Christian Democratic Party in order to form the *Izquierda
Cristiana* (Christian Left), which declared that: 'its task was to
contribute to the building of socialism through the contribution of
social and cultural elements of Christian inspiration . . .'[13]

When it came, however, this split was not as significant as
expected, for it failed to give the government the formal majority
that such a split had been intended to provide. Indeed the
government's position was in fact weakened. It now became
clear that there was no possibility of the government acquiring an
institutional majority. And the departure of the radical group
from the Christian Democrat Party left this party in a much better
position to pursue a stronger opposition line.

The split of course did not come at a good time for the government. In the same month of August, the 25th convention of the
Radical Party took place. The declaration issued by the convention
stated: 'Because we are socialists, we use historical materialism
and the class struggle as an interpretation of reality.' This declaration went too far for some members, and seven deputies and five
senators seceded to form the MRII, or *Movimiento Radical de
Izquierda Independiente*. They stated that the Radical Party
declaration 'had moved very far from the ideology of social
democracy of their party (as laid down in the declaration of
principles of 1969)'. Present radical policy no longer included the
'affirmation of democracy, which is no mere affirmation, but the
image of the aspirations and anxieties of those sectors and classes
to which our militants belong, and from which we draw our
support'.[14] But the MRII added that they would continue to give
moral and political support to Unidad Popular.

Not only did the Christian Democrats and the Radicals split.
But the secessionist groups of Christian Democrats, the MAPU,
at the time members of the government coalition, also split. They
gave up the ministry they held in the government, and their three
deputies now joined the Christian Left. In a statement, they underlined the fact that they had always regarded themselves as a force
on the left which 'inspired by Christian and humanist values, will

[13] *La Nación*, 8 August 1971.
[14] *Ibid.*, 4 August 1971.

fight for socialism'. But they felt that 'Unidad Popular, and the bulk of the present leadership of MAPU think very differently about it. They consider MAPU to be a party of strongly Marxist content'.

These developments signified a serious setback for the government. The various splits seemed to indicate that its problem was more a question of how to keep its own coalition united rather than of how to enlarge its support.

The lack of any coherent strategy with regard to the problem of achieving an institutional majority has its parallel in many other important areas of policy: land reform and nationalizations for example. This helps one to understand why from the beginning of Allende's term of office each political group in the coalition seemed more concerned with maximizing its own specific advantages than with developing a common strategy for the implementation of its programme. This not only led to a generalized atmosphere of indiscipline but also generated an exclusive and sectarian attitude to anyone outside the government. This has alienated many technicians, civil servants, workers and peasants from the government, and has served to promote cohesion among the forces of the opposition. The problem did not pass unnoticed by the government. More than a year after Allende took office, Unidad Popular declared in a self-critical analysis:

> We propose to eradicate sectarianism which finds expression in relations between the parties within Unidad Popular itself, and which obstructs the basis of common work and leads to harmful forms of competition in the recruitment of members or attempts to divide sectors of the public administration, enterprises in the same area of public ownership or spheres of influence.
>
> Equally we have decided to eradicate the sectarianism which extends beyond the Unidad Popular and which tends to exclude combined action with non-party workers or those which belong to organizations opposed to Unidad Popular: or which does not recognize or endangers the rights of the workers who, although not with us, carry out their work honestly; or conditions the recognition of individual merit for technical work or representation to partisan adherence.[15]

It is hard to believe that after this first year it might become easier for the government to develop a joint strategy to achieve

---

[15] The *El Arrayan* Report, February 1972, as translated by the Chilean Embassy in London.

that majority which 'the Chilean way has never had'. Where the government has been successful in carrying out its policies, as with a large part of its nationalization programme, it has done so by maximizing the possibilities open to it through its use of the executive power. But even in this field it is evident that it has failed to produce any 'qualitative changes' which would increase its support.

SOME CONSIDERATIONS ON THE FUTURE OF THE UNIDAD POPULAR

From the political point of view, one is led to conclude that the 'Chilean Way' has not yet really been tried in Chile, simply because a basic pre-requisite of this approach is the control of an institutional majority. The present government coalition, though presented with good opportunities to gain that majority has failed to do so. Unidad Popular's basic commitments therefore remain as no more than commitments. There seems to be no agreement among the government's constituent groups as to what the requirements for the 'Chilean Way' are, hence it is unlikely that they could ever find a common strategy. If this is the case they will continue to implement policies lacking in coherence without facing up to the fundamental political problems. In such a context, their policies will not be effective, and they will only contribute to the creation of circumstances likely to lead to political developments that are alien to Chile, and inimical to the 'peaceful road to socialism'. If the present Unidad Popular is to have any future, a very radical clarification process will have to take place among its members. If the collapse of the government's economic policy comes before the political clarification, then the prospects for the *vía Chilena* seem very gloomy.

H. Zemelman and Patricio Leon

5   Political Opposition to the Government of Allende

THE ANALYSIS OF THE PRESENT CHILEAN POLITICAL PROCESS MAY serve to underline some features of the Marxist theory of the state and of the relationship between social classes and institutional structures. Few countries offer such a clear example as Chile of the impact of the elements forming the ideological superstructure on the social and economic mechanisms which operate at the level of the infrastructure. Its long, bourgeois democratic tradition has led to the accumulation of many juridical and institutional elements, to which formal respect has been given, and which have built up a system of domination thanks to the acquiescence of other social sectors. The achievement of a high degree of consensus had been the other side of the face of a weak bourgeoisie, and in the blind logic of weak dominant classes, they have transformed their superstructure into their Achilles's heel. For the Chilean political process has shown how political power can transform itself into an instrument which will destroy the unity of the institutionalized power structure of the bourgeois state, when it is controlled by an alliance of social forces which escape the influence of the dominant class and its allies.

We shall attempt to analyse how a revolutionary process can develop when political power is in the hands of those who do not control the means of production. We must study the contradictions which arise when the struggle takes place simultaneously on the plane of legality and on the plane of the mobilization of the masses; we must try to understand how the consensus which has legitimized the traditional system of domination can be replaced by something else, and finally we must recognize clearly the role of the dominant ideology in the structural changes under way. In one word, our concern is with the correlation between social polarization and political polarization.

THE PROBLEM

On 16 January 1972, the head of the Christian Democratic Party declared 'We are not asking the government to compromise its programme. All we are asking is that he should not impose it on the other two thirds of the population.' His declaration came immediately after the united opposition had defeated the official candidates in elections for a deputy and a senator. Yet, days before, President Allende himself had announced his willingness to conduct discussions with other political sectors on the basis of the programme of Unidad Popular.

These events were the culmination of a long process of growing tension. The key factors which have characterized developments in Chile since 4 September 1970 are: first, the ideologically consistent application of the programme of the coalition government; secondly, the extent of the representativeness of the Allende government in carrying out its programme; and thirdly, the problem of the relationship between the executive and the other powers of the state, which amounts to the problem of the break up of the unity of the bourgeois state into antagonistic powers.

The very first steps undertaken by the executive led immediately to the definition of the two political lines which have dominated the period: (a) the defence of institutionality, beginning with the defence of the judiciary, and culminating in the defence of formal, abstract, consensus democracy, and of the liberty of expression, allegedly endangered by the government; and (b) the defence of private property, taken to be medium and small property, culminating in the defence of 'workers' ownership of enterprises', and the consecration of the principle that the economy must contain a 'private sector' – a principle which envisages the reversibility of the present process.

The government embarked on the formation of the sector of social property, making use of lawful procedures, which, without bringing into question the legality of the existing system, provided a short cut to ensure that the bourgeoisie should not be able to use existing institutions to mutilate the programme. From the moment that the Unidad Popular dominated the executive power, it was clear to the right, that unless the armed forces indulged in subversive action, it must seek refuge in the legislature, which it will dominate until the elections of March 1973. The by-passing of Congress which the government chose as its method was possible thanks to a decree law of August 1932, promulgated by the shortlived so-called Socialist Republic, and which was still in force. The executive thus started on the changes in the economic structure, without any legal need for parliamentary debate. But this opened it to attack on all sides, since the defence of oligarchic interests could shelter under the banner of the defence of institutions, and other groups could identify their interests with the political interests of the bourgeoisie. The Achilles's heel of the bourgeois state might become that of the Unidad Popular, should all fractions of the bourgeoisie unite under the slogan 'Democracy and Liberty in danger'.

The use of the institutional superstructure by political forces which are opposing the dominant interests inevitably poses the problem of the legitimacy of the various powers of the state. Faced with a policy which injures its interests, the right can only question the legitimacy of the executive's action in legal terms, above all because the system requires the co-operation of the three powers, executive, legislative and judiciary, in all great decisions. This is the consensus within which conflicts of interests must be solved. Thus, in the view of the right, all the measures taken by the executive without the consent of these powers are illegitimate. As *El Mercurio* put it, 'the foundation of liberty is the existence of a balance of powers'.[1] The dispute on the internal structure of the state undermines the image of the 'impersonal' state. And indeed, when legal mechanisms are used for purposes which oppose the aims of the dominant *status quo*, the identification between material and institutional interests, between moral and cultural values is broken. 'Disorder', 'dishonesty', 'incapacity' are alleged, and such calls serve to undermine first the image, then the legitimacy of the executive as the instrument of revolutionary power. The executive is the power which has the hegemony within the state. The object is therefore to force it to lose this hegemony, by contesting its representativeness, and hence its power to impose itself without exceeding the bounds of legitimacy. This has been the strategy of the right throughout the period under review.

Making use of Decree Law No. 520, of August 1932, the government proceeded with its programme of industrial expropriation. At the end of December the president announced on the

---

[1] *El Mercurio*, 17 January 1971. *El Mercurio* was founded in 1827; it represents the 'democratic' tradition in Chile. It is owned by the Edwards family, one of the great industrial, commercial and financial clans in the country, and is the 'classic' mouthpiece of the bourgeoisie.

radio that a draft law would shortly be sent to Congress to nationalize all banks, after which the public would no longer be able to make use of the facilities then provided by the government to buy up privately owned shares – a measure which really hit the bourgeoisie. Meanwhile the policy of rural expropriations advanced rapidly towards the aim of 1000 *latifundios* in 1971; Communal Councils were set up as organs of peasant power,[2] and in January 1971, a draft law, setting up Neighbourhood Courts was sent to Congress – a project which the right immediately attacked, alleging them to be popular tribunals of inquisition into people's private lives. None of these measures, except perhaps that concerning the banks, affected very powerful interests – and the land reform was carried out on the basis of the law voted during the Christian Democratic government. The reasons for the reaction of the right must be sought elsewhere.

One was the movement launched by the *mapuches* in the south.[3] The second was the way in which the left was solving the problem of the contradiction between its objectives and the formal limitations of the organs of power of which it disposed. Or to put it in more general terms: can the ideological power which makes use of institutionalized power transform it *before* it is itself captured by the ideology of that institutional structure? Or how to break the dominant ideology without losing legitimacy? How can the structure of and the functions of the state be changed without destroying consensus? According to *El Mercurio*, on 8 January 1971, it is the institutions themselves which define the possibility of change: change must therefore be legitimate; change itself is not rejected, provided it is legitimate.

The *mapuche* movement launched a massive campaign of occupation of estates, leading to a mobilization of the peasantry. In the summer of 1971 a powerful peasant/*mapuche* movement overthrew practically all legal limitations, but since its objects were specifically *mapuche*, it had but little echo among other peasants and could not spread throughout the country. Thus all hopes of mobilizing the peasantry have failed to materialize owing to the impossibility of overcoming their internal contradictions, and the Unidad Popular has lost influence among the peasants. This is reflected in the fate of the Communal Councils, which have flourished in Cautín, and particularly in the department of Lautero, but have languished elsewhere. In any case the policy of the

[2] Decree Law No. 481, December 1970.
[3] *Mapuches*, the Indian inhabitants of southern Chile.

Unidad Popular in this mobilization has been ambiguous – which may explain why the structures for mobilization, created too hastily, have failed to develop. Nevertheless, it was the *mapuche* movement, and the massive occupation of lands, which led the Christian Democrats in particular to take up for the first time the defence of private property in terms of the defence of landed property, and to put forward demands to participate in the making of decisions.

The second issue which, as noted above, has increased political tension is the manipulation by the government of the powers of the state. The use of the legal institutional superstructure for revolutionary ends has led to maladjustments and to disarray in the system. The use of such mechanisms as the sequestration of properties, which can be justified on the grounds of the existence of labour unrest, has enabled the agrarian reform to proceed more quickly. Sequestration implies the intervention of bureaucratic power in favour of the oppressed social sectors. Nevertheless, large numbers of medium and small proprietors feel themselves endangered. This has helped to enlarge the dominant alliance to include sectors of the small and medium bourgeoisie, which gives right-wing strategy a markedly mesocratic character. The defence of material interests appears more and more under the guise of the defence of ideological interests, involving many levels of the middle classes, among whom the medium and small landed proprietors, while the right and the Unidad Popular are rivals for the control of the rest.

The right argues that democracy is in danger. The government strives to win over these middle levels by stressing its anti-monopolistic and anti-oligarchic policies. The right operates on the ideological plane; the government on the plane of structural measures. But since these middle levels do not form a homogeneous economic class, they are more likely to be moved by ideological considerations. To prevent this, the left must not only use institutionalized power, it must be able to break up the dominant ideological patterns. This can only be achieved either by a revolutionary insurrectional movement, which will carry out economic change at the same time as it demolishes the apparatus of the bourgeois state; or, on the assumption that legality, legal security and order are values of the dominant ideology which the oligarchy will muster in its defence, by mobilizing the middle sectors around itself, these values must be demythologized. If this is not understood, then the legitimacy or illegitimacy of the process of change will count for more than its necessity or its justice. The struggle will no longer be one between classes but will be defined as the defence of a way of life, which would give free play to all social, economic and ideological interests.

Using the apparatus of the state does not imply destroying the dominant ideology. It must be used in a specific way, one which will not unbalance the distinct spheres of power revolving around the central planet, namely consensus. Any move must face the dissociation between what is legal and what is legitimate; it must recognize the difference between the spirit and the letter of the law. For the new legitimacy to work out its own legal expressions, a new consensus is necessary, which must be the result of a daily struggle for the conscience of workers, peasants, middle sectors, professional people etc. In this sense, political power, rather than being the instrument promoting change within the closed circle of the dominant ideology, must serve as a battering ram, to breach it, even if thereby the rate at which change can be introduced must be slowed down to the pace of the ideological-institutional offensive.

It must be noted in this context that one of the principal errors in the manipulation of state power has been the failure to understand that the effects which economic changes can have on the ideological plane have been distorted by the image created by the state bureaucracy. The state bureaucracy has traditionally formed the basis for the alliances between the oligarchy and other social sectors, mainly the middle classes. It has been the mechanism for policies designed to strengthen the dominant alliance by means of a wider consensus; here political power can easily show a disfigured visage.

If the reaction of the dominant groups is conditioned by passing events (e.g. in Cautín), or by the difficulties experienced by Unidad Popular in carrying out a policy on two levels, that of material interests which must be shifted and the ideological-institutional level, we can understand why the bourgeoisie itself is split. But it is a split which will be healed not by the common defence of interests but because of the contradictions within the system. One group in the bourgeoisie has refused to form a united front with the oligarchy, but demands a share in the political process through the observance of the constitutional system.

The polarization of the bourgeoisie into at least two fractions can be explained, as that of Chile itself, by a structure characterized by constant and effective state intervention. The bourgeoisie is thus composed of several fractions, including the political-bureaucratic, all of which rely on the economic support of the state. This explains why some sections of the bourgeoisie have supported policies opposed to the interests of other fractions, as for instance the agrarian reform of the Christian Democrats. It is thus difficult for the bourgeoisie to act as a single class. It is not strong enough to confront a government hostile to its interests, nor can it rally around one of the fractional groups, other than the dominant oligarchy, a policy which would run counter to the interests of the 'political bourgeoisie'. Hence the only policy which unifies all sectors is the defence of interests dressed up in the garb of the free play of democracy, provided that it is the populist political fraction which is in the van. Hence the defence of private property, when it enlarged its scope to include the defence of the small-scale shareholder 'who has invested in shares all his hard-earned savings', renders easier the strategy of concentrating on the institutional plane of struggle – and populism fades steadily into the background.

What is this political fraction within the dominant bourgeoisie? Its presence constitutes the most significant contradiction, since its participation in the process of transformation, though ostensibly an expression of consensus, rapidly becomes an obstacle to progress. At the same time it serves to aggregate the interests of other fractions, and acts in the interests of preserving the legitimacy of the system, which to survive must accept the equation: liberal democracy equals populism. In this context the populist fraction of the bourgeoisie takes on a hegemonic role, in spite of the many contradictions within the bourgeoisie. It acts by means of oligarchic control and delegation of power to intermediate sectors, and makes use of various mechanisms of participation.

The theme of delegation of power is well-known in the history of capitalism. When such a delegation takes place in a state already playing a large part in the productive process, a new social category arises, originally dependent on the bourgeoisie, but capable of attaining a high degree of autonomy. This category which we can describe as the 'service bourgeoisie' gradually increase in real power, and the dominant class has to share power with it. It is these groups, dependent on the bourgeoisie, yet with increasing institutional power which make up the progressive populist fraction of the bourgeoisie. They are drawn from different social classes, form part of the state apparatus or are linked with the bourgeois infra-structure. They are closely integrated with the organization of the state and with those whose function it is to legitimize the existing power structure (public administration, management of enterprises, institutions of government: judges, deputies, the military etc., technical and professional organizations, publicists, salesmen etc.), all of whom are in direct relationship one way or another with the dominant class, since the delegation of power takes place in various ways.

Precisely because this service bourgeoisie takes on the role of principal defender of the superstructure, it can objectively accept a much wider margin of change than can the dominant bourgeoisie. It can remain at an equal distance from all changes which do not affect the juridico-institutional organization, and thus tends to adopt a central position. This enables it to coordinate the other fractions of the bourgeoisie. Nevertheless this group is marked by a fundamental ambivalence, oscillating between the defence of its political and institutional interests, and its ideological links with other fractions of the bourgeoisie. It reaches maximum equilibrium and stability when material interests find their expression in the institutional structure. But when there is a risk of a confrontation between the dominant bourgeoisie and the popular classes, it is not surprising that the service bourgeoisie can be made use of by a political opposition to the government in power.

Thus, when a popular government takes power, sectors of this service bourgeoisie will seek the alliance of new groups, though this does not mean that they surrender their independence. They will act on behalf of different social interests, so long as their autonomy is respected. They become the instruments of their allies by means of the delegation of power. Thus the process of delegation of power has had the result that the representation of the interests of the oligarchy has been assumed by this *ensemble* of social strata, which depend on the oligarchy, even though they have acquired growing autonomy. This explains the role of Christian Democracy, which has aggregated the interests of the dominant bourgeoisie with those of large and heterogeneous popular strata.

THE POLICY OF THE RIGHT

The policy of the political fraction of the bourgeoisie is what we might call a 'populism of the right'; it is a populism which infuses power into the dominant alliance, but at the same time compels the oligarchic nucleus to subordinate itself to the strategical and tactical lines laid down by the fraction. On the other hand, because of its links with the dominant economic interests, it cannot follow a policy aimed at the overthrow of capitalism. Yet the autonomy it enjoys enables it to lean on an alliance with the people, since some segments of the service bourgeoisie are willing to accept state capitalism.

Thus, in any coalition formed by an alliance between classes, elements of this bourgeoisie will be present, and all the more in a country like Chile with its over-developed bureaucracy. In this context we can now examine the policy of the right, when Unidad Popular came into power. Its first object was to restore its links with the middle sectors, both with those who voted for Allende, and with those who supported Tomic. The method chosen was to spread uncertainty and to profit from any crisis: shortages, squatting, redundancy, foreign currency etc. Ideologically, the right's intention was to provoke the Unidad Popular to adopt measures which would shatter the 'agreement/mobility' model of the middle sectors, and replace it by a revolutionary model before Unidad Popular was effectively in control of power.

Thus Unidad Popular, in addition to promoting economic change, was faced with the challenging task of creating a new institutionalism, a new consensus, by means of a skilful and imaginative policy of mobilization and participation. This has not, however, happened. On the contrary, the efforts of the government to win over the middle sectors by means of a policy of structural changes have failed. Profound changes in the structure of the ownership of property need not necessarily be accompanied by a conviction that the foundations of co-participation in the exercise of power must be challenged. The redistribution of income, or the creation of the Sector of Social Property may have adverse effects on the bourgeoisie, but it does not ensure a realignment of forces, a displacement of classes, as long as the sectors who benefit continue to accept the ideological patterns of the dominant class. So true is this, that as we noted above, it is around the theme of the defence of democracy and of individual liberties that the whole class has rallied.

The failure to understand how and why one can accept a policy of change, but not a questioning of the institutions, has enabled the most backward elements in the bourgeoisie (represented by the National Party) to impose their political line on the progressive, populist fraction, represented by the Christian Democrat

Party. This has occurred because the relationship between the oligarchic nucleus and some elements in the service bourgeoisie has been based on their common interests in the superstructure, even when Unidad Popular has formulated no plans for a rupture. The relationship between the National Party and the Christian Democrats can be expressed in the formula: anti-communism equals anti-statism; in other words, not only must changes be legitimate, they must guarantee co-participation. They must be changes which preserve present institutions, i.e. they must take place with the participation of all classes, thus ensuring consensus and closing the circle. We noted earlier, that not change, but illegitimate change was rejected; this sentence can now be completed with the addition that all legitimate change which guarantees co-participation in power is acceptable. The circle may become wider, so long as it remains closed.

The political axis of the right has however moved to the centre. This is understandable, for its best policy is to force the Unidad Popular into a confrontation with the consensual values embodied in legal forms, so dear to the middle classes as the reflection of their constitutional history, their own accession to power. As Marx has pointed out, referring to the French bougeoisie, 'a whole superstructure of feelings, illusions, ways of thinking, conceptions of life arises above the different forms of property ...' The refuge of the right which it is most difficult to conquer is precisely this whole gamut of feelings, illusions, ways of thinking. To give battle in these conditions leads to a dilemma: either the revolutionary model is shattered in the effort to make it express such a superstructure; or the real root of the difficulty has to be faced: re-education by means of the diffusion of new values. But is there time for the new values to impose themselves before the dominant ideology can distort the effects of the policy of structural changes? The bourgeoisie has the advantage of operating with present values, and uses them to contain and circumscribe. Such values as mobility, profit, property, agreement and consensus are used to legitimize a hegemony, and not to promote an authentic democracy.

A policy of change related to the desire for social mobility in groups and individuals can be compatible with greater state control of the economy and with a policy of redistribution of income, but only so long as it preserves the social differences between different strata, which are concealed behind a technocratic façade. Most revealing in this context are the efforts both of the

National Party and of the Christian Democrats to mobilize professional and technical groups either by supporting their economic claims, when faced with the government policy of fixing maximum incomes, or by urging them to become pressure groups capable of standing up to the power of the state. Thus the College of Lawyers has undertaken the defence of the judiciary, demanding that the campaign of denigration should cease, since 'it hampers plans for collective progress' and 'accentuates the deterioration in the democratic regime and the state of law of which we are so proud'.[4] The engineers in turn claim the right to take part in the revolutionary process as leaders 'who must in no way be submitted to political changes'.[5] The College of Engineers protested against alleged violations of elementary human rights, echoed by businessmen.[6] On 22 July 1971, the College of Lawyers published a protest against the government's failure to include lawyers among those entitled to more than the fixed maximum income, and criticized the 'lack of consideration shown by the relevant organs to our Order...' and the 'unjustified and offensive contempt' with which they had been treated, which they were bound to resent in view of 'the dignity of their profession'.[7]

Shortly afterwards, the strike of the supervisors in the copper industry broke out. They demanded effective participation in management and in decisions concerning working conditions. It was to all intents and purposes a political movement, in spite of the denials of those who took part.[8] Shortly afterwards they were publicly supported by the Junta de Profesionales of Concepción, which united employees in various industries, together with lawyers and members of the university of Concepción.

The appeal to professional and technical groups acquired more consistency when these groups were publicly called upon to join the Confederación Única de Profesionales de Chile or CUPCH (United Chilean Confederation of Professionals). On 29 August 1971 the press published details of the aims of the confederation, notably 'to secure respect for the freedom to work ... and to ensure that professionals, technicians and specialists should play the part

[4] *El Mercurio*, 10 January 1971.
[5] *Ibid.*, 6 November 1971. See also *La Prensa*, 18 November 1971. *La Prensa* was founded on 28 October 1970, after the victory of Unidad Popular, by members of the Christian Democrat Party, and ex-members of the Frei government.
[6] *El Mercurio*, 28 November 1971.
[7] *Ibid.*, 22 July 1971.
[8] *Ibid.*, 16 August 1971.

in the national development for which they have been prepared'. 'Strength through unity' would ensure the achievement of these aims.[9] The campaign was maintained throughout September, and was extended to the medical profession.

The strategy of mobilizing the middle strata is designed to create a model of a 'centrist' society, politically dominated by an alliance of groups within the service bourgeoisie. On the economic plane its aims would be expressed in 'communitarian' formulas of popular capitalism, which it would be difficult for the bourgeoisie to reject, since in the first place it is too weak, and secondly they derive anyhow from the policy which the populist fraction of the bourgeoisie put through during the Frei government (agrarian reform based on middle or small property, co-operatives, social welfare for the middle sectors, improved agricultural wages, increased state intervention in the economy).

THE BOURGEOISIE, THE CHURCH AND THE ARMY

Two points must be noted concerning the weakness of the bourgeoisie. First, it lacks any ideological consensus of its own owing to its divorce from the Catholic Church. Secondly it has lost influence over the army.

The Church has frequently shown itself inclined to accept changes aimed at producing a more just society, at uprooting the idea that property should benefit only the few, and it has denounced false Christians. The group of priests associated ever more clearly with the revolutionary process is growing in numbers and influence. In an investigation on the attitude of Christians to Marxists carried out by a Jesuit sociologist, the following results were obtained: 52·8 per cent welcome friendly co-operation in concrete projects, leaving their differences open; 36·8 per cent reject Marxism, but wish to continue the dialogue with the Marxists; 3·1 per cent consider that in view of the present situation Christians should reach an understanding with the Marxists. That is to say 92·7 per cent of the Chilean priests show a positive attitude towards the changes. Only 5·3 per cent are prepared to fight Marxism as a perverse doctrine, and 1·3 per cent avoid any contact with Marxists.

The rise of the Christian Left (which has split from the Christian Democrats) in October 1972 provides another illustration of

---

[9] *Ibid.*, 29 August 1971; cf. *La Prensa* of the same date.

the way in which Christian ideology contributes to the legitimation of the political process, leaving the bourgeoisie leaderless. The following paragraphs from its ideological manifesto are worth quoting: 'The task of our party is to contribute to the construction of socialism in Chile, by the contribution of forces inspired in Christianity ... For us Christian inspiration means that we are committed to struggle for the liberation of the people, for the construction of a just society ... The Christian experience in our view embraces aspirations to socialism ... We seek the revolutionary convergence between Christians and Marxists.' With a Church inclining towards such positions, Catholic ideology has ceased to be an element of consensus for the bourgeoisie, which is left only with the traditional reverence for the institution.

As regards the armed forces, they have accepted the role of a professional-technical group; government policy has assigned a hierarchical position to their function in terms of their real importance for the social and economic development of the country. The armed forces do not have intimate relations with the oligarchic nucleus, nor are they moved by any sense of being an oligarchy. They are drawn mainly from the middle strata, and to this extent are the equivalent of the bureaucracy. If we agree with Lenin (in *State and Revolution*) that the principal elements in a state are capital, bureaucracy and armed forces, then in Chile the system suffers from an internal cleavage caused by the separation between capital, and its instruments, namely the bureaucracy and the armed forces. According to our model this has arisen because, owing to the considerable importance of state intervention, and the weakness of the bourgeoisie, the fractions of the bourgeoisie inserted in the superstructure have acquired greater autonomy.

In this fluid situation, the growing weight of the bourgeoisie is likely to lead it to a centrist position. The only possible answer for Unidad Popular is a policy of mobilizing peasants and workers, and the replacement of the middle strata by representatives of the popular classes – assuming of course that they have been uncontaminated by the dominant system. It is a risky operation. Breaking with the middle sectors would not only constitute the crime of *lèse révolution*; politically it would consolidate the alliance of the right with the centre. One can only therefore advance slowly in a policy designed to break up the traditional ideological patterns of these middle sectors, until the classes benefiting from the revolutionary changes should have become strong enough to offer the middle strata the possibility of alliance with them. The problem is not to displace the middle sectors, but to isolate, structurally and ideologically, the dominant class – the industrial, commercial and financial bourgeoisie, and the landowning oligarchy.

This is what has happened with the radical fraction, which has evolved to the point that it has accepted historical materialism. One of the two parties into which it split as a result, led by the deputy Morales Abarzua, seems to be ideologically closer to the Communist and Socialist Parties, but its real nature is revealed by its close dependence on the teaching profession (hence its demand to control the Ministry of Education); the other, which is directed by Senator Bossay, has rejected Marxism and stuck to secularism, rationalism and social reformism. The problem for the government is that only so long as it remains within the present institutional system can it count on these middle sectors; should it overstep the limits, these sectors would form a 'centre' front around the political-populist fraction of the dominant bourgeoisie. Classes would be polarized not in terms of interests but in terms of ideologies. We return therefore to the starting point. Unidad Popular must work with the middle strata, but it must break with the dominant ideology. According to the Communist Party and the Socialist Party, this could be achieved by inverting the axis of political activity towards the peasants and workers. But is it possible for workers and peasants to take over and preserve the direction of the state when faced with a powerful opposition, able to injure them in their weak spot, namely their inexperience of the bureaucratic apparatus? This is one of the first questions which arise in a democratic revolution: efficiency in the use of mechanisms which were created precisely in order to prevent it. A long apprenticeship is required so that the process should become irreversible.

The fact that government action and the evolution of political consciousness are out of step may strengthen the middle sectors unless new forms of mobilization and participation are devised. Thus when class conflict is disguised as a struggle between government and opposition, which can be solved by the executive making use of constitutional devices, the bourgeoisie wins influence. If the government solves these conflicts, within the institutions, it forestalls the trend to polarization against it, but it strengthens the trends towards consensus. In the words of R. Tomic, the leader of the Christian Democrats, 'when you win with the right, it is the right which wins'. The Unidad Popular's chances of maintaining its hold on workers and peasants would thus decline. The peasant is attracted by the bourgeois slogan, 'the land to him who works it', and sees land as private property. The slogan of the Christian Democrats, 'the firm belongs to the workers', introduces the same idea into the industrial sector, it is the answer to 'state property'. Can in fact the policy of expropriation without mass mobilization win the allegiance of the peasant and working classes? Of their bodies perhaps, but not of their souls, which still respond to the ideology of the populist fraction of the dominant bourgeoisie. The duel between Unidad Popular and the Christian Democrats for the alliance with the peasants and the workers becomes fiercer, and one must not leave out of account the strong union control exercised by the Christian Democrats both in the middle strata and among the peasants.

It is the *Movimiento de Izquierda Revolucionaria* (MIR) which claims to stand for radicalization by means of the preponderance of the workers and peasants. But without effective mass support it remains isolated in a system which admits of an active opposition. Fundamentally it disregards the strategy of the right, designed to bring about a realignment around a 'centrist' coalition which will displace the traditional oligarchy and leave no room for a combination such as Unidad Popular to present an opposing front. One must not forget that Unidad Popular, because of its socially heterogeneous character, tends to favour this trend. Hence we cannot completely discount the possibility of an understanding, agreement, or compromise between Unidad Popular and parts or the whole of the Christian Democrat Party. Who shall say where the dividing line must fall, in order to avoid falling into some Byzantine intrigue? To what mast shall we tie ourselves to be safe from the siren songs of the bourgeoisie? Will class consciousness protect us? But does class consciousness not recognize many gradations?

The strengthening of the centre, representing the preponderance of the political fractions of the bourgeoisie, gives greater weight to the superstructure, which carries out fully its functions of legitimation and stabilization. At the same time the popular movement is prevented from creating its own legitimating values by means of a policy of mobilization, since logically, these values would impair the stability, which has been agreed on. But one must not lose sight of the fact that within the ideology of consensus, there are elements – as yet inarticulate – of the ideology of the working class. These elements must be developed so that they may express in a more objective way the real interests of workers in general, faced with an abstract ideology, manipulated by the dominant class.

THE BEHAVIOUR OF POLITICAL GROUPS

Hitherto the policies of the bourgeoisie have been analysed in conceptual terms. We shall now turn to an analysis of its actual strategy, which can be divided into five phases.

First phase. This lasted from January to March 1971. The government began to apply its programme, using legal devices, and avoiding parliament. This posed the problem of legitimacy as opposed to legality.

Second phase. The election of local councillors in April. The most backward fraction began its campaign to impugn the representativeness of the government and its right to impose its programme without the consent of the nation. The discussion found its most extreme expression around the demand for a plebiscite, which the most conservative groups put forward from now on.

Third phase. From May to July 1971, a period during which expropriations in favour of the Area of Social Property were pushed forward. The opposition intensified its efforts to discredit the government by accusing it of anti-democratic and arbitrary attitudes. This phase culminated in the by-election of July in Valparaiso.

Fourth phase. Lasting from August to November 1971. The theme of 'the defence of democracy' dominated the political scene; the Christian Democratic Party took over the leadership of the bourgeoisie, which led to the secession of the Christian Left.

Fifth phase. From November 1971 to January 1972. With the shifting of the position of the Christian Democrats, political lines were more sharply drawn, and the institutional conflict came to the fore. The struggle between the executive and Congress was waged against the background of the campaign conducted by the middle sectors in the name of 'liberty', anti-statism and anti-Marxism. The phase culminated in the ministerial reorganization of 16 January 1972, when the fraction of the Radical Party most representative of these middle sectors was brought into the government of the Unidad Popular. The government was thus trying to widen its base, faced with the danger that these same middle sectors might be won over by the 'centrist' strategy of the bourgeoisie.

The following analysis of events is based on the division within the bourgeoisie. On the one hand the monopolist or pro-monopolist bourgeoisie has as its mouthpiece the National Party and the various interest associations (the Confederation of Production and Commerce, Chambers of Commerce, the SNA etc.). The political fraction of the bourgeoisie is less tied to the economic structure, and is concerned with the preservation of the institutional structure; its mouthpiece is the Christian Democrat Party, with its many professional, working class and peasant organizations (it controls two out of three of the Peasant Confederations). The two groups are in agreement only on some policies; on others they differ.

Both parties are critical of étatism, demand respect for persons and property, and the defence of existing institutions. But the demand of the Christian Democrats in the early stages to participate in the revolutionary process contrasts with the policy of the National Party of forming a united front against the government. Nevertheless they acted together occasionally, notably in the by-election in Valparaiso, and reached an agreement by August/September 1971. Thus, while the Christian Democrats began by defending their right to switch from defence of bourgeois democracy to participation in the revolutionary process – which in their view merely continued the policies of the years 1965–70, they were gradually won over to the anti-Marxist position implicit in the united front.

The traditional right wing launched its campaign for the defence of private property – in the guise of small and medium property – proclaiming that liberty and respect for institutions are indissolubly linked with property.[10] Without security of property, investment would cease, leading to unemployment. Equally they declared that thousands of small shareholders should not be deprived of their holdings.[11] The Sociedad de Fomento Fabril criticized the formation of the Area of Social Property on the grounds that more than 300,000 owners of factories and industries would be affected,[12] whereas in fact only some 100 firms were to be incorporated in the Area of Social Property and over 50 per cent of the capital of the banks was controlled by no more than 10 shareholders.

---

[10] *El Mercurio*, 22 January 1972
[11] *Ibid.*, 31 January 1972.
[12] *Ibid.*, 20 November 1971.

Nevertheless, *El Mercurio* argued[13] that those who would suffer from the formation of the Area of Social Property would not be the privileged and the capitalists, but the middle classes who had saved money, the craftsmen, traders, farmers, etc. The president of the Confederation of Production proclaimed that 'control of the banks means the loss of economic, social and political freedom'; and *El Mercurio* again stressed that the advance to socialism involved not only the incorporation of large areas of economic life into the sphere of state property, but that it led inevitably to 'limitations on the private life of individuals'. Thus 'the ending of the secrecy of the banks is one of the greatest changes introduced into the life of Chileans'.[14]

Meanwhile the Christian Democrats, though they also defended private property, stressed the demand for participation. On 23 January 1971, Senator Benjamin Prado 'demanded participation for shareholders and employees in banks', and rejected further state control.[15] The party attacked collectivism and accused the government of forwarding a policy of 'state socialism', which excluded the workers from participation, and which the party would totally reject.[16] The defence of participation, and the rejection of étatism were the main lines of Christian Democrat policy, with which they strove to preserve their own identity. Thus they resisted attempts to persuade them to join the National Party in a united front, and sought on the contrary to open discussions with the Unidad Popular on those points on which their policies coincided, maintaining however their determination not to accept what they regarded as illegality or anti-democratic methods. Their policy is illustrated in the speech of Senator Irureta, president of the party, at the plenum in May 1971, in Cartagena: 'There is a wide field in which we can reach agreement with the Marxists . . . We believe we should move from a purely negative opposition to an opposition which offers solutions . . . There is a possibility here of a wide ranging democratic dialogue which will contribute to the stability of the country . . . The Christian Democrats will not oppose a national, popular effort, in all those fields on which, because we coincide, a dialogue is possible, a minimum of consensus, a concerted action . . .'[17]

[13] 1 November 1971.
[14] 26 November 1971.
[15] *La Prensa*, 23 January 1971.
[16] *El Mercurio*, 10 May 1971.
[17] *Ibid.*, 9 May 1971.

This political behaviour expressed the thesis of 'the unity of the people', defended by Tomic when he stated that 'without the Christian Left (meaning the Christian Democrats as a whole, and not merely some groups) there cannot be in Chile a democratic revolutionary process . . .' It is the model of the populist alternative, opposed to the revolutionary, Marxist, 'anti-democratic' model, and as such attractive to the middle sectors. Revolution in Chile might follow two roads: a violent one, represented by the Marxist dominated Unidad Popular, or a democratic one, carried out by Unidad Popular together with the Christian Democrats. The reality behind this argument is that the Christian Democrats would enable the middle sectors to insert themselves into a popular revolutionary process which they would dominate ideologically.

THE CRUCIAL ISSUE

Such considerations lead on to a crucial question in the Chilean experience: is the process of socialization of the means of production carried out within the existing institutional system irreversible or not? The problem must be seen in terms of whether the structural changes are reflected quickly enough in the political field. The bourgeoisie has always insisted that other political alternatives should remain open. The Christian Democrats presented themselves as a popular and democratic alternative – but this will inevitably drive them into the position of being the 'centrist' leaders of the right. The 'defence of democracy' thus acquires a double significance: it becomes not only a demand to respect the national consensus, but a guarantee that other political options remain open. This explains why the right, by trying to form a United Front, is seeking to prevent the strengthening of the government coalition. Should the middle sectors join and 'democratize' the government, its real leadership, that of the Socialist and Communist Parties, will be concealed, and the polarization democracy/dictatorship will be less clear.

Meanwhile Unidad Popular has attempted to win the middle sectors, without reaching an agreement with the Christian Democrats. It has strengthened itself by the inclusion in government on 16 January 1972 of representatives of that wing of the Radical Party which refused to accept the modifications introduced in Radical Party policy at its last convention.

While the National Party continues its campaign to promote a

United Front, from May 1970, the Christian Democrats took up
the cause of public order, notably in connection with the assassination of Perez Zujovic on 8 June 1971. Their respective accusations
against the government can be followed in the columns of *El
Mercurio* and *La Prensa*. By July, when both parties joined to
support a common candidate in the by-election in Valparaiso, the
strategy of the most backward fractions of the bourgeoisie had
been imposed on the Christian Democrats. The ensuing secession
of the Christian Left was welcomed by the conservative sectors,
who saw in it the possibility of a further consolidation of the
Christian Democrats. In turn the Christian Democrats started to
use the language of the right, culminating in a defence of the
traditional methods of teaching law in the Faculty of Law: law
seen, of course, as the written expression of the dominant spirit in
society, expressing the co-existence of all in harmony. Beneath this
idea of consensus, universal values, natural law, juridical norms
intrinsic to human nature lies concealed the objective reality of the
existence of social classes, antagonistic to each other. If the law,
the political constitution of Chile, states that 'today there are no
privileged classes in Chile', then there are none.[18] Law, which is
the creation of the classes in power, is thus above objective
reality. The argument for consensus or social harmony is based on
juridical norms which transform classes into bodies which can and
should reach agreement with each other. Those who strive to
make law descend to the level of human interests compromise the
autonomy of legal science and of society itself, as *El Mercurio*
stated on 19 and 25 October.

Nevertheless the National Party and the Christian Democrats
did not always agree on tactics. The Christian Democrats in
particular, with their heterogeneous following, needed to maintain their identity, their greater willingness to accept change in
spite of the fact that they had now come out openly in defence of
the institutional regime coupled with a capitalist structure favour-
ing the middle sectors. The National Party accepted this tactical
divergence as inevitable; at the same time it took up, in modified
form the policy of participation of the workers in enterprises. It
announced its intention of presenting a draft law designed to
'renew economic structures and make them more efficient for
production and more just in distribution...by introducing workers
into the ownership and management of factories'.[19] On the other

[18] As was stated by the President of the Supreme Court on 1 March 1971.
[19] *El Mercurio*, 18 November 1971.

hand, when the National Party impeached the Minister of the Economy, it was not supported by the Christian Democrats, who preferred to seek an understanding with the president, on condition that a law should be submitted to Congress defining clearly the three areas of the economy. They rejected the National Party accusations on the ground that they were based simply on the defence of capitalist structures. The National Party in turn criticized the Christian Democrats, challenging them to prove that they were defending capitalist structures, and declared themselves to be defending 'the structures maintained by the Christian Democrat government'.[20]

A minor, accidental event, tactically mishandled, served to bring the two parties together again. On the occasion of the discovery of some alleged speculations by a well-known business man, the press of Unidad Popular and the government mentioned the name of Frei. Frei replied in a declaration in which he accused Unidad Popular of disregarding such permanent values as respect for property, people, tranquillity, order and discipline, a declaration which was also aggressively anti-communist: 'At this moment, when the Communist Party is imposing its will . . .' the public must not be daunted, but must defend what is most sacred.[21] Frei's reaction served to galvanize an anti-communist campaign, and polarized public opinion with the choice: either 'democracy, with or without changes', or 'dictatorship and change'. Unidad Popular replied with: 'either socialism or fascism'. From this moment, the Christian Democrats, led by their most conservative wing, the followers of Frei, took over the leadership of the right. 'Eduardo Frei cannot be omitted from the list of those who may succeed Dr Allende' declared *La Prensa* on 27 September 1971. And Senator Fuentealba noted some of the new Christian Democrat positions: 'The Marxist leaders are sectarians'; 'they do not accept the existence of the opposition'; 'for them pluralism exists only within the government'; 'the Communist Party and the Socialist Party wish to prevent any dialogue or *rapprochement* between the president and the Christian Democrats'.[22] It is clear from this that the Christian Democrats were pressing to be included in the decision-making process in view of their role as an alternative government.

It must be noted that the presence of the middle sectors in a

[20] *Ibid.*
[21] *La Prensa*, 25 September 1971.
[22] *Ibid.*, 29 September 1971.

combination of popular forces should not be confused with the representation within such a combination of the populist progressive wing of the bourgeoisie. Hence the participation of the Christian Democrat peasant, worker, or employee must be achieved without any political compromise with the structure of the party itself. The Christian Left accepts participation in the process itself, but plays no part in the political bargaining from within the camp of the bourgeoisie.

The Christian Democrats alleging that the government had failed to present a draft law to Congress defining the three areas of the economy, which had been their condition for refusing to support the National Party in its impeachment of the Minister of the Economy, now presented on 15 October 1971 their own draft law of constitutional reform. The debate on this draft was carried out, in the ideological sphere, in terms of 'communitarianism' versus 'étatism'. The latter was attacked on the grounds that it represented political dictatorship and economic inefficiency.[23] In addition the draft put forward the demand that enterprises should belong to the workers, who should have full powers of decision in management and control of surpluses – thus impeding a centrally planned policy of investment. Put forward in a society which still comprises a powerful private economic sector, and within the ideology of the dominant bourgeoisie, such a policy could lead only to the atomization of the working class and to increasing the mesocratic trends in society.

From another point of view, the draft law for constitutional reform forms part of the counter attack by the bourgeoisie, using one of the powers of the state, but different bourgeois interests are here interwoven. For the Christian Democrats, their attack on the government, based on Congress, is their reaction to a process which has broken the national consensus, and hence the possibility of reaching an agreement which might consolidate their position as an alternative government. They represent the political expression of those who wish to construct in Chile a 'communitarian socialism'.[24] The National Party however see the offensive based on Congress as helping to the formation of the United Front.

There are however deeper causes for this offensive. Until the victory of Unidad Popular, there were no serious internal contradictions in the structure of the state. Economic power controlled

[23] *Ibid.*, 30 October 1971
[24] *Ibid.*, 13 November 1971

political power. But when Unidad Popular came to power, these interests were separated, leading to an institutional crisis, which soon took the form of a conflict between the legislative and the executive. The loss of unity in the state was regarded by the bourgeoisie as a 'crisis of democracy', whereas it is in reality the loss of their political power, while they still have economic power. Since the bourgeoisie, however, is strongly dependent on the state, it has not the strength to resist the government. When it is forced to pay its debts to the state, to submit to the regulation of credit and production, to absorb some proportion of the rise in salaries, when it can no longer indulge in speculation, then it denounces 'spoliation', 'attacks on personal dignity', 'flagrant violations of essential rights'.

Faced with an institutional crisis, the reply of the bourgeoisie is: strengthen Congress. Faced with a political power which does not respect its interests, it replies: set up the private sector of the economy as part of the political constitution of the state.[25] Under the pretext of strengthening Congress and defending the maintenance of order, right-wing strategy is now being followed, under the leadership of the Christian Democrats. Having passed through the phase of negotiation/participation, the opposition enters the phase of 'co-power' (the Congress) capable of neutralizing the executive. A strong legislature will counter-balance the executive; hence the demand for longer sessions of Congress, during which deputies can put forward draft laws, without confining themselves to discussing drafts put forward by the executive; hence proposals for the approval by the Senate of appointments to high administrative office, where previously the president was free to appoint on his own initiative; hence the demand to increase the number of high officials who can be held accountable politically (e.g. the Director General of Investigations, the general in command of the Carabineros). Other proposals are made for procedural changes which would impede the consolidation of the left.

[25] Early in December 1971, a gathering of several thousand people was held to form the 'Front of the Private Area', under the auspices of the Confederation of Production and Commerce. All the principal firms were represented as well as the National Party and the Christian Democrats. A national committee was elected, under the presidency of a medium businessman, and it inaugurated a countrywide campaign to protect 'private enterprise' by means of the formation of a front of the masses, and by constitutional reforms imposed by the National Party and Christian Democrat majority in Congress.

The right sees in Congress the possibility of welding its pressure groups together, and reviving a new version of parliamentarism. For the populist progressive fraction access to the executive is still open. However, should Unidad Popular succeed in forming itself into one party, even this road would be barred to the Christian Democrats, unless they chose to fuse with the traditional right, and lost their identity. A weak and fragmented bourgeoisie can only find support in a collegiate power (parliament). But when it is based on one or several political fractions (such as the service bourgeoisie) it will inevitably proceed to the acceptance of a mesocratic society. One of the dangers facing Unidad Popular is that it might come to serve as a channel for this process.

H. E. Bicheno[1]

6 Anti-Parliamentary Themes in Chilean History: 1920–70

A SURVEY OF THE HEADLINES IN THE CHILEAN PRESS DURING THE first year of the Unidad Popular (UP) government might give the unwary observer the impression that the period has been characterized by a succession of subversive plots. Conspiracy theories have abounded and dramatic public announcements (like modern ceremonies of exorcism), have marked the official recognition of each theory while presaging its prompt disappearance from the front pages of the newspapers and from the view of an increasingly sceptical populace.

Events over the past year more than justify the alarm of the UP. The 'peaceful road to socialism' has been obstructed by the activities of groups of the extreme left and the extreme right which have each committed one major political assasination.[2] The result of this has been a very high degree of political polarization from which the UP is unlikely to benefit. It is the first of those assassinations which concerns us most here.

Chilean political development, long characterized by a relatively low level of physical violence, was abruptly re-routed on 22 October 1970, when General René Schneider, Commander-in-Chief of the Chilean army, was shot and killed in an abortive kidnap plot. This plot, if successful, might have closed the democratic door to power which the presidential election of 4 September had opened for the UP. The most immediate result was

[1] The author is an historian working at the Instituto de Ciencias Políticas of the Universidad Católica, Santiago, Chile. Grants from the Department of Education and Science and from the Foreign Area Fellowship Programme made possible the research for this article.
[2] General René Schneider Chereau, 22 October 1970; Edmundo Pérez Zujovic, Minister of the Interior under Frei, killed by members of the *Vanguardia Organizada del Pueblo* on 8 June 1971.

the adoption of personal security measures by the new president
of a kind previously unseen in Chile. In the ensuing months the
name of the unfortunate general was invoked so frequently by the
UP, and often for such seemingly petty and partisan ends,[3] that the
circumstances of the crime itself seem almost to have been for-
gotten in the welter of propagandistic interpretations placed upon
it.

Yet the truth of the matter, as it emerged during the long trial
that ensued, was sufficiently dramatic not to require embellish-
ment. Briefly, a number of very senior officers had conspired with
a well-known retired general called Roberto Viaux, and an *ad hoc*
group of anti-communist zealots that followed him, and had
decided to make a *coup d'état*. Though the government overthrown
would have been that of out-going President Frei, the aim was to
prevent the UP taking power. Schneider had to be removed from
his post because of his open opposition to the scheme.[4] The state
of emergency that would automatically follow the kidnapping
would leave one of the plotters, General Camilo Valenzuela, as the
de facto ruler of the capital and in a perfect position to take over the
government. The feasibility of the plan was never tested because
General Schneider drew a pistol when his car was halted and his
jittery would-be kidnappers mortally wounded him.

The plot which led to the death of General Schneider, and the
later emergence of a neo-fascist phenomenon have historical antecedents of a more profound nature than is generally recognized.
It is the purpose of this article to trace those antecedents and to
indicate that they represent a recurrent theme in Chilean politics
whose importance is often overlooked.

THE 1920s: ALESSANDRI AND THE REVOLT OF THE ELECTORATE

The political structure that has governed Chile down to the
present day was largely built between 1925 and 1930. The political
and social forces that brought about this re-structuring found
expression in the personalities of Arturo Alessandri and Carlos
Ibáñez, with other figures, principally those of Marmaduke Grove

---

[3] Reaching an all-time low when Edmundo Pérez was murdered and *Ahora*,
a UP magazine, printed 'La derecha detrás del crimen' on its cover when it
was already known that extreme leftists, including a man recently pardoned
by President Allende, were responsible. *Ahora*, 15 June 1971.

[4] *El Mercurio*, 7 May 1970.

and some Radical Party leaders, playing supporting roles to both.

The two main figures, however, were the flamboyant, vocal and excitable Alessandri and his antithesis, Ibáñez. While nobody doubts their historical importance, it is as well to emphasize the degree to which the two men completely dominated Chilean politics from 1920 to 1960 – the year when Ibáñez died, having outlived his great rival by over nine years. The extreme personalization of politics in Chile during this period is largely attributable to their contribution. Both were presidents for two terms, ruling for a total of 21 years. Alessandri stood as a presidential candidate in 1920, 1931 and 1932. He was a pre-candidate in 1946, standing down in favour of the compromise candidature of his son Fernando. Carlos Ibáñez was a presidential candidate in 1927, 1938, 1942, 1952 and was a pre-candidate in 1925. In effect, since 1920, only the presidential election of 1964 can be said to have been unaffected by either Ibáñez or Alessandri, as even in 1970 the Alessandri mystique was still strong enough to play an important role.

Alessandri has been considered the more important figure largely because his victorious presidential candidature in 1920 has been held to represent a middle-class revolution which overthrew oligarchical domination in Chile.[5] He is also held to have led the revolt of the same sector against the parliamentary regime and finally, with the constitution of 1925, to have put an end to the dominance of an aristocratic fronde[6] that overthrew national considerations along with President Balmaceda in 1891, in order to rule for the exclusive benefit of its own and allied foreign interests.[7]

However, the reality was rather more complex. The traditional rural oligarchy, for sixty years before 1920, had shown a great ability to accept new personnel while preserving its way of life. Weakened by the abolition of entail in 1857 and later by the economic depression of 1858–60, they recruited new blood and new economic power among those whose wealth had been earned in mining, industry and commerce. Though some scholars have

[5] R. J. Alexander, *Prophets of the Revolution*, 4th ed., the Macmillan Co., New York, 1969, pp. 53–74.

[6] Alberto Edwards, *La Fronda aristocrática*, Editorial del Pacífico, Santiago, 1945, pp. 173, *passim*.

[7] H. Ramirez Necochea, *Balmaceda y la contrarrevolución de 1891*, Editorial Universitaria, Santiago, 1969. For a critique see H. Blakemore, 'The Chilean Revolution of 1891 and its Historiography', *HAHR*, Vol. XLV (1965), pp. 393–421.

attempted to suggest a parallel between the European and the Chilean *bourgeoisie*,[8] the Chilean situation was rather different. Both economic sectors, either as producers of raw materials or providing services related to that economic activity, based their economic power on international trade. There was a corresponding lack of the economic conflicts which the term *bourgeois* implies. Rather there was an agreement on a policy based on economic liberalism and progressive monetary inflation. The rural aristocracy and the new urban groups combined their forces to form a new ruling oligarchy.

Nonetheless, the relative importance of the rural and urban oligarchs was undergoing a rapid and continuous change.

TABLE 1[9]

Population, Urban and Rural 1865–1960

Year	Total In thousands	Urban	Rural	Total Growth Rate
		In percentages		
1865	1819	25·0	75·0	100·0
1875	2076	27·0	73·0	114·1
1885	2250	30·6	69·4	137·3
1895	2696	38·0	62·0	147·8
1907	3231	43·2	56·8	177·0
1920	3703	46·4	53·6	204·2
1930	4287	49·4	50·6	235·7
1940	5024	52·5	47·5	276·1
1952	5933	60·2	39·8	326·1
1960	7374	66·5	33·5	405·5

Perhaps provoked by the relative decline in importance of the agricultural sector, the principal differences between rural 'aristocrat' and urban '*nouveau riche*' were related to the rigidity of the structure of social acceptance imposed by the former and the social barriers placed by established Santiago high society before the advance of pushing new men from the provinces who were occupying positions in the administration, the professions and the

[8] H. Ramirez N., *Historia del Movimiento Obrero en Chile. Siglo XX*, Talleres Gráficos Lautaro, Santiago, 1956. For a critique see Anibal Pinto Santa Cruz, *Chile, un caso de desarrollo frustrado*, Editorial Universitaria, Santiago, 1962, pp. 36–40. Also Edwards, *op. cit.*, p. 25 with another view.

[9] From a synthesis of all available sources in J. Tapia V., *Bureaucratic Power in a Developing Country. The Case of the Chilean Social Security Administration*, unpublished PhD. dissertation, University of Texas, Austin, 1969.

armed forces previously monopolized by the 'aristocracy'.[10] This in no way implies that the new groups doubted the values of the upper class – indeed, the use of the word *siútico* to describe some of the new men was born of their excessive emulation of the aristocracy in the hope of being taken as one of its members.[11] The problem of social acceptance, once a certain standard of wealth and power had been achieved, became one of style rather than of values.[12] A concomittant of a decline in real power in an aristocracy is often an over-emphasis on manners or birth. Terms such as *siútico* became a social weapon of those who, possessing the correct surnames, were less important than their fathers had been. It has been observed that 'The incorporation of the middle sectors of society into the structure of power did not seem to entail the complete replacement of the traditional elite; it simply meant that they had to share the power with these newcomers – to come to terms, to compromise or negotiate.'[13]

This does not mean, of course, that they enjoyed doing so. Unless one comprehends the extent to which personal likes or dislikes divided the ruling class in Chile, one is not likely to grasp the source of many of Alessandri's problems in his first presidency. If manners make man, between 1920 and 1924 in Chile they contributed to unmake a president.

It is quite clear that Alessandri had been one of the worst abusers of the parliamentary system, participating wholeheartedly in the game of making and breaking cabinets with which the political elite entertained itself in Congress. This irritated the conservatives but their irritation became fury during the 1920 campaign when Alessandri not only promised social reforms but also sought and received the fervent support of the lower classes, using the mob to pressure Congress when it seemed that his opponent might cheat him of victory. Since the masses were largely disenfranchised, it was felt that Alessandri, for reasons of

[10] R. Donoso, *Alessandri. Agitador y Demoledor*, Fondo de Cultura Económica, Mexico, 1952, Vol. I, p. 206. Donoso writes: 'These elements lacked . . . class consciousness and distributed themselves among the traditional parties.'

[11] F. B. Pike, *Chile and the United States 1880–1962*, University of Notre Dame Press, 1963, p. 284.

[12] Land was coveted by the *nouveau riche* as a symbol of social status, prestige and acceptance. See S. M. Lipset, 'Values, Education and Entrepreneurship', in Lipset and A. Solari (eds.), *Elites in Latin America*, Oxford University Press, 1967, pp. 9–10.

[13] L. Ratinoff, 'The New Urban Groups: the Middle Classes', in Lipset and Solari, *op. cit.*, p. 74.

personal ambition, was unjustifiably involving the plebs in a process that was not of their concern. It was his demagogic capacity, not his moderate reform programme, that earned Alessandri the absurd reputation of a bolshevik in some upper class sectors.[14]

However, while the two factions of the ruling class wrangled bitterly, a large portion of the electorate was quite clearly uninterested in either of them. Thanks to an intricate electoral system, in 1920 Chile saw 166,113 voters casting 1,717,656 votes to elect 354 electors who in turn decided who should be president. 83,100 voters with 819,892 votes gave 175 electors to the *Unión Nacional* and its candidate, Luis Barros Borgoño. 82,083 voters with 889,810 votes gave 179 to the *Alianza Liberal* and Alessandri.[15] Objections and accusations of foul play nearly left the matter in the hands of a Congress overwhelmingly favourable to the *Unión Nacional*, but a neutral tribunal finally adjudged Alessandri the victor by a margin of one elector.[16]

An analysis of the voters by provinces indicates an even distribution throughout the land, Alessandri winning because of his overwhelming strength in the North and in Concepción.[17] The vote distribution is what one would expect in a clash between two factions of the ruling elite and in an election where bribery, fraud and intimidation were rather more important than ideas.

What is even more clear is that not even those elements of persuasion were able to get a majority of the electorate to the polls. Of 341,872 voters registered in 1918,[18] only 48·6% cast their votes on 25 June 1920. It would seem likely that accompanying

[14] A complicating factor was the issue of concession versus repression – it would seem likely that the shift in population towards the cities and the resulting 'social question' must inevitably coincide with an increasing defensive social rigidity on the part of the sector whose relative power is declining.

[15] These are all figures relating to the elections of 1918, 1920 and 1921 and are from Oficina Central de Estadística, *Censo Electoral 1921*, Sociedad de Imprenta y Litografía 'Universo', Santiago, 1922.

[16] A. Alessandri, *Recuerdos de Gobierno*, Editorial Nascimiento, Santiago, 1967, vol. I, p. 51.

[17] In Tarapacá and Antofagasta the *Alianza Liberal* won 22 electors and their opponents only 2. Both of these provinces as well as Concepción had serious economic problems at this time, as well as a tradition of hostility towards Santiago.

[18] In the three congressional elections following the first up-dating of the voting registers since 1890, the abstention rate was: 1915: 18·67; 1918: 46·9: 1921: 46·77.

the political rise of the new men was a decline in voter interest. While Alessandri represented a movement for change within the system, a far larger movement was expressing, through abstention, discontent not necessarily with the Conservative Party as much as with the political system that the ruling class as a whole had chosen to install and misuse.[19]

The years 1920-24 were marked by a continuation of the political deadlock implicit in the extremely close results of 1920. Though the 1921 congressional elections witnessed a marked increase in the votes obtained by the Democratic and Radical Parties, with government sponsorship this was to be expected. More significant perhaps was the continued high abstention rate (46·7%). As the techniques he had employed in opposition were used equally effectively against him, Alessandri joined the ranks of those alienated from the existing system. Diatribes against the opposition, particularly the 'old men of the Senate', came to dominate the president's public utterances. He blamed the *Unión Nacional* for his inability to keep his electoral promises, and yet his personality was responsible for deepening the divisions among the liberal groups, some of whom supported him while others did not. His effect on the Radical Party was similar, as his behaviour was deeply offensive to the old guard,[20] particularly Enrique MacIver, the party's grand old man.

Alessandri's personal popularity also declined as a result of continued economic problems and of the repressive measures taken to control popular unrest.[21] At the same time, even those who were inclined to favour his cause felt that some of his ministers and his closest advisers were '. . . mediocre men and nobodies . . .'[22] Not only were some of these men known to be inept, they were also considered to be dishonest.[23] The matter of corruption in governmental spheres was clearly not a new one. The habits for which Alessandri's friends were condemned by the *Unión Nacional* were not new in Chilean politics – and if the

---

[19] R. Donoso, *op. cit.*, Vol. I, Chapter 4, 'La oligarquía Parlamentaria'.

[20] Enrique Oyarzún, *Unpublished Memoirs*, pp. 6–8.

[21] Carlos Vicuña Fuentes, *La Tiranía en Chile*, Imprenta O'Higgins, Santiago, 1945, Vol. I, pp. 114–19.

[22] *Ibid.*, p. 119.

[23] Vicuña, Donoso and Oyarzún, to name only three, concur on this point. Alessandri himself, attempting to refute the charges made against his confidants, lists his *ministers* – an unconvincing debating trick. See A. Alessandri, 'Rectificaciones al Tomo IX', Imprenta Universitaria, Santiago, 1941, pp. 15–21.

charges against these men were correct, they were guilty of mere pilfering when compared with the entire political elite which shared the responsibility for manipulating the national finances for their own private benefit.[24] Nonetheless, even in theft there are important differences in style, and the same men who had encouraged monetary inflation in order to borrow from the government at one price and repay less, were shocked by others who hired out their political influence to obtain favourable government contracts for foreign and domestic companies.

There was at least one powerful body of opinion, the army, which came to regard both practices as corrupt, feeling that the national interest should come first, and claimed as its own the *noblesse oblige* long conspicuous by its absence among the rulers of Chile.[25]

The deadlock between 1920 and 1924 led both factions to make advances to the military, strengthening the position of the one sector of society capable of overthrowing both. Meanwhile, by delaying interminably long requested reforms in the system of promotions and salaries, they tempted it to do so.

THE ARMY

While clearly an awareness of the decline of Chile's international importance played a part in both the conservative dislike of the new members of the ruling class and in the alienation of voters from the political process, the sector which most forcibly resented this decline was the army. With a tradition of martial glory second to none in South America, it was also the first truly modern army in the continent[26] thanks to the re-organization, amplification and re-equipment that the Prussian mission under Emil Körner

[24] The self-nominated patricians of the rural aristocracy were not above this. In 1925 the *Sociedad Nacional de Agricultura* (SNA) received a subsidy from the government at a time when the president of the SNA was also Minister of Agriculture. The SNA was a self-help society. See G. M. McBride, *Chile, Land and Society*, American Geographical Society, New York, 1936, p. 230.

[25] On the disparaging attitude of the middle and upper groups towards the *roto*, see F. B. Pike, 'Aspects of Class Relations in Chile 1850–1960', *HAHR*, XLIII, No. 1, February 1963, p. 17.

[26] During the early decades of this century, Chile sent military advisers to a number of South American nations – positions now occupied by US personnel

accomplished between 1891 and 1910.[27] During the latter half of the parliamentary period, however, the power of the Chilean army became more apparent than real. The growth in power and prestige of Argentina and Brazil naturally produced a relative decline in the importance of Chile. However, when a booming and militarily re-organized Peru seemed to threaten, in 1920, the absolute decline in the military preparedness of the army became apparent. The equipment was old, the ammunition scarce and the organization deficient.[28] Most of the blame for this was attributed by civilian and soldier alike, to the neglect of the Ministers of War. A man who knew most of them at too close a range to be hood-winked commented that '. . . with few exceptions, the most mediocre elements have been appointed as Ministers of War'.[29] The matter was made worse by the fact that the few ministers who attempted to achieve something were inevitably prevented from doing so by the frequent changes in ministerial combinations.

Military revolt against this state of affairs can be traced to an abortive plot in 1912 about which President Barros Lucco, as was his wont, did nothing. However, when the conspiracy named after General Armstrong was uncovered in 1919, wiser politicians than those ruling Chile might have seen the writing on the wall. Among the aims of the conspiracy was the creation of a military *junta* to run the country through a figurehead civilian president. Even more significant was the degree to which a number of officers believed that the institutional problems of the army required political solutions and their complete scepticism over the capacity of the politicians to find these solutions without being forced to do so. The aims of the 1919 conspiracy provide a blueprint not only for the events of 1924, but also for practically every movement of protest that has convulsed the army since then.

In public declaration, Generals Armstrong and Moore stated the five main objectives of the plotters. Points one, two and five are simply professional complaints – the need to consolidate the unity of the officer corps and to strengthen military discipline

[27] Though by expanding the officer corps against Körner's advice, the Chilean army created an over-officered situation that was to plague it for decades.

[28] L. Errázuriz, *La llamada movilización de 1920*, Escuela Tipográfica 'La Gratitud Nacional', Santiago, 1923, pp. xii–xxiii.

[29] Columbano Millas, *Los Secretos que divulga un secretario privado de los ministros de guerra...*', Imprenta Universitaria, Santiago, 1923. His information on the incompetence and irresponsibility of some ministers (pp. 15–102) is very revealing.

'. . . frequently undermined by political influence . . .', and the need for Congress to solve long-delayed problems of promotion and recruitment.[30] Considerations of a trade-union type played similar roles in army conspiracies in 1924, 1939, 1947–55 and 1969. Points three and four, however, grant us a clear insight into the minds of these officers and illustrate the degree to which institutional problems were felt to require far-reaching national solutions. The aims expressed were: 'To impel the industrial development of the country in order to obtain our economic independence and to ensure the national defence, supplying ourselves from our own resources, creating factories for military equipment and all kinds of industries to supply abundant work for the populace.'[31] Further, Congress was to be 'asked' to dispatch the laws demanded by the working class in order to end their anguish which '. . . affects the troops who should not be brought into contact with popular agitation'. Thus, because these officers felt a need for domestic sources of supply and did not like to use their men for internal repression, the nation had to industrialize thoroughly, guided by the most ample social legislation. To obtain these changes, the officers intended to strengthen the executive both against popular effervescence and against the legislative branch.

Though never proved in court, it seems that Alessandri was involved in the plot, retreating from further participation primarily because of the melodramatic behaviour of General Armstrong.[32] Whatever the truth of the matter may be, as president, Alessandri showed no small degree of favour towards the conspirators, promoting some and re-incorporating others.[33] General Brieba, marginally involved in the plot and Alessandri's appointee as army Commander-in-Chief, put an end to the investigations of the conspiracy in an order dated 5 September 1921. Three years later, to the day, a variety of birds came home to roost.

It should be remembered that in 1919, under a cloud of suspicion, Major Carlos Ibáñez was transferred from his post as

[30] See A. Walker Valdés, Revolución? . . . La verdad sobre el motín militar, Imprenta Selecta, Santiago, 1919.

[31] Ibid., p. 64.

[32] R. Donoso, op. cit., p. 238, Note 6; C. Millas, op. cit., p. 153; basing himself on the trial, Walker Valdés denies this: op. cit., p. 39.

[33] R. Donoso, op. cit., p. 237. Among those convicted were General Alberto Herrera and Major Ambrosio Viaux – both fathers of future leaders of army conspiracies.

Director of the Carabineros School to the humble post of Prefect of Police in Iquique.[34] There, he later admitted, he was a supporter of Alessandri in 1920, and as a result he was given the plum post of Director of the Cavalry School in 1921.[35] Regrettably, one can only conjecture about the early relationship of these men, but in December 1923, Alessandri chose the Cavalry School to make the first of several highly political speeches to the army.[36] Sitting next to his benefactor, Ibáñez listened attentively as the president blamed the opposition for the political deadlock and proposed a toast to a near future when the 'redeeming' reforms would be law and the nation could be at peace.[37]

Alessandri's appeals to the middle-ranking officers at the Cavalry School and his use of the army[38] and all the power of governmental intervention, in defiance of a prior gentleman's agreement, to obtain a majority in the congressional elections of March 1924, were countered by a conspiracy called TEA. The leaders of this movement were the conservative leader Ladislao Errázuriz and the leading anti-Alessandri liberal, Francisco Huneeus.[39] The plotters made contacts with senior army and navy officers of a traditionalist bent, attracting many others by concentrating their attacks on the decline of public morality which they attributed to a *camarilla execrable* that surrounded the president.

In a complicated sequence of events,[40] precipitated by the action of the newly elected congressmen in voting themselves handsome salaries in defiance of the constitution and of public opinion, the plans of TEA were pre-empted by a group of 57 young officers[41] in a spontaneous show of disgust on 2 September

[34] E. Würth Rojas, *Ibáñez. Caudillo Enigmático*, Editorial del Pacífico, Santiago, 1958, p. 18.

[35] R. Boizard, *Cuatro Retratos en Profundidad*, Imprenta el Imparcial, Santiago, 1950, p. 12.

[36] E. Würth, *op. cit.*, p. 23.

[37] *Ibid.*, p. 24.

[38] General Brieba in *Actuación del Ejército en las elecciones de 1924*, Santiago, 1927, insists that the supervising officers were legally under executive control. Similar pressure had sparked the 1891 civil war.

[39] E. Monreal, *Historia completa y documentada del período revolucionario 1924–25*, Imprenta Nacional, Santiago, 1929, p. 135.

[40] For a narrative of these events, see F. M. Nunn, *Chilean Politics 1920–31, The Honorable Mission of the Armed Forces*, University of New Mexico Press, 1970.

[41] Among those who acted were Marmaduke Grove, leading figure in the *coups d'état* of January 1925 and June 1932, and Ariosto Herrera who tried

1924. Though the president cheerfully used the pressure of the officers to obtain, at last, the passage of his social legislation, his opponents of TEA, using the navy as leverage,[42] forced him out of office. Alessandri discovered, to his intense chagrin, that even those officers who favoured his programme were perfectly capable of separating the man from what he had come to see as his cause.[43] He was replaced by a triumvirate of senior officers, his new laws were ignored and TEA appeared to have won.

The victors soon learned that they too were to obtain scant benefit from the Pandora's box they had opened. In the last effort made by the traditional oligarchy to impose one of its own members as president, they announced the candidature of Ladislao Errázuriz. Carlos Ibáñez, Marmaduke Grove and some leading radicals[44] deposed the ruling triumvirate and cast the *Unión Nacional* into as serious a disarray as the events of September had cast the parties of the *Alianza Liberal*. A caretaker government of civilians, with Ibáñez as Minister of War, ruled until Alessandri returned from exile, his popularity restored by the brief taste of conservative rule that Chile had experienced.

Thus, three revolts came together. That of TEA, remembering 1891 and reacting to continued sectorial decline, that of the electorate, disgusted by the degeneration of political behaviour, and that of the army, reacting against national and institutional decline. It is one of the ironies of history that the immediate beneficiary of these developments was Arturo Alessandri, who was to some extent the target of all three revolts.

THE INTERIM: JANUARY 1925–MAY 1927

From the time of the noise of sabres until Carlos Ibáñez finally held all the reins of power in his hands in 1927, the parliamentary oligarchy was kept uncomfortably aware of the presence of a new and genuine third force in Chilean politics. The charges of corruption, raised up for partisan ends by TEA, were used to castigate aristocrat and *siútico* alike. A short-lived newspaper edited by the poet Vicente Huidobro supported by Manuel

and failed in 1939. See R. Aldunate Philips, *Ruido de Sables*, Escuela Lito-Tipográfica 'La Gratitud Nacional', Santiago, 1970, p. 32.
[42] E. Oyarzún, *op. cit.*, pp. 21–6, contains Francisco Huneeus's account of the events of September. The TEA *coup* was planned for November.
[43] Carlos Saez Morales, *Recuerdos de un Soldado*, Editorial 'Ercilla', Santiago, 1934, Vol. I, pp. 93–4.
[44] Notably Oyarzún and his protegé Juan Antonio Ríos.

Hidalgo[45] and expressing the views of many young officers, especially Marmaduke Grove, gained notoriety (and its editor two weeks in hospital) by publishing the findings of a *Tribunal de Sanción Nacional*. This tribunal, allegedly formed by four army officers, four naval officers and four civilians, produced a list of 28 men held to be the main offenders against public morality and the national interest. First on the list was Alessandri's closest friend and sometime Minister of the Interior, Cornelio Saavedra. The tribunal declared him to be: 'A person totally discredited by public opinion, recognized as one of the most unscrupulous administrative "fixers".[46] He has used whatever ministerial and parliamentary positions he has occupied for illicit transactions. Intellectually negligible, inept as a ruler, his name has figured in every scandal there has been in the last few years. He has no political ideal other than a desire for personal enrichment. Disloyal to his friends when they are no longer of any use to him. Among those most responsible for the discredit which surrounded the government and precipitated its fall. He enjoys an economic situation which bears no relation to his work or to his inheritance.'[47] Later in 1925, Grove nearly precipitated a crisis by tearing up a presidential decree naming Saavedra as Chilean consul in Hamburg, declaring it to be an 'indecency'.[48]

Though the *camarilla execrable* headed the list, further down we find Francisco Huneeus, Gonzalo Bulnes and other aristocratic names. To the discredit of the self-righteous young officers, the names of the only two parliamentarians to defy the noise of sabres[49] were also on the list, probably for that reason alone. The party composition of the list was 14 radicals, 7 liberals, 3 conservatives, 3 democrats and one businessman.[50] The influence of TEA is manifest and is all the more notable for being shared by the leaders of the 23 January *coup* which overthrew TEA's pretensions.

The constitution of 1925 did not end the alienation of those

[45] A leader of the Communist Party, later Trotskyite presidential candidate (1931) and early member of the Socialist Party.
[46] The word 'gestor' in this context means the hired representative of private firms who uses his pull in governmental circles to obtain contracts for his principals.
[47] *Acción*: Diario de purificación nacional, 7 August 1925.
[48] E. Oyarzún, *op. cit.*, p. 181.
[49] Guillermo Bañados and Pedro Leon Ugalde.
[50] E. Oyarzún (p. 220) was pleased because most of the radicals named were *Alessandristas* and he was fighting them for control of the party.

sectors which felt unrepresented by the existing parties. Though a presidential system was established, putting an end to unrestrained parliamentarism, the document was to be instrumental in the long maintenance of the power of the traditional parties. The electoral system adopted was devised by D'Hondt in 1898 to guarantee the power of the Belgian right. The system is based on a simple majority vote in the rural areas electing few deputies but becomes increasingly proportional as the number of deputies elected in an area increases. Thus the ruling class was guaranteed not only its full number of rural deputies, it was also granted a proportion of deputies in areas where it was in a minority.[51]

Alessandri tried to rule during 1925 in the divisive, partisan and personalist manner that he had always enjoyed. As before, he attempted to use the military threat to further his own ends,[52] and persistently refused to co-operate with the radicals, the largest of the parties, on any except his own terms.[53] Alessandri did not accept Ibáñez's offers of resignation[54] as he hoped to use the Colonel. Eventually, when he wanted Ibáñez out of the Ministry of War, he found that he had helped to consolidate the position of his old *protegé* to a point where the man who had to leave was himself.

The immediate cause of Alessandri's second fall was an open letter, addressed to Ibáñez by some 200 businessmen who invited him to stand as a presidential candidate. Most, if not all, of the signatories were members of the exclusive *Club de la Unión*, but none were prominent in politics.[55] The invitation stated that it was evident that even a major political crisis had proved incapable of producing an agreement among the political parties. It asserted the need to assure that a man with strength of character, energy and disinterest, with an understanding of the needs of the times and a sincere concern for the future of Chile should become president. It ends: 'We consider that you combine these qualities

[51] E. Cruz Coke, *Geografía Electoral de Chile*, Editorial del Pacífico, Santiago, 1952, pp. 61–2. This work shows clearly how conservatives and liberals submerged their differences and co-operated electorally, maintaining a disproportionately high level of representation during the period 1938–48.

[52] C. Vicuña, *op. cit.*, Vol. II, Sociedad de Imprenta y Litografía, Santiago, 1939, p. 62.

[53] E. Oyarzún, *op. cit.*, p. 192.

[54] C. Vicuña, *op. cit.*, Vol. II, pp. 30–1.

[55] Among the signatories was Ibáñez's friend and admirer Carlos Zañartú. The killing of his son by *carabineros* on 24 July 1931 decided Ibáñez to leave the country without further struggle. See R. Boizard, *op. cit.*, p. 60.

and that you cannot and should not refuse the offer we make you . . .'[56]

Ibáñez did not refuse. Earlier in the year, the Colonel had used the argument that a government minister could not be a presidential candidate, to force Armando Jaramillo, Alessandri's *dauphin*, to leave office, thereby destroying his candidature. Alessandri used the same argument to suggest that Ibáñez should resign, and was obliged by his sense of personal dignity to resign himself when his minister refused to do so. Significantly, Alessandri's last act as president in 1925 was to appoint as his Minister of the Interior, and therefore successor, none other than Luis Barros Borgoño, the opponent he had defeated in the so-called revolution of 1920. The emergence of a political force that threatened real changes made the thin distinction between defender of the *status quo* and reformer in 1920 disappear altogether by 1925.

The civilian component of this new force organized itself as a new party, called *Unión Social Republicana de Asalariados de Chile* (USRACH). Ibáñez withdrew his candidature when the impossible happened and the main political parties agreed to present a common candidate, Emiliano Figueroa, for the presidential election of 24 October. However, USRACH, with the open support of Grove,[57] presented the candidature of Dr José Santos Salas, a close friend and later minister of Ibáñez. When one considers that USRACH was formed only 18 days before the election and that the omnipotent levers of bribery and corruption were out of its reach, one can only be surprised that the unknown Salas obtained 28·4% of the votes of a very restricted electorate – only 302,142 voters in a population of nearly 4 million.[58] Salas's programme had been to fulfil the objectives of the 'revolution' of September 1924 and its re-affirmation of January 1925. USRACH called for a minimum wage, cheap housing and the nationalization of the nation's basic resources. After Salas was defeated, USRACH's president, Carlos Contreras Labarca, a communist, called for a national strike to protest at the dishonesty of the election. Thereafter USRACH, with a generous complement of communists among its leaders (Contreras became an USRACH senator, Hidalgo a deputy) moved ever leftward. On 24 September 1926, it pronounced its main programme to be the fight against

[56] J. A. Ríos, *Durante el Gobierno del General Ibáñez – Actuación de la Junta Central Radical*, Balcells y cia, Santiago, 1931, pp. 10–11.

[57] C. Vicuña, *op. cit.*, Vol. II, pp. 82–3.

[58] Dirección del Registro Electoral, Santiago.

capitalism.[59] In its move leftward the party lost a vital supporter, Ibáñez, who persecuted the leaders of USRACH when he became president. The differences between populism and socialism were to cause the failure of two later reconciliations between Ibáñez and the communists.[60]

Perhaps with USRACH in mind, an observer attributed Ibáñez's rise to 'The follies and vices of successive Alessandri administrations [which] had brought the country into chaos and had opened the door to communism . . .' He continued: 'The aristocrats, absorbed in their own selfish intrigues and in enriching themselves from public funds, seemed to have lost the art and forfeited the right of government. If, indeed, they saw it at all clearly, they were manifestly incapable of meeting the danger that faced them. The tide of communism flowed on unchecked. It now fell to the middle class, and to the youth of that class . . . to take into their hands the conduct of government and to dam this flow.'[61]

IBÁÑEZ

President Figueroa proved to be ineffectual, and during his presidency some of the bad old habits of the parliamentarians returned. Lacking the courage and the prestige which might have enabled them to dislodge the military *incubus* they limited themselves to puerile insults which only served to unite the officer corps and strengthen the independent position of Ibáñez.[62]

When Ibáñez finally manoeuvred himself into the Ministry of the Interior, a moral purge of unprecedented proportions took place. Not even Figueroa's brother in the Supreme Court escaped the vigorous action of Ibáñez, Pablo Ramírez and Aquiles Vergara. Corrupt government officials went to jail, some preferring suicide.[63] The proud bearers of aristocratic names were among those who suffered the effects of this purge. Oyarzún, protesting at the arbitrary nature of most of the deportations, was told by Ibáñez that 'the people' had long felt that the rich always escaped their just punishment in the courts, and that his brusque

[59] Lia Cortes and Jordi Fuentes, *Diccionario Político de Chile*, Editorial Orbe, Santiago, 1967, p. 499.

[60] These contacts were during 1937–38 and 1951–52.

[61] Public Record Office, A 5574/2158/9, Clark Kerr to Henderson, 24 July 1930.

[62] Eulogio Rojas Mery, *Memorias de un joven octogenario*, Imprenta Roma, Santiago, 1957, pp. 251–5.

[63] E. Oyarzún, *op. cit.*, p. 86.

actions were designed to alter that situation.[64] Of the drastic purge of the judiciary, the same source cites names of notoriously corrupt judges and asks why they should escape the sanctions of '...these regenerators who hold the whip with which we are all lashed . . .?'[65]

The elimination of political opponents was not, however, even disguised as anything else. Ibáñez persecuted 'agitators' of all kinds and since he decided who was an agitator, communists, radicals, liberals, conservatives and even army officers were jailed and deported with great *élan*. Evidently the electorate was delighted by his actions, arbitrary and cruel though many of them may have been. In the uncontested presidential election of 22 May 1927, Ibáñez obtained 96·7 per cent of the votes cast, representing 74 per cent of those registered to vote, in probably the most honest presidential election to be held in Chile until 1958.[66]

It is not our purpose here to analyse Ibáñez's first presidency. Elected as president, he chose to rule dictatorially as more suited to his personality and training – though without organized support he could do little else and his differences with USRACH cut him off from any possibility of such support. The theme of the corruption of the established parties was taken up by the *Confederación Republicana de Acción Cívica* (CRAC), formed expressly to support Ibáñez, whose attacks caused the political parties to declare themselves in 'recess' during 1930 because they lacked the necessary guarantees to 'continue evolving'.[67]

The discredit of the political parties was further underlined by their meek acceptance of the *Congreso Termal* in 1930 in which they agreed to make use of a constitutional device and presented only as many candidates as there were congressional and senatorial seats up for election (132 deputies, 20 senators), thus obviating the need for a campaign or even for voting. Ibáñez had only to state his intention to hold elections in which bribery and fraud were to be eliminated, for the parties to accept his decisions concerning the candidates to be 'elected'.[68] We have only to compare the distribution by parties of deputies appointed to the *Congreso Termal* with a similar arrangement proposed by President

[64] *Ibid.*, p. 70.
[65] *Ibid.*, p. 77. Like the anonymous tribunal of *Acción*, the 'regenerators' did not feel the need for legal proof in order to condemn.
[66] Dirección del Registro Electoral. Basically a plebiscite, it was not accompanied by the usual bribery.
[67] L. Cortes and J. Fuentes, *op. cit.*, p. 106.
[68] E. Würth, *op. cit.*, p. 155.

Figueroa in 1925 and rejected by the Democratic Party and USRACH, in order to see who were the main beneficiaries and who the losers under Ibáñez.

TABLE 2[69]

Deputies 1925 and 1930

Party	1925 Figueroa Proposal deputies	%	1930 Congreso Termal deputies	%
Conservative	27	20·5	22	16·7
Lib. Democratic	16	12·1 ⎱ Liberal		
Liberal	25	18·9 ⎰ Unificado	} 31	23·5
Radical	41	31·1	34	25·7
Democratic	14	10·6	31	23·5
USRACH	9	6·8	—	—
CRAC	—	—	14	10·6
Total:	132	100·0	132	100·0

The president of CRAC summed up the essence of the Ibáñez appeal when he declared his party to be '. . . formed by the workers and employees of Chile . . . and all those intellectuals and apolitical independent men who do not seek public office as a reward for electoral services, but who desire effective guarantees that they will be able to work in peace'.[70]

Pike observes that '. . . he knew how to co-ordinate the seething forces of the era into an effective whole, and how to dash down extremists of all types so as to prevent disparate energies cancelling each other out. Because of these abilities, Ibáñez managed to preside over the four most active fruitful years of national existence that Chile had enjoyed since the War of the Pacific. The institutional structure that has governed Chile down to the present day was fashioned by Ibáñez between 1927 and 1931.'[71]

Perhaps the most significant results of those four years, however, lay in the things Ibáñez did not do. He did not abolish Congress or outlaw the political parties. He did not attempt to create any institutional outlet for the forces that supported him.

---

[69] Sources: L. Cortes and J. Fuentes, p. 498; E. Würth, p. 153. Ibáñez demanded the right to *name* the congressmen while Figueroa merely allocated seats, leaving the names to the parties.

[70] Cámara de Diputados, Sesiones Ordinarias, 2 June 1930. Cited by L. Cortes and J. Fuentes, p. 106.

[71] F. B. Pike, *Chile and the United States* . . . , p. 188.

Like a TEA conspirator, he did not blame the political system for the faults of the men who operated within it. Though, through CRAC, he toyed with the idea of corporativism and the replacement of political parties with trades unions, he never attempted to implement those ideas. His mild dictatorship, though increasing the power of the central government and involving it in the economy of the nation, respected the *status quo* to a remarkable degree, as Table 2 indicates. Perhaps his greatest contribution to Chilean development was that the nation felt the violent effects of the economic depression while under overtly authoritarian rule. In Brazil, Argentina and Germany, to mention only three of many examples, the crisis discredited formal liberal-democratic *régimes*. In Chile it discredited dictatorship while leaving intact the apparatus of authoritarian rule which has played so large a role in later Chilean history.[72]

The fall of Ibáñez was precipitated by the activities of landowning and professional elements '. . . who had grown tired of Ibáñez and the high-handed methods of his entourage and who raised the parrot-cry of "Liberty" throughout the land. That revolution was essentially the work of the members of the Union Club and those whose dream it is to belong to that institution . . . the return of constitutionality was regarded as the sure vanguard of the millennium'.[73]

1931–33: POLITICAL BREAK-DOWN

It soon became apparent that Ibáñez had postponed rather than precipitated political fragmentation. After his fall the full weight of the economic crisis was felt in Chile. President Montero, a radical and ex-minister of the late dictator, took the unpopular deflationary measures at that time in vogue for dealing with the crisis. After enduring mounting popular unrest and a major naval mutiny, brought about by his pay cuts, he fell before a daring *coup* administered by Marmaduke Grove, egged on by Arturo Alessandri.[74] Of Montero it was rightly commented that: 'While

[72] By Decree No. 5115, 26 December 1932, two days after assuming the presidency again, Alessandri separated the detective *Investigaciones* section from the corps of *Carabineros* and made it directly dependent on the president for orders, personnel and promotions. Though the 'dictator' Ibáñez created *Investigaciones* and was much condemned for using it as a political police force, the 'democratic' Alessandri confirmed it in that role.

[73] PRO, A 4492/86/9, Thompson to Sir John Simon, 4 July 1932.

[74] R. Donoso, *op. cit.*, Vol. II, pp. 88–103. A common persecutor had made many of the enemies of 1925 into friends and fellow conspirators.

it is difficult not to sympathize with Montero as a man who meant well and was imbued with a strong sense of duty, it is only too clear in retrospect that he was one of the weakest and most uninspiring leaders any nation can ever have been cursed with.'[75]

As we have indicated above, 'constitutionality' was the surest and safest way of guaranteeing the *status quo*. It should not surprise us, therefore, that those demanding fundamental changes were left by default of the professional politicians to rally around the figure of another military *caudillo*.[76] The essence of Grove's attraction lay in the fact that 'From his earliest adolescence ... this individual has made himself an intolerable nuisance to all constituted authority and will continue to do so.'[77] Under the slogan '*Pan, Techo, y Abrigo*'[78] the new master of Chile did away with Congress and announced a socialist republic – it lasted 12 days and endured four different revolutionary *juntas*. Grove's enlightened militarism,[79] Eugenio Matte's freemasonry[80] and primitive socialism[81] fought for control against the *ibañista* Carlos Dávila. Armed force decided the issue temporarily in favour of the latter.[82] Dávila's '100 days' were terminated by another *coup* and the army, deeply divided[83] and under hysterical civilian harassment first crushed a revolt led by the Commander-in-Chief of the air force and then handed over the government to the president of the Supreme Court. The ensuing election saw the return of Arturo Alessandri to the Moneda.

Montero's failure had reduced the prestige of the civilian politicians to so low a level that mere squads of soldiers could make and depose rulers with ease. The populace did not appear to

[75] PRO, A 4107/86/9, Thompson to Sir John Simon, 19 June 1932.
[76] J. C. Jobet, *El Partido Socialista de Chile*, Prensa Latinoamericana, Santiago, 1971, Vol. I, pp. 65–7.
[77] PRO, A 4313/86/9, Thompson to Sir John Simon, 24 July 1932.
[78] J. C. Jobet, *op. cit.*, p. 49. 'Bread, a roof and clothing', better known as the election slogan of the Popular Front in 1938.
[79] J. R. Thomas, 'The Evolution of a Chilean Socialist', *HAHR*, Vol. XLVII, No. 1, February 1967, p. 22, *passim*.
[80] Matte was the Grand Master of Chilean masonry.
[81] Some early members of Matte's *Nueva Acción Pública* (NAP) left in anger after 4 June because NAP was not, in its essence, socialist.
[82] Ibáñez, expecting Dávila to step down for him, returned on 6 July; three weeks later, disillusioned, he returned to exile, after a failed *cuartelazo*. See R. Montero, *Confesiones Políticas*, Empresa Editora Zig-Zag, Santiago, 1958, pp. 80–9.
[83] The call for '*civilismo*' was originally launched by General Vignola from Antofagasta.

care. An observer thought it '. . . ominous that Grove . . . is the only individual who has stirred up any popular enthusiasm worth mentioning since the beginning of the revolution'.[84]

The period between Ibáñez's fall and the return of Alessandri saw the birth of at least sixteen new political movements, each with its own special formula for the redemption of Chile. Of these, seven called themselves socialist[85] and were eventually to unite in April 1933 to form the new *Partido Socialista* (PS) which stepped in to the place abandoned by the communists in their bitter divisions between Stalinists and Trotskyites.[86]

During its brief existence the Socialist Republic found time to issue a pamphlet containing a 30 point revolutionary programme.[87] A pastiche of APRA, USRACH, free-masonry and what we could call 'social militarism', the programme contained propositions that by now are familiar to us. The *coup* had been made against 'Oligarchical and clerical oppression, political corruption and the disdain of the late rulers for the misery of the Chilean people, . . .'[88] It promised a purge and a re-organization of the judicial system and proposed the creation of the *Tribunal de Sanción Nacional* which we last saw in 1925. The document overflowed with drastic solutions for the crisis, most of them to be paid for by those best able to afford it.[89]

The traces of Grove's political formation are to be found in all the early *Partido Socialista* literature. It would be hard to over-estimate his impact on the party during its first decade of existence. Though he admitted that he had never read the works of Marx, he had read and was deeply convinced by the works of Mazzini and of Carlyle. He felt that nations, races and great men were the dynamic forces of history. A commentator has called Grove a precursor of Justicialism[90] and certainly the influence of Grove aids us in understanding the solidly Chilean roots of the later so-called 'peronist' period of the Socialist Party.

However, despite various later moves towards *caudillismo*, from

[84] PRO, A 5074/86/9, Thompson to Sir John Simon, 28 July 1932.

[85] J. C. Jobet, *op. cit.*, Vol. I, pp. 65–6.

[86] Each faction presented a candidate in the presidential election of 1931.

[87] Junta de Gobierno Socialista, *Los 30 puntos*, Librería e Imprenta 'Jordan' Talcahuano, N.D.

[88] *Ibid.*, p. 2.

[89] This had been an aim of the naval mutineers, whom Grove freed from prison. See, J. M. Cerda, *Relación Histórica de la Revolución de la Armada de Chile*, Sociedad de Imprenta y Litografía 'Concepción', Concepción, 1934.

[90] E. Halperin, *Nationalism and Communism in Chile*, M.I.T. Press, Cambridge, Mass., 1965, p. 123.

1933 onwards the PS entered the existing political arena and has
operated within it to this day. Jobet, commenting on Grove's
legacy, says that 'Alongside its revolutionary position, in its
evolution there arises and co-exists an undeniable fondness for
popular representation and a corresponding electoralist mentality'.[91] As he says, it has been a difficult dichotomy to overcome.

Another large group of new political movements, destined to
fade away leaving little trace, but symptomatic of the times, were
a number professing a desire to create a new politics inside the
existing framework.[92] These groups felt that the dictatorship had
been the result of the corruption and unrepresentative nature of
the traditional parties.

A reaction to the 'tropicalization' of Chilean politics was the
Milicia Republicana (MR), created in emulation of similar groups
formed in Portales's time which had helped to establish civilian
government in Chile at a time when military *caudillos* were
deciding the politics of her neighbours. The MR expressed no
political aim other than to guarantee constitutionality – as such, it
received the firmest moral and material support from President
Alessandri. Units of *milicianos* made insolent tours around some
army barracks. Provoked by this, and by the fact that the *jeunesse
dorée* of Santiago were harassing his cadets, General Vignola, by
this time Commander-in-Chief of the army, wrote a stern warning
to the Minister of Defence. Bored by the military pretensions of the
'*milicianos*', he wrote, 'I do not wish to elaborate upon what would
be the consequences of a clash between the Army and any other
armed organization, as you will understand perfectly where this
would lead the country.' He asked only that the army be left in
peace.[93] The idea that a group of part-time soldiers could in any
way stand up to the professional army, was of course, absurd.[94]
However, the MR, by definition, also stood ready to crush
'bolshevism' and as late as 1936 its use in strike-breaking was
considered.[95] To a certain extent, the *Carabinero* Corps made it

[91] J. C. Jobet, *op. cit.*, Vol. I, p. 99.
[92] The most long-lived were: *Unión Republicana*, formed in 1931 to be *Un
Partido político sin politiquería*; *Partido Agrario*, formed in 1932 to represent
agriculture in a future corporativist state.
[93] *El Debate*, Santiago, 14 December 1933. Alessandri distorts this incident
in his memoirs, perhaps to justify sacking the leader of the *civilista* movement
that ended the chaos in 1932. See *Recuerdos . . .*, Vol. III, pp. 20–1.
[94] Its military effectiveness was not worth the bitterness, remembered to
this day, that it created in the army.
[95] PRO, A 1483/74/9, Sir R. Michell to A. Eden, 14 February 1936.

difficult to justify the existence of the MR, and it eventually died when prolonged inaction led to internal divisions.[96]

The last section of the groups formed at this time was based on European fascism. Two of these were formed as a reaction to the Socialist Republic[97] and were so rabidly anti-communist that even the frightened middle classes were repelled by them. The third was rather different.

The *Movimiento Nacional Socialista de Chile* (MNS) though born of the same chaos as other fascist and militarist groups, predated the Socialist Republic and proved to be like the *Partido Socialista* in that it was a uniquely Chilean variation on an international theme. Founded by Jorge González von Marées and eleven others on 5 April 1932, the MNS proclaimed the moral degeneracy of Chile to be the fruit of unchecked individual and collective egoism, itself a product of the general decay of the democratic ideal in the world.[98] The theme is familiar.

It should be noted that the early programmes of both the MNS and the socialist groups have quite marked similarities. Nationalism and the need for a hierarchy based on merit are important themes in both. Respecting private property only if it were utilized for the common good, both recommended the nationalization of foreign holdings in Chile. Insofar as members of each group identified US domination of Chile's main sources of wealth as Jewish exploitation, there was even a common denominator of anti-semitism.[99] Of course, nationalism and racism are practically inseparable and these similarities were inevitable in two new ultra-nationalist movements. Also, the *caudillos* of the respective movements shared a formative experience – González had been a member of TEA[100] and the two men, though differing in the

---

[96] J. de la Cuadra Poisson, 'La Verdad de las Incidencias Milicianas', *La Nación*, Santiago, 1935.

[97] Formed by retired General Javier Díaz and by Aquiles Vergara, terror of the judiciary in 1927. See *Ideología de la Acción Nacionalista de Chile*, Editorial 'La Cruz Svástica', Santiago, 1932.

[98] *El Movimiento Nacional Socialista de Chile*, Imprenta 'La Tracción', Santiago, 1932.

[99] Cf. (i) 'Un grupo sórdido, arribista y judío, resíduos de los duros días de dominio de los Guggenheim, se mantienen aferrados a la dirección del mineral'; p. 51 in R. Latcham, *Chuquicamata Estado Yankee*, Editorial Nascimiento, Santiago, 1926. Latcham was an early PS deputy. (ii) 'Nuestra industria salitrera agoniza bajo las garras del judaismo internacional.' Headline in *Trabajo*, the MNS newspaper, 27 July 1933.

[100] *Trabajo*, 20 July 1933, p. 5.

treatment to be prescribed, agreed that the disease was the corruption and selfishness of the political elite.

The main early division between one group of nationalists who knew little of Marx but who embraced socialism, and another group that emulated German national-socialism, was the issue of religion. The MNS founders were mainly dissident conservatives who felt that the Church should be kept out of politics and that Leo XIII and Pius XI provided better examples than Pius IX and Pius X. To these men, the masonic influence in the early socialist groups was anathema.

It should be borne in mind that much of the political activities of the younger army officers in the mid 1920s was co-ordinated in the masonic lodges.[101] Clearly one can sink, as the MNS did, into a swamp of conspiracy theories over this matter. The importance of free-masonry in the Radical Party and in Chilean positivism was clearly very great, but during the 1930s, the main division among progressive forces became that of socialism versus corporativism, the classic political issue of religion rapidly declining in importance after the 1925 dis-establishment, thanks to the moderating influence of Archbishop, Crescente Errázuriz.

Nonetheless, for most of its brief life, the MNS fought against the world judaeo-masonic-capitalist-bolshevik conspiracy as outlined in *The Protocols of the Elders of Zion*. This position was gradually abandoned because, in Chile, violent anti-semitism was not well received.[102]

1932–38: A NEW POLITICS

Similarities in tactics and membership,[103] more than ideological differences, led the MNS and the PS to clash repeatedly throughout the second Alessandri government. The process culminated in 1936 with three MNS troopers killed in a huge street-battle in Valparaiso on 13 June and the young socialist poet Barreto shot down in a *nacista* reprisal in Santiago on 23 August.

[101] Particularly the *coup* of 23 January 1925. E. Oyarzún, *op. cit.*, p. 105. A more general picture can be found in F. Pinto Lagarrigue, *La Masonería. Su influencia en Chile*, Editorial Orbe, Santiago, 1966.

[102] Genteel anti-semitism was and is common, but the same gentility prevented such people joining a pugnacious organization like the MNS.

[103] Charges that the MNS was based upon German immigrants were unfounded. The MNS resented the racial exclusivity of the *Bund* and declared the two movements incompatible. *Trabajo*, 22 June 1935. Like the PS, the MNS drew a great deal of support from students and young workers.

In a reversal of the situation prevailing in the 1920s, the defenders of the *status quo* had finally realized that their common interests far outweighed their differences while the insurgent forces were bitterly and bloodily divided. The liberal-democratic system, repeatedly pronounced dead and needing only burial by socialist and *nacista* alike, showed signs of remarkable vigour.

Political fragmentation had left the Conservative and Liberal Parties as virtually the only party pillars upon which Arturo Alessandri could base his government. The majorities that their support gave him in Congress and Senate permitted the president to rule in a firm and dynamic manner without a recurrence of the 1920–24 conflict between executive and legislative. The Radical Party was too divided and vacillating to adopt a consistent policy either of participation in government or of opposition during this period.

Surprisingly, the actions of the new revolutionary parties strengthened the system they sought to overthrow. On one level, their violent conflicts were a permanent incentive to maintain the unity of the government coalition and provided justification for the extremely authoritarian measures adopted by Alessandri.[104] At another level, once the extremists decided to participate in elections, the parliamentary institutions were enhanced by their improved representativeness and the principle of liberal democracy was strengthened by the *de facto* recognition of its professed foes. Finally, the Radical Party showed the flexibility which traditionally strengthens established parties by co-opting the PS through its adoption of the Popular Front strategy.[105]

There remained, however, two groups which resolutely refused to come to terms. One was the MNS, which condemned the Popular Front as both a communist plot and as a cynical sell-out to the establishment. The other group were the *ibañistas*. In February 1936, a number of civilian conspirators, including Juan

---

[104] A gun-battle involving *nacistas* in Rancagua was the immediate justification of the 'Law for Internal Security of the State' which was and is the main legal weapon with which Chilean governments have defended themselves against verbal or physical extremism on the part of their opponents. For a survey of this and other strongly repressive legislation see K. Loewenstein, 'Legislation for the Defense of the State in Chile', *Columbia Law Review*, Vol. XLIV, May 1944, pp. 366–407.

[105] See J. R. Stevenson, *The Chilean Popular Front*, Oxford University Press, 1942. The first electoral victory of the PF was the election of Cristóbal Saenz, multi-millionaire landowner, in a senatorial election in 1936.

Antonio Ríos[106] and René Silva Espejo,[107] together with some
discontented army officers, failed to bring about a *coup* which was
to begin with the removal of General Novoa, the army Commander-
in-Chief and a fierce opponent of any such initiative.[108]

Three trends, therefore, presented candidates for the presidential election of 1938. Two of these, the liberal-conservative
block and the Popular Front, respected the electoral process. The
third, an alliance of *ibañistas* and MNS with dissident groups of
socialists and democrats, revived the protest against the party
system that had helped to enthrone Ibáñez in 1927. The essence of
this protest is to be found in a speech made by Jorge González in
1936: 'You, conservatives, liberals, radicals, democrats and the
rest of the old parties; you who dare to raise your voices to condemn our attitudes, you are the sole authors of national destruction. You have made of politics, in its essence a noble art, the
filthiest of occupations; you have sunk a race, once magnificent
in its energy, into the most appalling state of degeneration; you
have miserably exploited a trusting people from your parliamentary and ministerial positions; you have handed over the state
schools to the most iniquitous and corrupting of sects; you have
used the church and religion for political ends, driving faith from
the hearts of the people . . . '[109]

Yet the *caudillo* chosen by these evangelists was already showing
a taste for the *politiquería* which he so roundly condemned. Assisted
by Juan Antonio Ríos, he made repeated efforts to become the
candidate of the Popular Front. His hopes were sabotaged by the
fact that the MNS was his most vociferous supporter[110] and by
the hatred of Marmaduke Grove.[111]

[106] Leader of the Radical Party during the dictatorship, later president of
Chile 1942–45.
[107] An early MNS member, expelled after a failed *putsch* against González.
Today the extremely respectable editor of *El Mercurio*.
[108] R. Montero, *op. cit.*, pp. 94–7; A. Alessandri, *Recuerdos*, Vol. III,
pp. 70–80; R. Donoso, *Alessandri*, Vol. II, pp. 182–3 and p. 188, note 6.
[109] J. González, 'La Violencia nacista y los partidos políticos', Radio
speech, 28 August 1936, Imprenta Eyzaguirre, Santiago, N.D. See also,
Tribunal de Sanción Nacional, quoted at p. 363 above. Cornelio Saavedra himself became the main target of MNS attacks on governmental corruption, the
word 'Cornelio' becoming *Nacista* slang for 'crook'.
[110] The MNS had been the first group to declare Ibáñez's candidature and
clung to him unflinchingly, despite his public announcements that he was
anti-fascist (*Trabajo*, 29 January 1938). Unfazed, *Trabajo* declared that the
word fascist in Chile meant reactionary and that therefore the MNS too was
anti-fascist (30 January).
[111] Grove swore he would vote for Ross before he would vote for Ibáñez.
See E. Oyarzún, *op. cit.*, Appendix p. 31.

Despite his failure to be nominated by the Popular Front, Ibáñez and his supporters waged a war on two fronts during 1938. The main front was the battle against Alessandri, but a less known battle was the one which aimed to destroy the candidature of Aguirre Cerda[112] by massive demonstrations of *ibañista* strength. The 'March of Victory' on 4 September 1938 was to be the last blow, after which the Front would fall apart and Ibáñez would receive the support of those groups which had already made contacts with him behind Aguirre's back.[113] The march itself was huge and carefully orchestrated by the MNS.

However, in his battle with the hostility of Alessandri, Ibáñez had twice planned a *coup* in self-defence. By August 1938, a plan had been established whereby a select group of MNS troopers would seize two central buildings in Santiago and barricade themselves well enough to prevent dislodgement by *carabineros*. Alessandri would be forced to have recourse to the Santiago garrison, and they, supposedly, would deny their assistance until a less partisan figure replaced Alessandri in the Moneda.[114]

Irritated by Ibáñez's vacillations, fearing discovery after an indiscretion by one of the leading plotters and perhaps afraid that if the Popular Front did collapse he would lose his hold over Ibáñez, Jorge González decided to precipitate matters and on 5 September 1938, Alessandri faced the most serious attempt to overthrow him since the day, 14 years earlier, that he had left the Moneda for the first time.

The failure of the *coup* and its extremely bloody suppression undoubtedly gave the victory in 1938 to Aguirre Cerda.[115] The wholesale massacre of surrendered *nacistas* left an indelible mark on the memory of Alessandri, who used all his powers to protect the *carabineros* who perpetrated the crime.[116]

However, the man who won as a result of this event first made a deal with González to obtain *nacista* support by promising that justice would be done and then made another with the man

[112] Aguirre, leader of those radicals who opposed the PF strategy, had been defeated by its proponents led by J. A. Ríos. A few dozen deals later, Aguirre defeated Ríos to become the radical nominee for the candidature of the PF. Radical party politics have never been boring.

[113] R. Montero, *op. cit.*, p. 101.

[114] Though some details emerged in the two trials that followed, the conspiratorial background was revealed in *Trabajo*, 24 March 1939.

[115] He won by 2111 votes, less than 1 per cent of the vote.

[116] Leonidas Bravo R., *Lo que supo un auditor de guerra*, Editorial del Pacífico, Santiago, 1955, p. 90.

responsible for the massacre, *carabinero* General Arriagada, to obtain his recognition of the Popular Front victory in exchange for an eventual presidential pardon.[117] Thus the young MNS troopers who battled against Ross's agents so successfully on 25 October 1938,[118] saw the executioners of their comrades pardoned by the man they helped to elect.

THE RADICAL PARTY IN POWER: 1938–52

Inevitably, the revolutionary nationalist parties did not continue to support the PF for very long. In a reversal of the situation under Alessandri when 'The radicals wasted their prestige, wore themselves out politically and wiped their mouths while their liberal and conservative colleagues ate and drank'[119] it was now the communists and, especially, the PS which discovered the disadvantages of being the junior partner in a government. The brief (1938–41) socialist interlude in the government left the party divided and bitterly hostile to both radicals and communists.

For the radicals, the hunger of the 1930s was assuaged and, by opening new horizons for government employ and filling the new posts almost exclusively with the faithful, it established an awesome reputation which remains with it to this day. In the process of expanding its area of patronage, it reinforced the tendency, established in 1925 in the Chilean social security administration, of increasing the benefits of the white collar employee at the expense of those least able to pay the cost.[120] As in 1920, part of the middle sectors of society had mobilized the lower classes, forgetting about their allies of the election campaign once the desired object had been achieved.

As we have seen, the clientelistic basis of party politics had been selected more than once for attacks by sectors which neither participated in the working of the parties, nor benefited from their actions when in power. In the absence of a general solution

[117] See Ismael Edwards Matte, 'La Historia de un Indulto', *Ercilla*, 1 March 1949.

[118] Tito Mundt, *Las Banderas Olvidadas*, Editorial Orbe, Santiago, 1965, pp. 89–90.

[119] Eudocio Ravines, *La Gran Estafa*, Editorial del Pacífico, Santiago, 1957, p. 103.

[120] See Charles J. Parrish and Jorge Tapia V., 'Welfare policy and administration in Chile', *The Journal of Comparative Administration*, Vol. I, No. 4, February 1970, pp. 455–75.

to social and economic problems, the benefits accruing to the few were condemned by the many, especially since the few were inevitably selected according to the imperatives of party patronage, seemingly without regard to their efficiency or suitability for the posts to which they were appointed.[121] We have used the word *politiquería* to describe the target of the condemnation to which we refer above. The man in the street, regardless of social and economic status, felt a common revulsion against the man in the political organizations because of the latter's unresponsiveness to his needs. In a situation of economic prosperity, the irritants of the spoils system are less noticeable. In times of crisis (the early 1920s, the early 1930s and the early 1950s) the knowledge that those who were supposed to find solutions did not feel the spur of personal privation became unendurable. It has been observed that 'The decisive difference between the North and Latin American spoils systems resides in their relative importance to other avenues of wealth. In the US the proceeds obtainable through politics have always been and remain negligible; in contrast throughout Latin America political power has always been the surest and quickest way to wealth; . . . '[122] It is this point of view which is to be found in the electoral programme of any opposition party in Chile during this period. For the charges of corruption, favouritism, nepotism etc. are, *par excellence*, the tactical weapons of those parties in opposition, and tend to increase in importance the longer the party is out of power. The natural hunger of those tasting the fruits of power after prolonged abstinence is coupled with a desire to have men of confidence in important administrative and diplomatic posts. With sharp political differences between the parties this inevitably leads either to the replacement of men who have learned their job with others without experience, or else both groups are found space in an ever more bloated bureaucracy.[123] Against a back-drop of intractable national problems, this

[121] We have only to read Marmaduke Grove's articles in *La Nación*, October to December 1924, to see how important this issue was in the movements we have discussed. Repeatedly he urged the need for government appointments to be made on the grounds of merit alone. For a soldier accustomed to taking examinations continuously in his career as a means of hastening promotion, the suggestion was an obvious one.

[122] S. Andreski, *Parasitism and Subversion. The Case of Latin America*, Pantheon Books, New York, 1966, pp. 10–11.

[123] Laws of *inamovilidad funcionaria* seem to be aimed more at protecting a government's appointees against possible future political dismissal than at creating a professional civil service.

behaviour has been singled out for attack time and again by parties which do exactly the same when they come to power.

We have used the word *party* to describe any organization formed for political ends, but 'Until recently, when discussing Chile it was preferable to replace the words classes, parties, organizations and programmes with the words crowds, clienteles, clans and promises'.[124] Even the author cited, however, is forced to ignore his own important semantic definition because it is in terms of class and party, however regrettable the imprecision, that political issues in Chile have been discussed. When we talk of the Conservative and Liberal Parties we are referring to a small number of men who administer a large electoral fund with the help of collaborators hired for the duration of a campaign. The classic Radical and Democrat Parties used clubs, neighbourhood circles and a more personal level of association in order to bring together their alliances of workers and middle sectors – though the radical election chests would be filled by wealthy land-owners and merchants in the same manner as that of the two older parties. For all of these, 'Intense political activity coincides with the campaigns for the renewal of parliament or the election of a president. Between two elections, it is the distribution of the national budget which is the main preoccupation of the [party] directorate.'[125]

During its fourteen years in power, the Radical Party developed an internal bureaucracy and a systematization of patronage which was wholly new in Chile. The party developed away from the extended family towards Tammany Hall. However, Chile could not continue indefinitely being ruled according to the patterns laid down in a less complicated age. The increased government sphere of activity demanded that those in power do more and more and that their actions be more noticeable. It is against this background that we must consider the development of the second revolt of the electorate, the presidential election of 1952.

There are four developments during the period under discussion of a clearly subversive nature, all of which are connected by one common factor – Ibáñez.

On 25 August 1939, General Ariosto Herrera attempted a *cuartelazo* against President Aguirre Cerda. This officer had been

---

[124] Luis Mercier, *Mécanismes de pouvoir en Amérique Latine*, Editions Universitaires, Paris, 1967, p. 173.
[125] *Ibid.*, p. 88.

approached by a group of conspirators after he had refused to march his troops past the Moneda palace until a red flag was removed from under the president's balcony. Originally pleased at the triumph of the Popular Front[126] as he believed it would reform Chilean politics, he was disillusioned by the voracity of the new rulers and was easily persuaded that Chile needed his firm guidance to help her recover from the disastrous earthquake of January 1939. The revival of the TEA postulates on the part of the civilian group in question was now summed up briefly – Chile needed less *politiquería*. The preparation for the *ariostazo*, as it came to be known, was a very last minute affair, precipitated by the general being called into retirement. Though a group of officers were persuaded that the action was intended to dramatize internal problems in the army, the late and uninvited arrival of Ibáñez made it clear to them that something more extensive was planned. The movement fell apart from that moment.

A new nationalist movement was formed with Herrera as its figurehead after this event. Composed primarily of *nacistas* alienated from González and the VPS in his move to the left,[127] the *Movimiento Nacionalista de Chile* (MNCh) revived the old MNS formulas under the direction of Ariosto Herrera's lawyer, Guillermo Izquierdo. Neither MNCh nor VPS prospered, uniting in 1942 in the *Unión Nacionalista* led by Juan Gómez Millas, and this eventually joined with the *Alianza Popular Libertadora*, Ibáñez's party, and the *Partido Agrario* to form the *Partido Agrario Laborista* (PAL) in 1945. Almost the only thing that united *nacistas*, *ibañistas* and *agrarios* was a common lip-service to corporativism.

Meanwhile, Ibáñez and his friends continued to subvert the army. He found fertile ground for his efforts because of a recrudescence of problems concerning promotions and salaries.[128] The plotters chose melodramatic names (*Grupo de Oficiales*

---

[126] Letter of November 1938 in the possession of Guillermo Izquierdo Araya. For other information on Herrera, I base myself on two interviews with Guillermo Izquierdo, supplemented by the text of the trial and the press of the period.

[127] The more rabid anti-communists and the anti-semites had split off earlier to form the *Partido Fascista*. A linear descendant is the *Partido Nacional Socialista Obrero*, blamed for setting fire to various synagogues during the 1960s.

[128] A problem in fact created by Ibáñez by his undue expansion of the officer corps in the fat days between 1927 and 1929. An 'over-officered' situation had been an important factor in 1919 and 1924.

Seleccionados – GOS, formed in 1941; *Por Un Mañana Auspicioso* –
PUMA, formed in 1951), were promptly discovered, and their
leaders transferred away from temptation.[129] PUMA was allegedly
formed to prepare for an intervention if Ibáñez did not win the
presidential election in 1952. His victory, for Colonel Abdon
Parra, was indeed an auspicious dawn – promoted over the heads
of the entire General Staff, he later became Minister of Defence.
The resignations of his superiors which ensued temporarily
'solved' the problem of promotions.

Finally in 1946, after Gabriel González Videla won the presi-
dency with the support of a rapidly growing Communist Party,
the *Milicia Republicana* was resurrected under the name of *Acción
Chilena Anticomunista* (AChA).[130] Created on militaristic lines by
Arturo Olavarría,[131] Jorge Prat,[132] and some leading ex-members
of the MR, the organization counted with the support of Julio
Durán[133] and Oscar Schnake[134] as well as large numbers of ex-
MNS and MNCh activists. Following President Gabriel González
Videla's outlawing of the Communist Party in 1948, only the hard
core of ex-MNS/MNCh members remained in AChA, and they
wanted to act against the government – Olavarría forestalled this
by seizing the AChA arsenal and disbanding the organization.

Some of this group, fanatic *nacionalistas* all, were organized in a
subversive movement called *Los Condores*[135] which came close to
toppling President González Videla in the *Colliguay* plot in 1951.
They kidnapped two important leaders of the trade union movement[136] with the idea that the government would be blamed for the

[129] See Ercilla, 22 March 1953, p. 5. Leonidas Bravo, *op. cit.*, p. 146;
R. Montero, *op. cit.*, p. 78 and pp. 104–19.
[130] A. Olavarría Bravo, *Chile entre dos Alessandri*, Editorial Nascimiento,
Santiago, 1962, Vol. II, pp. 41–53.
[131] Campaign manager for Aguirre Cerda (1938), Ibáñez (1952) Alessandri
(1958) and Allende (1964). In essence, a radical.
[132] Conservative youth leader, later unwilling candidate of the nationalistic
Acción Nacional in 1964, after gaining a reputation as an Ibáñez minister.
[133] Radical presidential candidate, 1964.
[134] Founder member of the PS and leader of the anti-communist socialists
after 1941.
[135] D. W. Bray, 'Peronism in Chile', *HAHR*, Vol. XLVII, No. 1, February
1967, p. 40. Leonidas Bravo, *op. cit.*, p. 238.
[136] The trade union movement had recovered so well from the fragmentation of the mid 1940s that by 1950 a strike led by Clotario Blest and his
union ANEF (*Asociación de Empleados Fiscales*) had caused the fall of a
cabinet. *Los Condores* were convinced that a greater provocation could force
the trade union movement into a revolutionary general strike. (Izquierdo
interview).

outrage. The hiding place of the kidnap 'victims'[137] was discovered before popular anger was properly aroused and the plan failed.

All these factors, revealing in retrospect, still seemed so removed from the world of party politics that many experts shared the view that the control over public opinion exerted by the parties could not be broken even if popular feelings '…were to be aroused by the most powerful movement of negative reaction or by an impulse toward renovation'.[138] Using the symbol of a broom, and a programme which singled out the party system and *politiquería* as the sole authors of all national problems, Ibáñez won the presidency and 46·6% of the popular vote in September 1952 without the backing of any major party.

THE COLLAPSE OF IBAÑISMO AND POLITICAL RE-ORGANIZATION

So totally negative a political philosophy, though lethal in opposition, proved to be a disaster in government. President Ibáñez proved a shattering disappointment to those who had seen in him a latter-day Portales – the promised authority, nationalism and social progress materialized as whimsical arbitrariness,[139] nepotism and stagnation.

The political fragmentation of the early 1930s returned to plague Chilean politics. The *ibañista* majority in Congress, gained in the 1953 congressional elections, broke down into the following groups of congressmen:

TABLE 3
Ibañista Congressmen[140]

PAL	26	Socialcristianos	2
Partido Socialista Popular	19	Movimiento Nacional del Pueblo	1
Movimiento Nacional Ibañista	5	Asociación Renovadora de Chile	1
Democráticos del Pueblo	5	Partido Laborista	1
Nacional Cristianos	4	Democráticos de Chile	1
Union Nacional Independiente	4	Liberal Progresista	1
Radicales Doctrinarios[141]	3	Independiente	1

Total 74 in a chamber of 146

[137] They were not averse to the scheme.
[138] E. Cruz-Coke, *Geografía Electoral*, p. 94. Published May 1952.
[139] A. Olavarría, *op. cit.*, pp. 292–3.
[140] R. Montero, *op. cit.*, p. 187.
[141] Olavarría's group.

Without a majority in the Senate (14 out of 45) and with his majority of one in the Chamber of Deputies dependent on the whim of even the smallest of the groups that had climbed on the bandwagon, Ibáñez was presented with two alternatives. He could either attempt, by plebiscite or *coup d'état*, to rule dictatorially, or else he could spend his presidency indulging in that *politiquería* he had attacked so violently throughout his political life. He chose the latter, to the shocked disgust of his most fervent supporters.[142]

During his government, Ibáñez made an effort to bring the *Central Única de Trabajadores de Chile* (CUTCh) into the political arena by inviting CUTCh to participate in the government during 1955. Though CUTCh had been formed in 1953 with Ibáñez's blessing, Clotario Blest was not prepared to risk newly found unity by supporting Ibáñez, nor was he unaware of the disastrous effect a similar development in Perón's Argentina had had on organized labour in the neighbouring republic.[143] We must attribute this initiative more to Ibáñez's need for political support of any kind after the *Partida Socialista Popular* went into opposition, than to any serious effort to adopt the long-promised corporativism.

It was necessary that the populist phenomenon should burn itself out before a re-grouping of political forces could take place. To Ibáñez's discredit, his promises of legislation to end electoral corruption and to return the Communist Party to legality were not kept until 1958, and then the initiative was taken by a group of progressive parties briefly united as the *Bloque de Saneamiento Democrático*.[144]

The presidential campaign of 1958 saw the candidature of the three ensuing presidents of Chile. All of them received the support of some portion of the *ibañista* coalition. Jorge Alessandri

---

[142] See particularly René Montero, *op. cit.* Also D. W. Bray, *op. cit.* For a more complete study see the same author's Ph.D dissertation, *Chilean Politics during the Second Ibáñez Government 1952–8*, Stanford, 1961. A civilian-military conspiracy called *Línea Recta*, reviving some of the Armstrong plot's aims, planned to 'strengthen the executive' and to oblige the executive to be strong. A participant was Major Roberto Viaux, *Ercilla*, 22 March 1955, p. 5.

[143] For the events of 1955, see articles in *Ercilla*, Nos. 946–60, April–September 1965.

[144] Formed in March 1958 by those parties averse to the candidature of Jorge Alessandri, supported by the traditional rightist parties. It was believed that the elimination of bribery would cause Alessandri's candidature to collapse.

(1958–64), combining an image of authority and personal austerity with the appeal of technical competence, received the support of the PAL right-wing and was adopted as a new figure-head by the *portalianos*.[145] Salvador Allende (1970–) benefited by the reunification of the PS, *ibañista* PSP leaders like Clodomiro Almeyda, Raúl Ampuero overcoming their dislike of the Communist Party to form the *Frente de Acción Popular* (FRAP) which combination was strengthened by other small groups which had formed the more progressive wing of PAL.[146] Lastly, Eduardo Frei (1964–70) and the Christian Democrat Party (PDC) attracted those progressive elements of the *ibañista* constellation which were repelled by Marxism and attracted to the corporativist elements in PDC ideology.

There remained the gad-fly Radical Party, still the major party in Chile in the elections of 1957 and 1961, which stood alone in 1958, allied unsuccessfully with the right in 1964 and, after a deep division, with the UP in 1970.[147]

It would appear that all the major political alternatives offered to the Chilean electorate today have benefited in some way from the breakdown of the political force we have studied. Given the heterogenous elements that went to form Chilean neo-fascism, only the Communist Party is in a position to accuse others of fascism – and it is not surprising that it is the CP's internationalism and obedience to Moscow[148] which is cause of reserve even among its present allies, given the fierce nationalistic element in their formation.

The collapse of Ibañismo had a four-fold impact on the structure of Chilean politics. Temporarily, at least, it reduced the power of personality, giving way to presidential campaigns characterized by party programmes which showed serious preparation for government.[149]

[145] Julio von Mühlembrock, leader of the right wing of PAL led that section into the Liberal Party.

[146] Oscar Jiménez Pinochet, right-hand man of Jorge González in the tragic *coup* of 5 September 1938, was briefly Minister of Health in the first government formed by President Allende after his victory in 1970. Tarud, Allende's campaign manager in 1970, had been the leader of the progressive wing of PAL.

[147] Julio Durán, *achista* to this day, leads a dissident anti-communist section of the party, the *Democracia Radical*.

[148] It was the first CP in Latin America, if not the world, to applaud the invasion of Czechoslovakia.

[149] Though the completely personalist candidature of Jorge Alessandri in 1970 still showed the power of an appeal to end *politiquería*.

From a constitutional and legalistic view, Law No. 14851 of 15 June 1962 made the formation of new parties very much more difficult[150] while the view that parties are an expression of interest groups is made a great deal more coherent by the elimination of multi-group and across-class nationalist populism.

Finally, the weakness that established political organizations showed by their inability to parry the *ibañista* thrust was a contributing factor in the re-structuring of some of those organizations in order to meet new social and political demands. The growth of the PDC at the expense of conservatives and liberals forced the traditional parties to unite as the *Partido Nacional* (PN) in 1967, with a more formal organization and a more populist appeal[151] which has led to a revival of the political right. In the face of national modernization and restructuring undertaken during the 1960s, the traditional parties must change or be absorbed by the newer parties.[152]

CONCLUSION

In the broad spectrum of Chilean political parties, with a middle-class leadership and a popular base, there is room for every political persuasion except one – and that is the one we have studied. Be they Marxist or fascist, the groups which seek to abolish parliament, patronage and the spoils system without which the parties cannot function are, somewhat naturally, the common enemies of all the parties regardless of ideology.

Until the appearance of the Guevarist *Movimiento de Izquierda Revolucionaria* (MIR) in 1966 there had been no significant violent anti-parliamentary leftist movement since the early 1930s. In contrast, there has always been an anti-parliamentary neo-fascist right which has gradually eliminated the socialist from its national-socialist ideological base.

This element barely survived the crushing Ibáñez disappointment, only to revive and strike in 1970. The events leading up to General Schneider's murder are truly stunning repetitions of past

[150] The constitutionalist argument is expressed in A. Silva Bascuñan, *Tratado de Derecho Constitucional*, Editorial Jurídica, Santiago 1963. His views on party proliferation are to be found in Vol. III, p. 388, *passim*.

[151] Sergio Onofre Jarpa, the president of the PN has led the party towards a posture which combines the 'Travaille, Patrie, Famille' of Pétain and de Gaulle, with a leaning towards the example of the present Peruvian regime.

[152] The decline of the Radical Party must be attributed, in part, to the fact that its fabled machine is out of date.

events. On 21 October 1969, a general called Roberto Viaux, graduate of *Linea Recta*, occupied the barracks of the *Tacna* regiment in order to dramatize some institutional demands of the army. This action had been precipitated by his being called to retirement. The events of that day needed only the presence of Ibáñez to be a repeat performance of the *Ariostazo* of 1939. In the months following the *Tacnazo*, General Viaux became the object of attentions by diverse political forces, both of the left and of the right.[153] A small group of *nacionalistas* formed around him and it was these who, after the UP electoral victory of 3 September 1970, were organized to kidnap the Commander-in-Chief of the army. This group first exploded numerous bombs, leaving leaflets which attributed the explosions to a revolutionary Marxist group. The similarities to the *Colliguay* plot of 1951 are not surprising, as Juan Diego Dávila, a participant in that plot, was the man who planned the Schneider kidnapping. Finally, before the plot failed and Viaux was imprisoned, a lawyer called Pablo Rodríguez formed a movement called *Frente Nacionalista Patria y Libertad* (FNPL) which later adopted Viaux as its figurehead. The similarity to the MNCh of 1940 goes further – just as Izquierdo was Herrera's lawyer, so Rodriguez is Viaux's.

The FNPL, using a pseudo-swastika as its symbol, has engaged in street battles with leftist groups and has continually poured a flood of insinuating flattery in the direction of the armed forces.

So that no historical parallel should be missing, Jorge Prat and Arturo Olavarría have once again formed a party to prevent the dissolution threatened by Marxism and *politiquería*.[154]

It should be of little consolation to the rulers of Chile that these movements have usually had limited success and a brief life, for they have traditionally been the symptoms of a more generalized political malaise – a loss of faith in the ability of the parliamentary system to respond to a crisis.

Today, the existing party and parliamentary system is the object of attack from the MIR, which condemns it as an obstacle to

[153] For an account of the events in 1969 and 1970 see Eduardo Lebarca Goddard, *Chile al Rojo*. Ediciones de la Universidad Técnica del Estado, Santiago, 1971. He refers to the ambivalent attitude that the socialists adopted towards Viaux on pp. 62–5.

[154] See proclamations of the *Union Cívica Democrática* in the press of 13 December 1971. Prat died shortly afterwards, his funeral being attended by Onofre Jarpa, fellow leader of Acción Nacional in 1964 and by the *nacionalista* Mario Arnello, both leaders of the PN in its search for a new ideological posture.

fundamental social and economic changes and from the more extreme rightists who see it as a Marxist Trojan horse. However, neither the government nor the opposition parties have diverged very far from the traditional rules of the political game. Significantly, during the 1970 campaign, both Alessandri and Allende promised to call an immediate plebiscite to renew or change the composition or structure of the parliamentary institutions. Equally significantly, the victor has not kept his promise and a conflict between executive and legislature is building up.

It would require only an economic crisis, on top of the continuous problems of underdevelopment, in order to create a situation which, judging by previous appearances, has had somewhat unpredictable results.

Gonzalo Martner

7 The Economic Aspects of Allende's Government: Problems and Prospects

CHILE IS A LONG AND NARROW COUNTRY; SITUATED AT THE extreme south-west of South America, with a continental territory of 742,000 square kilometres and a population of 9·8 million, of which 74% are city dwellers. In 1970, the GNP reached 7,403 million dollars, of which agriculture accounted for 7%, mining 11%, industry 29%, construction 4%, electricity, gas and water 2%, transport and communications 4% and services 43%.

The contradictions which the dynamics of the Chilean economy have shown during the 1960s have led to a disordered functioning of its mechanisms. It is useful to examine the outlines of Chilean development during these last ten years, so that the programme of transformations and development undertaken by the Government of the Unidad Popular since 1970 can be understood.

THE CHILEAN ECONOMY IN THE 1960s

The year 1970 represents the culmination of a process of gradual stagnation in the growth rate of economic activity, visible from 1967. The available figures clearly reveal that the economy experienced a retrocession from that year: the average growth rate between 1961 and 1966 was 5·4%, double the 2·7% average for the years 1967–70, which was scarcely greater than the 2·3% growth in population.

Comparing these figures with the corresponding growth rates in other countries of Latin America, one concludes that in recent years, the Chilean economy expanded at a slower pace than Latin American economies as a whole, where annual growth rates exceeded 5%. According to studies carried out by CEPAL, per capita production for the entire region in 1969 was 471 dollars. With an average per capita production of 593 dollars in that year, Chile had been overtaken during the 1960s by Panama and Mexico, and now occupies sixth place, after Argentina, Venezuela, Uruguay, Panama and Mexico.

In like fashion, the Chilean economic system could not create the necessary employment to absorb the workforce during the 1960s. The active population, or workforce, has been growing annually by about 77,000, and the annual absorption of labour by the economy fluctuated around this figure, with unemployment being maintained thus at a level close to 6% of the workforce.

On the other hand, if one examines the distribution of the annual labour intake, one finds that as much as 66% of the intake went into services and other sectors which are not directly productive. Industry provided only 22% of the new jobs created during the decade. During the 1960s, there was only a 17·1% increase in employment in the productive sectors, whilst there was a 46% increase in the service sector – figures which illustrate the incapacity of the system to provide productive work.

The way in which the annual labour intake has been distributed among the different sectors of the economy indicates the lack of opportunities for work. One of the principal symptoms of the problem of unemployment and under-employment is the high percentage of the intake which enters the service sector.

This situation can largely be explained by the inadequate rate of economic development, by the orientation of investment towards projects which require little labour, by the indiscriminate incorporation of technology which substitutes machinery for labour, by the absence of lasting concern for the employment problem in the fixing of tributary or labour policies, by the low level of development in skilled activities associated with agriculture, forestry or the sea – important sources of employment, by the inherent contradictions of the system, etc. All these factors have contributed towards maintaining an important contingent of the workforce in a position of permanent unemployment.

The fundamental characteristics of this unemployment are the poor qualifications of the unemployed, its level, which has remained more or less constant throughout the 1960s and its localization in certain regions of the country. In this last respect, one finds that the Concepción and Lota-Coronel areas have maintained the highest levels of unemployment in the country during the last ten years.

Unemployment affects production capacity as well as the workers. It has been estimated that the manufacturing industry under-utilized its installed production capacity to the tune of 32% towards the end of the 1960s.

Gross investment was relatively stable within the GNP, about 17%, taking into account the changes in stocks, and just below 16% when these changes are removed. Nevertheless, from 1966, the increases in gross fixed capital investments began to be less than they were before this date, with the exception of 1968. Construction accounted for the most important part of fixed capital investments, and the rest, less than half, was accounted for by machinery and infrastructural works, followed in importance by the construction of dwellings. In the second group, imported components represent about 80% of the total, a reflection of the incipient national industry in capital goods.

In the 1960s, investment from the public sector represented on average 50% of gross national investment, but towards the end of the decade, direct and indirect government investment exceeded 70%. Most of this investment was what one might catalogue as productive, in the sense that it directly increased the productive capacity of a given production unit. Other investments generally took the form of infrastructural works and were less important in terms of volume, representing about 10% of gross national investment.

Existing figures reveal that infrastructural works were increasing up till 1964 and that after that date, their importance began to decline, particularly in 1967 and 1968. In 1968, they constituted only 72% of what they had been in 1964. The decline indicated is a direct consequence of the emphasis which the government at that time gave to each type of investment, since, in parallel fashion, directly productive public investment was increasing in importance.

Evident throughout the decade was the increased concentration, monopolization and denationalization of national production. In the industrial sector, the high degree of concentration reached is significant; only 3% of the business establishments generated 51% of the aggregate industrial wealth, employing 58% of the capital and 44% of the workforce, besides controlling 52% of the gross surpluses. The banking sector also showed a growing concentration of credit within the private sector. Studies demonstrated that in 1969, 0·4% of the borrowers controlled 25% of all bank credit whilst at the other end of the scale, 28% of the

borrowers only had access to 2·6% of bank credit. During the late
1960s, the income growth rates of financiers and banks were
enormous: in fact, the financial services within the GNP increased
at an annual accumulative rate of 9%, and in recent years went as
high as 26% (1969).

The concentration of property led to the concentration of
income: in 1968, 3·2% of the remunerated population received
42% of the national income, whilst at the other extreme, 47% of
the population only earned 12% of the income and had salaries
below subsistence level. In short, 90% of the wage-earning population received only 45% of the income. Agriculture constitutes
the poorest sector in the country, with 82% of the population
with incomes below subsistence level; at the same time, the 1%
at the other end of the scale acquired 18% of the income from
this sector.

Together with economic stagnation, unemployment and the
unequal income distribution, went acute inflation. Whilst the
price index for consumer goods rose by 5·4% in 1960 and by 9·7%
in 1961, the price increases for 1968, 1969 and 1970 were 28%,
29% and 35% respectively. Much as the country displayed a
capacity for imports hitherto unknown in its economic history,
largely due to the increased price of copper, the national bourgeoisie was neither able to elaborate nor to practice a policy of
price stabilization, preferring to raise prices as an instrument
designed to maintain intact the unequal income distribution.

The price policies followed in recent years consisted of un-
loading all the increases in the first months of the year, thereby
taking back the real gains the workers were obtaining with their
increased wages, which thus became merely nominal. Among the
effects of this policy, one might point out that the economic
system itself restricted effective demand right from the beginning
of the year, and with it, impeded the formation of a stable market
for industrial production, thus generating the industrial stagnation the country has had to endure.

As a result of the long, historical process of conformation of the
Chilean economy, the concentration of economic activity and
population in the central zone has come to constitute one of the
basic problems which obstruct development, especially if one
compares this disproportionate growth with the depression of the
other regions. The historical roots of this geographical con-
figuration are to be found in the way the Chilean economy
attached itself to the international capitalist system. As the political

and administrative centre, the capital city was the mechanism through which were channelled the surpluses generated by the agricultural and mine workers throughout the country. These surpluses went abroad or were earmarked by the ruling bourgeoisie for the creation of an urban infrastructure in tune with its requirements and standards. In all dependent countries, capitalist industrial development is uneven and centralized. The same mechanisms which lead to the monopolistic concentration of capital favour industrial concentration in certain areas, leaving the rest of the country at a disadvantage with regard to raw materials, foodstuffs and labour.

Industrialization in Chile was directed by sectors of the bourgeoisie directly or indirectly linked with international capital, guided by the limited horizon of private profits from sectorial investment and protected by the state, whose control they used extensively for their own ends. Industrialization thus conceived exaggerated the existing centralization and converted Santiago into almost the only real industrial centre in the country. In 1970, Santiago contained about 54% of the country's urban population, and almost 37% of the total population. In 1967, 45% of the GNP and about 58% of the industrial product came from Santiago. 70% of the national production of manufactures takes place in the central provinces of Valparaiso, Aconcagua, O'Higgins and Santiago.

The geographical concentration of the economic activity co-exists with inequality of incomes and bureaucratic centralism. The administrative apparatus of the state, the financial system and the industrial services adapted to the economic structure, uphold the unequal geographical distribution. By way of example, on 30 June 1970, 56% of all national monetary deposits in commercial banks were concentrated in Santiago, as was also 68% of the total of deposits in the country. With their centre of operations in Santiago, the private commercial banks controlled about 87% of all deposits, a proportion which rises to 92% if one includes the State Bank.

Not only are production, decision-making and management concentrated in Santiago; there is an enormous mass of poverty, represented by people who sought better living conditions in the capital and who remained incorporated in city life, carrying out services with a very low productivity and receiving the meanest of incomes. In the 1960s, the population of the central zone of the country rose from 49% to 52% of the national total, despite the fact that the respective proportion of industrial work remained constant between 1957 and 1967.

Along with this migratory process there has arisen a demographic phenomenon of great consequence. As from 1963 and 1964, the country's population growth rate began to drop. A series of measures calculated to control the birth rate explains this phenomenon; there has been a notable drop in the birth rate. One consequence of this is that the age structure of the population has begun to change. This means that in fifteen or twenty years' time, the country's population will have a larger proportion of adults, that is to say, the population as a whole has begun to get older. The impact of this phenomenon on the workforce will probably not be noticed in the 1970s, given the roughly fifteen-year time-lag between birth and incorporation into the workforce. From that date on, however, it is probable that the growth rate of the workforce will diminish.

UNIDAD POPULAR'S FIRST YEAR IN POWER

4 November 1971, marked the first anniversary of the rule of President Allende's government. The economic policy undertaken in the course of the year was inspired by the Unidad Popular Programme and the 1971 Plan. The results achieved in the course of these twelve months can be examined in the light of the central directives of the established economic policy.

The progress made towards the establishment of the 'new economy', that is to say, a transition stage on the way to socialism, has been truly substantial. The social ownership sector has been formed and will play a leading role in the development of the country. Into this sector copper mining has been incorporated, by means of constitutional reform unanimously approved by the National Congress, as well as iron ore mining, the saltpetre operations and the production of steel. In this way, Chile has come to own its fundamental natural riches. We are striving to liquidate the *latifundios* which comprise about three million hectares of land. We are nationalizing commercial banking and we have succeeded in controlling more than 80% of credit for social ends; and about fifteen banks have been taken into the social sector. In the industrial sector we are progressing with the taking over of various monopolies: cement, textiles and other fabrics, and in one year, more than seventy enterprises have been expropriated. In order to rationalize the commercialization, we have set up the National Distribution Company.

The policy of increased wages and strict price controls in the course of 1971 enabled a redistribution of income in the popular sectors to be carried out, reactivating the economy and bringing about greater employment in the abundant unused capacity of the industrial sector. Within the economy, wages were readjusted about 45% on average, whilst profits were checked through the price controls policy. It has been calculated that the wage-earners' share of the national income would rise from 51% in 1970 to 59% in 1971.

The increase in popular demand has created a dynamic internal market which has enabled production to expand. The manufacturing industry, which accounts for about a third of the national product, had grown by 10·2% by September 1971, compared with an equal decline in 1970, and this heralds an over-all increase of more than 12% for 1971. Copper production, nationalized in July 1971, and now in fact managed by Chilean technicians, will exceed 580,000 tons, an increase of about 9%. Production in the agricultural sector will increase by 5% in 1971. Construction will expand by 9%, 83,000 dwellings having been started in 1971 in contrast to 25,000 in 1970. ODEPLAN[1] predicts that the national product will grow between 7% and 8% in 1971 as against 2·7% from 1967 to 1970.

One consequence of the policy followed has been a fundamental increase in the levels of popular consumption. Food consumption in the first six months of this year has increased noticeably; the consumption of beef has increased by 15%, pork by 18%, lamb by 5%, poultry by 16%, potatoes by 55%, onions by 54%, root crops by 21%, lemons by 56%, condensed milk by 10%, sugar by 37%, noodles by 28% and beer by 20%. The passage from a depressed to an expanding economy has produced some upheavals in supplies, but these are being overcome. The supply of basic foods like beef, chicken and fish has been made difficult by the greater demand and by the effects of the earthquake on 8 July in the central zone, where the majority of the country's inhabitants live and where the greater part of the national product is generated.

The Popular government has succeeded in drastically reducing the rate of inflation in Chile. In 1970, the consumer price index

[1] Oficina de Planificación Nacional

rose by 35%, and up till October 1971, the same index displayed
an increase of 15·8%. ODEPLAN estimates that by the end of
1971, price increases will fluctuate between 15% and 17%, that
is to say, inflation has been cut by half, in spite of the fact that the
country has been affected by the drop in world copper prices.
The previous government was blessed with an exceptionally high
copper price which rose as high as 84 cents per pound, whilst in
1971, the average price will not exceed 50 cents. The policy of
liquidating the monopolies and *latifundios* has permitted the effective control of prices and financial trends, forcing a change among
economic agents previously used to open inflation.

Part of the government's inheritance was the enormous level
of unemployment. In Santiago, unemployment ran as high as
8·3% in December 1970. The reactivation of the economy which
took effect in the first six months of 1971 reduced this rate to
5·3% by June and to 4·8% by September; we foresee that by the
end of 1971, unemployment will have been cut by half, thanks to
the home-building programme and industrial reactivation. By
the end of the year 1971, this government foresees a labour shortage in Iquique and Llanquihue, and a scarcity of qualified workers
in provinces like Valparaiso, Concepción and Santiago.

In 1971 we saw the start of greater workers' participation in the
running of the economic processes. Six workers' representatives
were included when the National Development Council was set up
to discuss development policy at presidential level; workers' representatives are also included in the Regional Development Councils, organized at provincial level. Standards for popular participation have been established in the enterprises of the social and
joint ownership sector, giving workers responsibilities in the
management and operation of the enterprises. For the first time
in Chilean trade-union history, the CUT[2] Congress will discuss
the Six Year Development Plan formulated by the government in
consultation with the people. Educational services have been
increased substantially in 1971. 94% of the population between
the ages of six and fourteen and 35% between the ages of fifteen
and nineteen attended school. There has been a reduction in
the infant mortality rate as a result of the improved living
conditions of the people, the government's programme of distri-
buting half a litre of milk to children and various types of health
campaigns. Within its first year, the government has completed

[2] Central Única de Trabajadores.

some 33,000 dwellings for the people, and at the same time, in three months, some 18,000 emergency dwellings have been erected in the areas affected by the earthquakes. A tourism programme has been started for the people, with the creation of bathing resorts and, for the first time, workers' children have been able to ski in the extensive mountain ranges of the Andes.

Until 1970, the fiscal, monetary and credit policies belonged to the orthodox school, but because of the existence of idle production resources, vast unemployment and abundant natural resources, the government resolved to pursue a policy of over-spending (planned deficitary spending) designed to generate purchasing power in the economy, substantially extending public investment in order to get the national economy going.

The increase in public investment in the industrial sector, in public works, and especially in housing, has greatly compensated for the expected decline in private and foreign investments. The investment rate for 1971 will be approximately 14% of the national product, which will expand more than 7%, thanks to the increased utilization of the existing capacity.

Conscious of the fact that in their first year of office, the fundamental tasks of economic transformation and production reactivation have been fulfilled, the government's economic policy for 1972 will have a different character from that of the preceding year, emphasizing more the process of accumulation based on the collected external and internal surpluses, and the economic cooperation of the socialist countries, Western Europe, Japan and other nations, whilst at the same time hoping for a recovery in private investment, after the law for the delimitation of economic sectors has been passed, the project for which is pending in the National Congress.

THE OBJECTIVES OF DEVELOPMENT

After his first year in office, President Allende announced his economic development programme for the six years to 1976. The programme of the Unidad Popular not only reflects a change in economic organization but also a vigorous drive for economic development. The basic lines of the 1971–76 Plan for the National Economy can be summarized in the following points:

To gain greater economic independence. This goal will be reached through the incorporation of the country's basic riches into the national patrimony, like copper, iron, saltpetre, finance, industry

and commercialization. Similarly, the Chilean economy will be
linked to every country in the world by a new imports and
exports policy, freeing itself from its traditional markets and
integrating itself more firmly with new areas, like the socialist
countries, Western Europe, Asian, African and other Latin
American countries.

Copper will continue to be the principal export, for which
purpose its physical volume will increase 60% by 1976, which will
mean an income of about 1,200 million dollars for the country at
an estimated average price of 50 cents per pound. The country
will also increase its exports of manufactures and agricultural
products, which together will mean an increase from 400 million
dollars in 1970 to 560 million dollars in 1976. Annual exports
would thus total some 1,760 million dollars in 1976. Imports will
reach a more or less equivalent figure in 1976; intermediate goods
will account for 50%, capital goods for 23% and consumer goods
for 27%. The proportion of imports to the GNP will be reduced
from 15·4% in 1970 to 13·6% in 1976.

*To pass from an exclusive economy to an economy of popular partici-
pation.* It is the intention of the Plan that by 1976, the Chilean
economy should be able to provide employment for 3,940,000
workers. This means the creation of 944,000 new jobs. Since
Chile's population will have reached 11·2 million by 1976, it
is of paramount importance to expand those activities which
absorb the workforce. The target is to increase the 30·7% active
population in 1970 to 36% by 1976. One basic aim of the Plan is
to provide remunerative work for 479,000 women; thus, of the
total active population between the ages of fifteen and sixty-four,
the present 26% female proportion will grow to 41% by 1976.
That is to say, the Chilean woman will be fully incorporated into
the production process. Similarly, during the six years, racial
minorities like the *Araucas* will come to possess the same rights as
other Chileans, and will likewise be incorporated into the production process. Organized workers, women, young people and the
largest sectors of the Chilean population will participate in
decision-making, through the mechanisms of popular participation, assuming the management of the economic process.

To improve national income distribution. The Plan provides for an
increased share of the national income for the wage-earner; from
the 51% they received in 1970, they will come to control 60·7%
by 1976. To balance this, the share of proprietors and entrepre-
neurs will decrease from 18·6% to 8·3% over the same period.

The government will maintain its share at about 16%, whilst the share of enterprises in the social sector will grow from 4·9% in 1970 to 10·1% in 1976, the share of private businesses will drop from 6·1% in 1970 to 3·2% in 1976, and the share of foreign businesses will fall from 3% to 1·2% over the six years. By 1976, Chile will have a more equitable income distribution, making the lives of its inhabitants more just and honourable and, at the same time, creating a greater purchasing power in the wage-earning sectors, which will facilitate the formation of a growing market for national industry.

To reconstruct the productive apparatus in order to raise the standard of living. The changes which can be foreseen in the demand structure make it necessary to create an economy based on the prosperity of the people. To this end, substantial increases are envisaged in activities like construction, the output of which will increase by 92% over the six years, accounting for 5·3% of the national product in 1976 as opposed to 4·2% in 1970. The timber, furniture, paper, printing industries, etc., will increase their output by 66%, whilst the foodstuff, beverage, tobacco, textile, clothing and leather industries will increase by 52%. Education, health and other services will also expand to the tune of 57% over the six years. The infrastructure will also be greatly expanded, especially transport and electricity, with a 50% increase in output. Intensive efforts will be made in the fishing industry and in the agricultural sector to increase production by 47%, and in mining by 49% over the six years. The readaptation of the productive apparatus to the requirements of a popular economy supposes the production within every branch of goods designed specifically for the people. The design of cars, televisions, refrigerators, houses, etc., will be modified to conform with the needs of the Chilean people.

To increase savings and reorientate their use. To enable the increases in production already indicated to take place, investments will grow from 16·6% in 1970 to 18·2% in 1976. In six years 125,000 million *escudos* will be invested, equivalent to 10·7 thousand million dollars; 52% of this will go towards the productive sectors (agriculture, mining, industry), 23% towards the physical infrastructure (transport and energy) and 25% towards social investments (housing, schools, hospitals). To facilitate the accumulation rate indicated, the country will mobilize for its own benefit those surpluses which left the country before or were diverted towards luxury consumer goods by the monopolistic and financing sectors. The formation of the social ownership sector is the key factor in the mobilization of these surpluses, and in 1976 it will contribute 10·1% of national savings as against 4·9% in 1970. At the same time, it is envisaged that there will be a decline in savings from private enterprise and the government, which will be compensated for by increases in the social sector and by foreign assets.

To extend the social ownership sector and transform its function into a leading role in development. The formation of the public ownership sector is one of the basic objectives of the government programme, and the Plan has considered the production increases which will be necessary in the six years to enable it to acquire the role of leader in economic development. The social sector, which generated 10% of the GNP in 1970 will grow to generate 40% by 1976, to which end about 100 industrial enterprises of a monopolistic nature will be incorporated and their surplus used for the benefit of the bulk of the people. The government's aim is to restructure the social sector, creating 'operational sectors' to raise standards of efficiency and improve planning in the social ownership sector. The restructuring of the social sector will as a matter of principle involve the active participation of the workers in the management and administration of the enterprises in the social ownership sector. The workers' responsibility and discipline is the safeguard for the transformation of this sector into the vanguard of the Chilean productive process.

To increase national production by changing from a stagnant economy to an economy of sustained development. The production battle, whose contents and aspects form the substance of the Plan, will enable production to be increased by 50% over the next six years, thereby improving the standard of living for the estimated 11·2 million Chileans in 1976. This production goal will be achieved by means of Annual Plans, orientated by the present Six Year Plan, enabling national production to grow annually at least 7% on average. The important part of the Development Plan is not the stated targets, but the transformation which the economy and Chilean society will undergo in the six years.

Essential to the Plan is that this transformation can be made together with the degree of economic growth indicated above. Whether this target can be reached will to a large extent depend on the degree of mobilization of the working masses and their capacity to overcome the obstacles of the sectors which stand to lose by the progress of the people.

To create a more spatially balanced economy. One basic aim of the

Plan is that development must be in harmony with the regional economies. The twelve Regional Plans involved are designed to achieve a better utilization of natural resources in every province of the country. To this end, the investments' plan will be decentralized, so that new economic activity can be created in the most backward regions. Industries, roads, social and urban facilities will all come gradually to every province, thereby generating overall development of the whole of Chile with proper attention to the frontier zones.

Luis Quiros Varela

8 Chile: Agrarian Reform and Political Processes

CHILEAN DEVELOPMENT BETWEEN THE 1930S AND THE 1960S HAS been chiefly characterized by the extreme inequalities between the various social sectors of the country. However, during the past decade the accumulated inequalities have given rise to a growing instability which has necessitated efforts to carry out a transformation of the system, designed to reduce the tensions created between the various social and political forces, and to overcome the obstacles which stand in the way of accelerated development. More than any other socio-economic sector, agriculture was responsible for the greatest inequalities. The recognition of this situation is not a recent phenomenon; the prevailing conditions of Chilean agriculture have been the object of harsh criticism for more than forty years, and this criticism included pessimistic predictions for the future development of the country and its political stability, if a land redistribution programme were not carried out.[1] In the face of the changes experienced throughout the country, agriculture remained an economically stagnant sector in which traditional conditions of exploitation and life-style continued to dominate, without fulfilling the role assigned to it by the economists in the economic development of the country.[2]

[1] See, among others, George Macbride, *Chile, su tierra y su gente*, ICIRA, Santiago, 1970.

[2] The role of agriculture in economic development has been defined by economists as follows:

(a) as a source of labour
(b) to provide foodstuffs for the growing urban population, and especially, to compensate population increases
(c) as a source of foreign currency
(d) as a source of revenue for the government
(e) to generate savings which will then contribute to the growth of investments

See Charles Kindelberger, *Economic Development*, McGraw-Hill, New York, 1963, pp. 218–19.

From 1930 onwards, Chile has been undergoing rapid industrialization with an annual population growth of 2·2% and an increasing trend to urbanization. In 1930, the urban population accounted for 49·2% of the total population of 4,120,000, but by 1970, 71% of the ten million population were urban dwellers.[3] These figures imply a greater demand for agricultural produce, but productivity within this sector increased on average only 1·8% each year, which was inadequate to satisfy the rise in demand caused by the population growth.[4] So the country started to import agricultural produce, totalling as much as 190 million dollars in 1963, a sum which could have been significantly reduced by home production.[5] At the same time, agriculture's share of exports declined from 20% to 3%.[6] This was partly due to poor utilization of the scarce productive resources – land and capital – which meant that the workforce was under-employed. In 1965, there was a 32·5% surplus of rural workers.[7] This decline of agriculture was partly due to the lack of entrepreneurial ability. In spite of the favourable price, credit and tax incentives awarded to agriculture, these advantages merely protected 'inefficiency and resource wastage'.[8] Lastly, the stagnation of agricultural production was the result of structural obstacles in two ways: the excessive concentration of land ownership (*latifundio*), the origins of which take us back to the traditional *hacienda* system, and the large number of small properties (*minifundios*). Both are anachronistic and inadequate forms of land tenure. The situation is described in Table 1.

In social terms this situation concealed extreme injustices, in that given the political and social organization of the country, land was looked upon as a source of power and social prestige for its owners, or seen as a means of protection against inflation.[9] This also explains the absence of any significant rural middle class. By

[3] CIDA, Chile: 'Tenencia de la tierra y desarrollo socio-económico del sector agrícola', Talleres Gráficos Hispano Suiza Ltda., 1966, p. 12.

[4] ODEPA, 'Plan de Desarrollo Agropecuario, 1965–1970' (Synthesis), Impr. Camilo Enríquez, Santiago, 1968, p. 4.

[5] S. Aranda and A. Martínez, 'Estructura económica: algunas características fundamentales', in Aníbal Pinto, *et al.*, *Chile Hoy*, Siglo XXI Editores, Santiago, 1970, p. 120.

[6] ODEPA, *op. cit.*, pp. 8–9.

[7] *Loc. cit.*, p. 9.

[8] Aranda y Martínez, *op. cit.*, p. 120.

[9] ODEPA, *op. cit.*, p. 9.

the side of the great landowners and dependent upon them there existed an unorganized, poor, illiterate mass of peasants with no opportunities for social mobility – except the scant hope that migration to the cities offered. The small farmers found themselves in an identical situation, under-employed and with no access to financial facilities or technical assistance. In 1965, more than half the total of landholdings and more than a quarter of their total area was in the hands of renters and sharecroppers, with the resulting instability and incapacity to programme their productive tasks in the long term.[10]

TABLE 1

Size of Holding	Number of holdings	% of the total	area in 000 hectares	% of the total
Less than 5 hectares	123,636	48·8	207·0	0·7
5 to 50 hectares	92,408	36·4	1556·0	5·1
51 to 200 hectares	23,959	9·5	2284·0	7·5
201 to 1,000 hectares	10,158	4·0	4310·9	14·0
1,001 to 5,000 hectares	2,601	1·0	5495·4	17·9
more than 5,000 hectares	730	0·3	6795·4	54·8
National total:	253,492	100·00	30,648·7	100·00

Source: S. Aranda and S. Martínez, op. cit., p. 121.

The domination of the peasantry by the landowning class in rural areas meant that the organized latifundistas had unlimited access to government institutions and the processes of policy making in all fields.

The large landowners' most effective articulation was carried out under the direction of the National Agricultural Society (SNA), the oldest pressure group in Chile, formed in 1838. There were also regional pressure groups like the Northern Agricultural Consortium, the Southern Agricultural Consortium and other similar provincial groups, all with less political influence than the national organization, to which however they were linked.

The political power of the SNA until the 1960s came from the interweaving of its leadership with the Liberal and Conservative Parties, and to a lesser extent, with the Radical Party. It is symptomatic that throughout this period, 75% or more of the SNA's leadership consisted of individuals whose main activity had

[10] ODEPA, op. cit., p. 10.

nothing to do with agriculture, but with politics or other non-agricultural activities.[11]

Similarly, the SNA's free access to government was reinforced by the fact that nearly all the Ministers of Agriculture, from the creation of the Ministry in 1929, were connected with agriculture and were members of the SNA.

The SNA also managed to secure representation on the executive councils of newly created institutions like CORFO and its dependent enterprises set up by the 'Popular Front', and later with Ibáñez, and charged with the promotion of the country's development.[12] This allowed the SNA to participate directly in the management of the country, and in any case, gave it access to information about government programmes, which doubtless enabled it to promote and/or defend the interests of the large landowners. At least one reason for the government's incapacity to carry out a more effective agrarian policy, even when it was dominated by the 'Popular Front', can be put down to the political influence of the SNA. Some government attempts at reform, like the setting up of the Agricultural Colonization Bank in 1929 by General Ibáñez, with the object of dividing up and colonizing state and unused lands, were little more than symbolic gestures with very little impact. In the thirty-three years of its existence this Bank distributed lands totalling one million hectares to 4,206 settlers, but only 15% of the settlers were sold land in the central zone of the country, which is considered to be the most fertile region.[13]

The limitations on the action of the state are also reflected in the degree to which the state remained one of the largest agricultural landowners, its lands being controlled by government organizations and rented out by them to private owners, with rather negative results.[14]

---

[11] See Margarita María Errázuiz, 'Los grupos dirigentes agrícolas', (unpublished thesis) Santiago, Universidad Católica de Chile, 1970, pp. 98–104.

[12] In 1964 the SNA had representatives on the executive councils of, among other institutions, CORFO, the Central Bank, the State Bank, the Agrarian Reform Corporation, the Bank for the Amortization of the Public Debt, etc.

[13] See CIDA, op. cit., p. 250, and William C. Thiesenhusen, Chile's Experiments in Agrarian Reform, The University of Wisconsin Press, Madison, p. 36.

[14] In 1965, agricultural land belonging to or used by state institutions totalled almost 14 million hectares. 4,670,000 hectares of forest were also under their patronage. Agricultural lands belonging to or used by autonomous

152   LUIS QUIROS VARELA

The peasantry remained on the margin of the political system,
and this situation was reinforced by their illiteracy, or, if they did
participate in elections, by the fact that their votes were controlled
by the landowners. Such for a long time was the basis of the
Conservative Party's power, and to a lesser degree, of that of the
Radical Party in the agricultural provinces of the Norte Chico
and in the south of the country.[15]

The lack of peasant organization was legally justified by the
prohibition of unionization based on an interpretation of a
presidential directive on labour legislation. Later a law on peasant
unions (Number 8911, 1947), drawn up under the presidency of
Gabriel González Videla, established a system of peasant unions
so cumbersome that its provisions were almost inapplicable.[16]
In 1953, there was a total of 14,021 organized peasants, grouped in
fifteen unions. One of the first peasant strikes which took place in
that year (in Molina, a town situated in the vine-growing region in
the centre of the country), illustrates how the lack of peasant
organization necessitated the support of non-peasant elements for
its success – in this case, principally the Christian unions and
the Church.[17]

The political marginality of the peasantry is the result of
the conciliatory nature of the Chilean political system,[18] which
during this period achieved a consensus by emphasizing industrial-

----

or semi-governmental institutions totalled 650,000 hectares, of which
441,000 belonged to CORA and were liable to be assigned for redistribution
in the programme of agrarian reform. CIDA, *op. cit.*, pp. 356–60.

[15] See E. Faletto and E. Ruiz, 'Conflicto político y estructura social', in
Aníbal Pinto, *et al.*, *Chile Hoy*, pp. 213–54. For the 1969 election, they find a
positive connection between the National Party and agricultural activity of
0·5. For the radicals this connection is 0·3; for the PDC the connection is
zero, as it is for the Socialist Party; and for the Communist Party, the connection is minus 0·6.

[16] See Almino Affonso, *et al.*, 'El movimiento campesino Chileno', ICIRA,
Santiago, 1970, Vol. 1, pp. 49 ff.

[17] See F. Canitrot and H. Landsberger, *Iglesia, intelectuales y campesinos*,
Edit. del Pacífico, Santiago, 1968, an important study of this strike.

[18] See David Apter, *The Politics of Modernization*, University of Chicago
Press, Chicago, 1966, pp. 36 and 392 ff. At least up till 1964, the Chilean
political system displays all the characteristics of Apter's category – especially
in the reference to the low level of political participation and the form in
which political differences are resolved, the kind of decisions which result
from this, and the inequality which emerges.

ization with the approval of all the political parties, including those to the left. By harnessing urban labour sectors, political participation gradually increased, without significantly affecting the bases of economic and financial power of the upper classes, which in fact gained greater relative benefits from the increase in income over the period than the middle classes and labour groups.[19] On the other hand, the left-wing parties accepted the objective conditions and customs imposed by the Chilean institutional framework, and were incapable of consistently mobilizing the masses because of internal dissensions which plagued the Socialist Party, because of the communists' alienation from national problems, and because of traditional rivalry between both parties. These parties in the end strengthened the conciliatory nature of the system by accepting the electoral path as a means of achieving power, and holding to their electoral support with a defensive attitude towards the economic and social victories won by the workers' movement under their control. In those years, the peasantry was abandoned to its fate.[20]

FIRST ATTEMPTS AT AGRARIAN REFORM

The imbalances generated by the agricultural sector were drawn into the general trend which the Chilean political system began to show in the 1950s, in that it began to seek new solutions to break the obstacles to development. One of the first indications was the election, in 1952, of General Ibáñez, a populist leader, who, promising to bring about a 'Peaceful Revolution', expressed the frustration of the Chilean electorate with the fourteen years of government by the Radical and traditional parties. It was the first sign of peasant independence from political manipulation, and important groups within the sector gave their support to the victorious candidate. However, the populist character of 'Ibáñismo' prevented integral government action solving the

[19] Aníbal Pinto, the Chilean economist, maintains that between 1940 and 1953 the real income of all groups increased by 40%. Each group got a different share however, with the workers (57% of the active population) getting only a 7% real increase, the agricultural white-collar workers a 46% rise and the peasants a 60% increase. See Aníbal Pinto, *Chile, un caso de desarrollo frustrado*, Edit. Universitaria, 1959, p. 185.

[20] See, among others, A. Pinto's analyses, 'Desarrollo económico y relaciones sociales', in A. Pinto, *et al.*, *Chile Hoy*, pp. 51-4, and E. Faletto and E. Ruiz, *op. cit.*

problems. The growing frustration eroded the support of huge sectors for the regime, and only accentuated its inflexibility.

But during Ibáñez's six year term of office, several events of great importance for the future of the country, especially in relation to agrarian policy took place. Firstly, the union in 1956 of the left-wing parties headed by socialists and communists in the Popular Action Front, and the rise of the Christian Democrat Party, on the base of the former National Falange, created new forces. The election platforms of both forces in the following years helped to mobilize the electorate towards new goals which would bring self-sustained development for the country. Secondly, towards the end of Ibáñez's period of office, in 1957 and 1958, electoral reform expanded the bases of electoral participation, by making the vote obligatory. This greater participation was increasingly won by the new forces, especially after 1960, and implied the gradual transfer of power from the traditional to the centre and left-wing parties. The right succeeded in regaining power for the 1958–64 term of office with Jorge Alessandri. Though democratic, yet tied to the past, the government refused to listen to the public demand for more daring reform policies. But the Radical Party's demand that the government should carry out 'structural reforms' as a condition of its entry into the coalition, led to a series of laws for the agrarian sector. The most important was law Number 15,020, on 'Agrarian Reform', which deserves the name only insofar that it was intended to speed up a very limited programme of colonization and land tenancy reform. Basically, it was a question of a compromise between the interests of the landowning sectors and the demands of those groups which deemed the implementation of more radical measures to be necessary.[21]

This law allowed for the expropriation of abandoned or notoriously badly utilized holdings; of up to 50% of lands irrigated as a result of state financing, of lands with outstanding credit repayment debts, of *minifundios* for the purposes of consolidation, and of lands which, in spite of being well exploited, were needed for certain redistribution programmes. To carry out this programme, regional plans for expropriation were prepared. Landowners were to be awarded compensation, and they were given the right to retain part of their lands. Special tribunals were set up to examine

[21] See Robert R. Kaufmann, 'The Chilean Political Right and Agrarian Reform: Resistance and Moderation', in A. von Lazar and R. Kaufmann, editors, *Reform and Revolution*, Allyn and Bacon, Boston, 1969, pp. 159–228.

the grounds for expropriation and to determine the amount of compensation. The amount was fixed by the commercial value, and not by the fiscal valuation of the property for taxation purposes. Subsequent constitutional reforms allowed for deferred payments, with 20% to be paid in cash and the rest to be paid over a maximum of ten years, with allowances for fluctuations in inflation and an annual interest rate of 4% – all very favourable conditions for the landowners.

The expropriated land would be reassigned as economic units which would enable 'a family to prosper and maintain itself through the rational application of its labour' (Article 116 of the law). The *latifundio* was defined as a property exceeding twenty of these units, and in the event of expropriation, the landowner would be permitted to retain ten of these units. All these limitations drastically reduced the state's capacity to complete its programme, and reduced the peasants' hopes for improving their situation. For this reason, Alessandri's reform was disparagingly christened 'the flowerpot reform' ('la reforma del macetero').

The main contribution of this legislation was to create a state institutional structure to carry out the agrarian policy, principally CORA (the Agrarian Reform Corporation), and INDAP (the Institute of Agricultural Development). CORA was charged with carrying out the expropriation and redistribution programmes, and INDAP was responsible for providing credit and technical aid for the new landowners.[22]

At the same time, the symbolic gesture of approving an 'agrarian reform law' not only legitimized the concept and the policy itself, but also opened the way to increased activities by social institutions and political parties which were designed to strengthen the government's weak programme by demanding a more radical agrarian reform programme. The Chilean Catholic Church in particular, which had been moving away from the traditional sectors since the 1930s, broke with them and took up the cause of the marginal sectors. It divested itself of the lands it possessed in favour of the tenants who worked them, by means of an actual programme which even contemplated appointing assessors for the division of these lands, the installation of the new owners and the initial stages of production.[23]

[22] See James Becket, 'Problemas de la Reforma Agraria' in Oscar Delgado (ed.), *Las Reformas Agrarias en América Latina*, FCE, Mexico, 1966, pp. 574–79.

[23] An excellent study of land distribution by the Church in Chile is to be found in William C. Thiesenhusen, *op. cit.*

156156   LUIS QUIROS VARELA

But as had happened in the past, it was the dominating groups
which were responsible for the formulation, without peasant
participation, of labour legislation, and they thus benefited from
the peasants' lack of organization. So there was no interest in
promoting the limited degree of peasant unionization permitted
under the 1947 law, and the hopes of the peasantry remained
subjected to state action. Thus greater peasant unionization
depended on the action and support of elements outside the
peasants' control, principally the PDC and the left-wing parties.
But their success was slight: in 1960, the number of unions rose
to eighteen with 1,424 members; by 1964, after two years of
Alessandri's reforms, the number of unions had only increased
to twenty-four, with 1,658 members.[24] The limitations of Alessandri's reform programme were reflected in the achievements
of the regime: between 1958 and 1964, 1,066 families benefited
from the redistribution of 69,365 hectares.[25] The landowners'
organizations, principally the SNA, preferred to yield to the
government's agrarian policy of land division – in view of the
possibility of violence from the peasants, and the more symbolic
than real advantages which the law offered to the peasants, and in
view of the programme's limitations and the favourable terms of
compensation for expropriated property. For the rest, the new
state institutions strengthened the position of the large landowners on the executive councils, assuring their participation in
decisions taken with regard to reform. The government coalition
also planned confidently for the 1964 presidential elections with a
candidate acceptable to the three parties which it comprised
(radicals, conservatives and liberals). On the basis of a majority
expressed by the electorate in previous multi-party elections, it
could hope to remain in power and thus control the evolution of
agrarian reform. But the 1964 election campaign revealed the
frustration of the electorate which would not now be satisfied with
vague and limited promises from a coalition of conservatives and
liberals. Months before the election, the government front broke,
and the conservatives and liberals supported Frei and the programme of the Christian Democrat Party, which called for an

[24] In comparative terms, in the urban sectors, over the same period, the
number of professional unions had increased from 1,116 with 108,687 members to 1,154 with 110,669 members. In 1960, there were 608 industrial
unions with 122,306 members, and in 1964, 632 unions with 142,958 members. See CORA, *Reforma Agraria Chilena*, unpublished, Santiago, 1970, p. 24.
[25] CORA, *op. cit.*, p. 20.

integral plan of reform, and particularly, an accelerated, drastic and massive agrarian reform.

CHRISTIAN DEMOCRAT AGRARIAN REFORM, 1965–1970

The electoral victory of the Christian Democrat Party implied that it would be possible to carry out a complete development programme, of which agriculture would be a fundamental part. On the basis of law No. 15,020, drawn up by Alessandri, a new legal body was formed, together with a constitutional amendment, which gave the government greater powers and flexibility to expropriate, thereby initiating the most radical reform of the land tenure system. During the Christian Democrats' six year term of office, a collection of laws on various aspects related to the peasantry were drawn up with the aim of fulfilling much wider goals; these laws were complementary to the land tenure reform and were designed to promote the mobilization of the peasants and their integration with the system.

The legislation for agrarian reform was backed up with constitutional reforms which provided for a speeding up of the legal transactions for determining the amount of compensation, the establishment of deferred payment, and the legalization of when and how expropriators might take possession of the properties concerned. Finally, it established that all waters within the national territory were the property of the state, and cancelled all private claims to such ownership.[26]

Three laws provided legislation on agricultural ownership. The first (No. 16,465 of 1966) checked the possibility of escaping expropriation by subdividing property larger than the basic 80 hectare unit. The second (No. 16,640 of 1967), adopted the following basic criteria:

(*a*) Vesting the peasants with the ownership of the land they work.
(*b*) Facilitating the integration of the peasants and their families into the social, cultural, civic and political life of the nation.
(*c*) Improvement of productivity at all levels of agriculture.
(*d*) Reform of the systems of control and use of water.
(*e*) Reconstruction of public organizations which carry out duties related with agriculture.[27]

---

[26] *Loc. cit.*, p. 20.
[27] But at intermediate levels, officials stuck to the routine and made the

Finally, the third law (No. 17,280 of 1970) speeded up the taking over of properties scheduled for expropriation by CORA. Social legislation for the peasants was directed at the following points:

(*a*) Levelling up the minimum wage of agricultural workers to that of industrial workers and the establishment of an eight hour working day.

(*b*) Giving security and stability to the agricultural worker by laying down the conditions in which his contract can be terminated.

(*c*) Establishing the right of union affiliation for all agricultural workers, eliminating the obstacles in former laws.

By legislating on both land ownership and water resources, the Agrarian Reform Law potentially paved the way for the expropriation of all lands. In any case, a basic maximum limit of 80 hectares or its equivalent (depending on the quality of the soil) had been established. Landowners whose lands had been exploited efficiently were given the right to retain land corresponding to these 80 hectares or its equivalent. However, no parallel proposals were drawn up for the *minifundio* in this law; at the same time, the regional plans for the expropriation programme under Law No. 15,020, which now needed CORA's agreement, were put aside. The system of payment for expropriated property became less favourable, since in accordance with the new constitutional reform, the cash payment could now vary between 1% and 10% of the fiscal valuation – which included improvements carried out after 1964, installations and orchards, depending on the individual case – and the rest was to be paid over a period of up to thirty years in readjustable bonds and with a 3% annual interest. The co-operative was the system of ownership adopted, to be formed by peasants who benefited from the reform; nevertheless, the law set up a transitional stage on the way to definitive land ownership, called *asentamiento* (land settlement).

All these legal dispositions symbolized the state's new attitude to the agrarian problem in Chile. Over the six years of the Christian Democrats' term of office, the discussion of these

tasks defined from above more difficult. The lack of co-operation between various professionals working in the same organizations was particularly noticeable, and the problem grew worse when other public institutions had to take part, and professional cliques were in evidence. See Jacques Chonchol, 'Poder y Reforma Agraria', in A. Pinto, *et al.*, *Chile Hoy*, pp. 295 ff.

problems by all the groups affected by the programme expressed all the ideological elements of one of the deepest conflicts produced in the Chilean political system. Aims were put forward which necessarily required a changed outlook and the emergence of new attitudes on the part of both landowners and peasants in order to be fulfilled. However, given the characteristics of the Chilean political system, especially its conciliatory nature, it is not surprising that the implementation of the reform met with obstacles which, within the general context of the system, increasingly affected the effectiveness of the programme.

In view of its redistributive character, agrarian reform affected not only the agricultural sector, but directly or indirectly, the entire system. We shall therefore briefly examine the effects of agrarian reform on the government, the political parties, the pressure groups and the system as a whole.

For the government, controlled by a single party (the Christian Democrats) for the first time since the 1925 constitution, the basic problem in agrarian policy was to act quickly, mobilizing the peasantry towards the proposed goals and counting on peasant support for government action. So the Ministry of Agriculture and the autonomous organizations of Agrarian Reform (CORA and INDAP) were directed by militants of the Christian Democrat Party, ideologically firmly committed, and with experience in agricultural affairs. INDAP was directed by Jacques Chonchol (the present Minister of Agriculture in Allende's government), and was dedicated to the task of organizing the peasants at union level, through the action of 'promoters' in the agricultural sector.[28] The government attempted to incorporate the agricultural union confederations into the processes of political decision-making, but only after the reform legislation had been approved. In this sense the state once again undertook the task of promoting social and economic development from above by using its authority. This can partly be explained by the marginal state of the peasantry at the outset of this process, but it implied that the further development of the organization of this sector would remain under the control of the state in the future. Consequently, its effectiveness came to depend more than anything else on the authorities' attitude towards the new organizations. The relationship was accentuated by the *asentamiento*, a form of self-managed exploitation of the land by the peasants under the supervision of an Administrative Council guided by

[28] CORA, *Reforma Agraria*, pp. 36, 39.

CORA. In this way, it was hoped to prepare the peasants both for the tasks of administration and for the problems arising from the exploitation and commercialization of their property. After a period of three years, and eventually after five years, the *asentamiento* would become the co-operative of agrarian reform.

From 1965 to July 1970, the application of agrarian reform involved the expropriation of 1,319 properties with a total area of 3,408,788·3 hectares and more than 35,000 potential beneficiaries.[29] 45·7% of the expropriated properties were abandoned or badly exploited, 29·8% were offered to CORA by their owners, and 13% exceeded the basic 80 hectares. The rest came from land belonging to public or private companies and from estates which had been subdivided illegally, to escape expropriation.

The total number of *asentamientos* set up between 1965 and July 1970 reached 910, with 29,139 beneficiaries, totalling roughly 170,000 people. Ninety-eight properties were also apportioned over this same period, with a total area of 450,000 hectares and benefiting 5,668 families.[30] These gains achieved by state action in the agricultural sector were however limited to the extent that state apparatus for the sector was not reorganized. This led to serious obstacles in respect of all those aspects directly related with support for an ambitious agrarian reform programme like that planned by the Christian Democrats. In one way or another, twenty-one state institutions had a hand in the processes of agricultural production, with the resulting inefficient use of governmental resources through the absence of supervision, control and adequate coordination, and through the retention in other institutions of attitudes, aims and objectives which did not fit in with a process of transformation as complex as the agrarian reform. This has been particularly noticeable in the field of credit, commercialization and technical assistance for production. As a result, the peasants have suffered serious difficulties in adapting themselves to the process of integration into the market.[31]

The real cost of Agrarian Reform to the state, up till 31 December 1969, is shown in Table 2.

The percentages of expenditure and investments have varied over the period; thus in 1964, administrative expenditure accounted for 40·5% of the total, but only 14·3% in 1969; similarly,

[29] *Ibid.*, p. 38.
[30] *Ibid.*, p. 44.
[31] See J. Chonchol, *op. cit.*, p. 270.

infrastructural expenditure fell from 31·54% in 1964 to 14·64% in 1969. Expenditure for land acquisition over the same period dropped slowly from 18·9% to 6·74% over the same period, whilst on the other hand, expenditure and investment in the productive sectors quickly rose from 6·39% in 1964 to 54·13% in 1969. In 1968, the organizations' share was 7·6%, falling to 6·7% in the following year, and other investments accounted for an annual 3·5%, on average, over the period.[32]

TABLE 2

Real cost of Agrarian Reform up to 31 December 1969, in thousands of escudos (1969 value)

	1964	1965	1966	1967	1968	1969	Total
Spending and Investment (1)	63,830	93,048	186,425	319,944	413,446	582,093	1,658,486
Revenue (2)	12,537	30,748	59,359	95,591	126,745	244,000 (3)	568,980
Real Cost	31,293	62,300	127,066	224,353	286,401	338,093	1,089,506 (4)

Source: *CORA: Reforma Agraria Chilena*, p. 74.

Notes
(1) Budgeted balances for each year, with the corresponding expenditure on credit debts deducted, this being reflected in the annual expenditure.
(2) Corresponds to the revenue produced in the year following the expenditure and investments. This situation arises because the agricultural year does not coincide with the budgetary year.
(3) Estimated revenue for 1970. It represents repayments from the 1969 production programme (estimated in escudos, 1969 value).
(4) Real cost includes what has *effectively been paid*, but not (a) the balance of sums due for expropriated properties to be paid over thirty years and (b) liabilities from 1969 which must be paid in 1970 and which total 55 million escudos.

The programme was financed by CORA's own funds, which represented about one fifth of the total revenue. Over the period, the government contribution varied: from 64·5% in 1964 to its highest point of 81·84% in 1965 and back to 52·67% in 1969. External credit played a relatively small part in financing the operation, 13·68% in 1964 and only 7·89% in 1969. From 1967 on, internal credit played a more important role, contributing 11·5% in 1967 and rising to 22·24% in 1969.[33]

Two points sum up the agrarian reform policy of the Christian Democrats: the first is that expropriations gradually decreased towards the end of their term of office, and the second is that

[32] CORA, *op. cit.*, p. 71. It must be noted that during 1968 and 1969, Chile suffered one of its worst droughts, which severely affected agricultural production.

[33] *Ibid.*, p. 72.

resources were increasingly dedicated to improving agricultural productivity. Thus, the redistribution of land fell below the goals laid down by the Christian Democrats' presidential programme. This was the result of an optimism which failed to take into account the limitations of the political system, and the growing costs of a process of change directed at a rural marginal minority, whose interests only partly coincided with the interests of urban groups and political parties.

THE LANDOWNING GROUPS

The pressure groups representing the interests of the landowners underwent quite significant changes during the Christian Democrat period of reform. The 1965 parliamentary elections left the Conservative and Liberal Parties poorly represented in Congress, facing a Christian Democrat majority which on specific aspects of agrarian reform, could call on support from the left-wing parties, thus ensuring overall approval of the reformist legislation.

After 1965 the SNA had to face a total breach between its economic power and its political power which it had maintained for a long time through its corporative institutionalization within the governmental framework.[34] The loss of political power meant that it became one more pressure group, changing its aims and the articulation of its interests, and broadening its representation to include more than merely the large landowners. In the event, its aims became more compatible with government policy, since it had to accept the principles of social justice and the social function of agricultural property, in order to maintain the existing democratic regime, although at the same time it emphasized the need for maximum efficiency in production. This led the SNA to accept the 1965 constitutional amendment which sanctioned expropriation with deferred payment of compensation, inasmuch as 'it was essential for the preservation of the constitutional regime, it was of positive benefit to the agricultural sector's interests, and the nature of the amendment did not constitute a real threat'.[35] Thus the SNA no longer defended without question the traditional structure of landowning and the interests of all landowners. By distinguishing between efficient and inefficient landowners, it made an indispensable concession towards maintaining social stability.

[34] See M. M. Errázuiz, *op. cit.*, pp. 82–104.
[35] *Ibid.*, p. 111.

Because agrarian reform affected the large landowners whose interests it represented, the SNA broadened its base to include the small and medium-sized landowners, who in fact accounted for 99% of the total of landowners. It thus assumed the representation of the entire agricultural sector, identifying itself with a policy of agricultural progress within the private sector, 'it aspired to represent all those whose wish was to "produce", who were ready to work and fight for the progress of the sector, within the political possibilities and conjunctures which arose.'[36]

The search for broader representation meant that the SNA increased its membership by about 60% from 1966, and by 1969 had reached a total membership of 4,221, distributed as follows:

TABLE 3

SNA Membership (June 1969)

Agricultural Co-operatives	18
Employers Unions	7
Property Administrators	388
Students	81
Ex-farmers, agricultural schools	
Small farmers and agricultural engineers	467
Large and medium-sized landowners	3,260
	4,221

Source: M. M. Errázuiz, *Los Grupos Dirigentes Agrícolas* (Leading Groups in Agriculture), p. 98.

In view of the controversy over the figures of large and medium-sized agricultural properties, it is not possible to make a very exact assessment of how representative the SNA actually is. It is reckoned that such estates number some 31,000. Clearly therefore the SNA had not become really representative of these types of owners by the date indicated in Table 3 above. Furthermore, between 1958 and 1970, two-thirds of the leadership of the SNA were persons whose main activities were in no way agricultural; half of them were politicians; only 27% were farmers, and 3·87% were experts in public employment. The Confederation of Agricultural Employers' Unions (COSEMACH) was established in 1967, on the basis of law No. 16,125, which not only laid down rules for peasant unions but also regulated the unions of agricultural employers. The SNA took an active part in the creation of

[36] *Ibid.*, p. 115.

COSEMACH. It participated in the drafting of the law, and once it had been enacted it obtained funds and helped to draw up the rules and procedures for COSEMACH. COSEMACH unites 20 provincial federations, with 124 unions and more than 10,000 members, and another 20,000 associate members who subscribe but do not actively participate. COSEMACH's general objective was to promote the development and legitimate defence of the common interests of the member federations, especially regarding the economic management of agricultural enterprises, price policies, commercialization costs and technical assistance; to develop the sense of common purpose among farmers so that they might be capable of developing themselves, and achieving equality with the urban worker.

COSEMACH has made its mark as a mobilizing agent of the producers and of organized protest at the problems the producers have had to face, in contrast with the SNA's more conciliatory attitude. It has sought direct confrontation with the government, refusing to carry out instructions which it believed were harmful to its interests, disturbing public order by blocking roads and offering armed resistance to CORA's expropriations and to peasant occupation, an attitude which culminated in the murder of a CORA official in Linares.

With the intensification of agrarian reform, this group has drifted more and more towards the defence of the small and medium-sized agricultural property, which suggests that the larger landowners would be prepared to yield part of their property if that would guarantee the survival of their enterprises. This change can be explained by the precarious situation in which agricultural enterprises found themselves when faced with the conflicts which arose out of the process of agrarian reform, and by the fact that the interests of these groups were not represented by other organizations, such as the SNA. The radical defence of the rights of individual ownership have thus transformed COSEMACH into the most powerful spokesman within the land-owning sector.

THE PEASANT MOVEMENT

One of the most important aspects of Agrarian Reform has been the massive awakening of the peasantry to political consciousness, as reflected in the explosive growth of unionization after 1965 (see Table 4).

TABLE 4

Peasant Unions and their membership (1)

Year	No. of unions	No. of members
1965	32	2,118
1966	201	10,647
1967	211	47,473
1968 (2)	325	71,721
1969	385	101,232
1970 (3)	488	127,688

Source: *CORA, Reforma Agraria Chilena* (Chilean Agrarian Reform), p. 26.

Notes
(1) As on 31 December of each year.
(2) Data only up to September 1968.
(3) Data only up to June 1970.

Other types of organization covered the small farmers, the co-operatives and the *asentamientos*. (The figures in Table 5 do not go beyond July 1970.)

TABLE 5

Organization of the peasant movement in July, 1970

	No. of Entities	No. of Members
Peasant unions	480	127,000
Committees of small farmers	2,100	71,000
Peasant co-operatives	220	30,000
Asentamientos	910	29,139
Totals	3,710	257,139

Source: *CORA, op. cit.*, p. 28.

As has already been indicated, peasant organization had long-standing antecedents, but only when the government's attitude was favourable could it attain any degree of rapid development. Once again, it was forces outside the peasantry which were concerned to mobilize and unionize them. Thus it was political parties like the Christian Democrats and the communists together with officials of past government acting through INDAP who exercised the main influences on peasant organization. Because of this, the peasant movement was split into three confederations of unions: *Triunfo Campesino* (Peasant Triumph), *Libertad* (Liberty) and *Ranquil*; the first two were oriented to the Christian Democrats, and the third was Marxist and controlled by the Communist Party. Both trends were clearly concerned with agriculture and sought to improve the conditions of the peasants along similar lines, through their economic, political and

social integration. They differed however in their ultimate objectives, and in the tactics and strategy which were to be employed
to attain them. The Christian Democrat influenced movements
saw in Agrarian Reform a means of integrating the human being,
whilst the Marxist movement saw it as a weapon in the class
struggle to end the exploitation of the peasant.

External agents – political, intellectual and religious – had been
fundamental factors in the development of the peasant movement
in Chile in the first years of Christian Democrat reform; they
provided ideological orientation, financial assistance and legal
help, when pressures began to be brought to bear on the landowners or the government by means of petitions, strikes and other
methods. After 1965 the activity of these external agents was reinforced by the state's promotion of peasant organization through
the activities of the Agricultural Development Institute, until the
approval of the Peasant Unionization Law in 1967.

The political effectiveness of the peasant movement in Chile
depended on the government's agrarian policy, which in the case
of the Christian Democrats, was formulated without peasant
participation at top political and administrative levels. Because of
this, relations between the peasant movement and the government were characterized by divergent orientations between the
goals as defined and implemented by the Christian Democrats and
the aspirations of the peasantry, and so resulted in the failure to
integrate the peasants into the system. When the programme of
Agrarian Reform was initiated, the level of the peasants' discontent and their awareness of government action were different in
the various groups within the sector. The rural wage-earners (the
tenants, sharecroppers and migrant workers), who represented
about half of the active agricultural population, registered a lower
level of discontent with their conditions than the small farmers,
and so consequently, they also registered a lower level of aspirations for improvements and progress. At the same time, awareness
of state action in agriculture was also less among the wage-earners
than among the small producers.[37] In practical terms, this meant
a relatively weak demand for land over the initial stages of

[37] *Ibid.*, p. 101. Up till 1958, when the change noted above occurred, politicians always occupied more than half the leadership of the SNA; it could
have been the result of the increased hardening of the SNA's position towards
the government, especially in the implementation of Agrarian Reform, on
which politicians found that they could exert no influence after the election
defeat in 1965 when they lost their power base.

the programme (except in the case of small Indian producers), and pressure to improve wages and conditions by means of legal petitions, strikes and illegal occupation of land. 'Squatting' was mainly provoked by the need to ensure continued employment in the face of the landowners' attempts to sell or subdivide their properties in order to evade the application of the Agrarian Reform Law. However, the principal aim of the Law was the division of the *latifundio*, and so state action was almost wholly directed towards promoting the establishment of a system of communal ownership by the rural wage-earners. Co-operatives were the means to this end, with the *asentamiento* as a half-way stage, so to speak. But the imposition of this system of communal ownership and land exploitation was opposed by increasing numbers of the beneficiaries and peasants in general. They had now acquired a greater degree of political awareness, and demanded the fulfilment of election promises, namely individual or family land ownership. The growing expectations of the peasants towards the end of the Christian Democrats' term of office, led to the rural wage-earners' greater radicalization, and they began to reject more forcefully the agrarian policy imposed on them by the government. So peasant protests intensified, as did the number of illegal occupations of lands by peasants who demanded their expropriation in favour of those who worked them. This partly explains why the rate of expropriations dropped during the last years of the government.[38]

At the same time, the mounting peasant dissatisfaction was being used by extremist political groups like the Revolutionary Peasant Movement (MCR), a peasant organization under the auspices of the Left Revolutionary Movement (MIR), whose aim was to establish the bases of a revolutionary movement in the rural areas. Other groups, like the MAPU, which arose out of a division in the Christian Democrat Party in 1969, began to compete for peasant support to carry out the 'non-capitalist' path of development, rejected by the Christian Democrats.

More aware of their marginality and in spite of their greater dissatisfaction and their higher aspirations, the small producers were induced to form agrarian co-operatives, which were however relatively unsuccessful (see Table 5). The lack of policy for this sector of the peasantry can be explained by the greater problems

[38] See the studies of Almino Affonso, *et al.*, *op. cit.*, Vol. II, Raúl Urzúa, *La demanda campesina*, Ediciones Nueva Universidad, Santiago, 1969, and DESAL, *Tenencia de la tierra y campesinado en Chile*, DESAL, Santiago, 1969.

which the satisfaction of its needs would produce, because of its special characteristics: the age level seems to be much greater than the average for the overall agricultural population, they are strongly bound up with their property, which they would defend at all costs and their integration into the productive process led them to reject co-operative forms of production.[39]

To conclude, the Christian Democrat process of agrarian reform, could be said to have brought about the gradual disappearance of the great agricultural landowner; it had aroused the political awareness of the peasantry which emerged as a social and political force of some magnitude. But the peasants were still not integrated into the political system because of the differences between the aims and objectives the regime established in relation to the new land tenure structure and the expectations of the rural population with respect to land ownership. These expectations were in any case less extensive than those of the government, since basically they were directed at achieving individual land ownership. Certainly by 1970, the growing pressure of the peasants suggested that if the Christian Democrats remained in power, a family farm mentality might take hold of the peasantry, a mentality based on a relationship of client/patron between the peasants and the state or the political parties.[40] With the triumph of the Unidad Popular, such a possibility has been removed, or at least seems more unlikely.

The success of the political parties, including the Christian Democrats, in achieving peasant mobilization, has been only partial, in that they have not resolved the tensions which arose with the aspirations of the peasant leaders within those political parties whose aims were not individual or family land ownership, such as the Communist Party and the MIR. The problem of political parties manipulating the dissatisfaction of the peasantry has been projected onto the present Unidad Popular government.

UNIDAD POPULAR AND AGRARIAN REFORM

Unidad Popular's Basic Programme laid down as a fundamental political aspiration of the governing coalition the initial construction of socialism; its first, provisional, objective was the solution

[39] James Petras, *Social and Political Forces in Chilean Development*, University of California Press, Berkeley, 1969, esp. pp. 257 ff.

[40] E. Faletto y Ruiz, *op. cit.*, in *Chile Hoy*, p. 244.

of the immediate economic problems of the majority groups.[41] The enunciation of revolutionary goals by a coalition dominated by Marxist parties, and the action of the government to implement these goals over the fourteen months of its rule, has transformed Chilean political processes; the reconciliation of opposing interests as a means of achieving consensus has been replaced by the growing confrontation between the government and the opposition parties which feel threatened by the changes which have taken place. This general context applies to the agrarian reform policy of the present government, which in turn has contributed to the conflict between the Unidad Popular and the opposition.

Unidad Popular's Basic Programme conceives agrarian reform 'as a process simultaneous and complementary to the general transformations which are desired in the country's social, political and economic structure'; it is thus regarded as an integral part of political transformation in general.[42] Based on past experience and the inequalities and vacuums created by the Christian Democrat agrarian reform, Unidad Popular reformulated the following points of agrarian policy:

(a) The speeding up of Agrarian Reform with the expropriation of all properties exceeding the maximum limit of eighty hectares or their equivalent, withdrawing the landowners' rights to retain part of their property or including in the expropriation all or part of the expropriated land's assets.

(b) The immediate cultivation of all lands belonging to the state.

(c) Expropriated lands to be organized as co-operative properties. Peasants will be given full rights of ownership of their houses and garden plots and of their corresponding rights in the co-operative. Only in certain cases will land be allotted to peasants as individual property, and even in these cases cultivation and marketing will be worked on a co-operative basis. Similar measures will apply to small farmers, renters, sharecroppers and agricultural employees qualified for agricultural work.

(d) The reorganization of the *minifundio* on a co-operative basis, with a co-operative approach to work.

(e) The incorporation of the small and medium-sized farmer into co-operatives in order to obtain technical and credit assistance.

[41] *Programma Básico de la Unidad Popular*, Impresora Horizonte, Santiago, 1970.

[42] *Ibid.*, pp. 21–2.

(*f*) Lastly, Unidad Popular recognizes the rights of Indian
communities and incorporates them into the system, in order
to prevent the usurpation of their lands, and ensure them
sufficient land, technical assistance and appropriate credit.

The energy of the government in carrying out the measures for
the country's development within the Chilean institutional framework is reflected in the policy of accelerated agrarian reform, as a
result of which more than 2·5 million hectares have been expropriated all over the country, in the one year of Allende's rule.
These expropriations have not been achieved without problems.
Far from it, for besides constituting one of the general objects of
criticism from the opposition, the farmers in particular have
resisted with all the means at their disposal, from boycotting
production to the use of violence. This has occurred in the
province of Linares and in the south of Chile, where one of the
principal results of the policy has been the growing opposition of
the medium-sized farmers, who have joined the provincial unions
run by COSEMACH. With the authorities' decision to expropriate
all the *latifundios* in 1972, the landowners' pressure groups have
lost their access to the government. The dialogue, precariously
maintained until then, was broken in October 1971, after the president of the SNA had attempted to present the farmers' protests
and demands to the governing authorities, on the occasion of the
opening of the SNA's annual fair.

With the aim of avoiding the production losses arising from
the attitude of the farmers and from the strikes or illegal occupation of lands by the peasants, the government has taken over
estates, and assumed the administrative burdens. As a result, a
growing number of large and medium-sized landowners have
opted to hand over their property to CORA for expropriation.

As far as land tenure is concerned, the Unidad Popular has
abandoned Frei's programme and the transitional *asentamientos*,
and replaced them with the newly created Agrarian Reform
Centres (CERA). Under this new system, property is allotted on a
co-operative basis. The peasants own their houses and gardens,
but in exchange for their work, they receive a wage which is
graded according to the level of productivity they achieve. One
part of the surpluses produced is distributed to the peasants, a
second share is allotted to the community and the third is destined
for the capitalization of the property. The National Council for
Agrarian Reform approved this new system of land exploitation,

by interpreting the stipulations of the Agrarian Reform Law which allows 'other kinds of ownership' besides co-operatives. The implementation of this decision has already become a source of conflict with the opposition parties, especially the Christian Democrats and the peasant movements they control, who protest at the illegality of such an agreement, or see in it the frustration of their hopes for obtaining individual land ownership.

The Agrarian Reform Centres provide an alternative policy in view of the low economic viability of the *asentamiento* system as a means of transition. They also take into account the employment problem raised by the scarcity of land resources in relation to the over large rural workforce, since they offer incentives for productivity, capitalization and redistribution of the surplus within the sector.[43]

During the Unidad Popular's year of office the activity of the peasant movement, relying on the government's favourable disposition towards it, has been intensified through the presentation of petitions, strikes and the illegal occupation of land. But the differences between the Christian Democrat led movements and the Marxist controlled movements have grown. As a result of the measures indicated above, the Christian-Democrat movement has been pushed into defending the *asentamiento* and the co-operative forms of ownership developed by the previous regime. At the same time, they have found access to the government more difficult, and they have had to contend with the Ranquil Confederation and the Revolutionary Peasant Movement which have taken the initiative and demanded the speeding-up of the process.

The Marxist orientated movements are also in fierce competition among themselves. The Ranquil Confederation, which is integrated into the Communist Party, has put forward its demands within the programme of the Unidad Popular, emphasizing peasant organization and production tasks. The Revolutionary Peasant Movement, on the other hand, has tried to go further than the government's programme by mobilizing the peasants to fight for land. Here, too, their demands are more radical, since they propose expropriation 'with no holds barred', the reduction of the unexpropriated quota from eighty to forty hectares, no compensation, the elimination of the landowners' right to retain part of his land, the incorporation of the migrant workers into the reform programme, and a rapid drive for the peasants' organization and

[43] 'Quién reemplaza al patrón del fundo?', *Panorama Económico*, Special Edition, December 1971, pp. 28-9.

integration into the institutions charged with implementing the Reform.[44] The MCR is strongest in Linares and in the provinces of Cautín and Malleco; in these two provinces, their greatest success has been the mobilization and organization of numerous native communities for the restitution of lands which were taken from them by settlers and landowners. It is in these provinces that violence has broken out between farmers and peasants, with tragic results. It is also here that the officials of Agrarian Reform and its related institutions have given greatest support to peasant demands, leading the SNA and other organizations, which represent the large landowners, to protest and apply pressure to have them dismissed. These are recent developments which render difficult a complete evaluation of the Unidad Popular's first year of agrarian reform. The confrontation between the government and the opposition groups has grown sharper in the agricultural sector, but this is only one aspect of a conflict between government and opposition, on a national scale, a conflict involving the orientation, objectives and means the government is using in the process of change. The specific demands of the agricultural groups merge into more general policy statements which deal with this process.

CONCLUSION

After almost seven years, Agrarian Reform continues to be an important issue in Chilean politics. To date, policy has been implemented within the framework of the legislation previously enacted by the Christian Democrat regime, but this legislation is being interpreted and applied in accordance with the established goals of the Unidad Popular's government.

For the Unidad Popular, agrarian reform policy is a weapon in the class struggle, and so it is directed at the total disappearance of the large *latifundio* as an effective power base for the economic elite. At the same time, attempts are being made to correct the errors and limitations of the Christian Democrat policy, such as the paternalistic relationship between the government and the peasants, and the productive inefficiency of the *asentamientos*.[45]

[44] In mid-December 1971 the Confederación Triunfo Campesino (Christian Democrat) declared a national twenty-four hour strike in protest against government policy. The strike took place on 28 December.

[45] Gustavo Canihuante states that the Christian Democrats' management of agriculture was inefficient, and led to reduced agricultural production.

But Allende's government is faced with obstacles posed by its own definition of what must constitute the transition to socialism: by the reaction of groups opposed to its programme, and by the conditions and attitudes of the peasants themselves when faced with reform. These are all factors which affect future agrarian policy.

The fact that the transition to socialism must be made through the existing institutional channels means that the conciliatory system must be maintained and the rules of the game respected. But a programme of total change, as proposed by the Unidad Popular, is vulnerable by reason of its great complexity and its diversity of aims. This increases the opposition's chances of forcing the government to negotiate on specific policies. Hence, agrarian reform policy is one of the battlegrounds in the conflict between the government and the opposition, and this situation of total conflict must condition the execution of this policy.

Finishing with the *latifundio* is no longer a source of controversy; both the farmers and the opposition parties have yielded on this point. But the policy for the small and medium-sized landowners has still to be defined. Uncertainty in this field has been seized upon by the opposition parties and by COSEMACH, that is by those who defend the interests of these sectors against expropriation by the government. Indeed, their position in this respect seems to have been strengthened, since it is clear that the expropriation or the reduction of the land area of the medium-sized properties would not produce a significant increase in the land available for redistribution to the peasants.

The crux of the political debate concerns the creation of the Agrarian Reform Centres (CERA), which the Christian Democrats regard as the bases of future state farms. The newness of the Centres and the debate they have engendered impede a clear vision of the problem. In any case, the Minister of Agriculture, J. Chonchol has declared that the allotment of lands for co-operatives will be pursued through the Centres, as soon as the 'peasants' property mentality' has been broken; at present their principal point of reference is either their patron or the property

---

This was reflected in prices of commodities, and as a result, in the peasants' indebtedness to the state. He estimates that every settled family owes the state 70,000 escudos, or approximately 2,500 dollars at the present rate of exchange. See Gustavo Canihuante, *La Revolución Chilena*, Edit. Nascimiento, Santiago, 1971, p. 117.

on which they work.[46] In any case, apart from attempting to correct the errors of past policy, the Centres constitute an experiment which was sanctioned without the participation of those who are affected by it, and all this will, to a certain extent, influence future peasant demands.

The peasant movement views this process from three ideological standpoints: the Christian Democrat, opposed to this policy; the communist, supporting the government's plans; and the MIR, which is demanding the acceleration of agrarian reform, and its total state control.

The effectiveness of the peasant sectors is only partly conditioned by their mobilization and organization. To a great extent it depends on the action of their respective allies, principally the political parties at national level. Even when the conflict between the government and the opposition has centred on the question whether to maintain the formal democratic system of a mixed economy or to transform it into a socialist state, the support the peasants will get from their allies is going to depend on the overall strategy of the latter, and the relation between these strategies and the goals of the peasantry.

This is the initial problem which makes the integration of the peasantry into the political process a difficult matter. There is no doubt that the peasantry is still in a position to choose its allies, but there will always be an imbalance between the objectives of the government and the political parties, and the hopes of the peasants. Both in the programme of the Unidad Popular, and in that of the Christian Democrats, there is an implicit demand for a 'change in mentality' among the peasants; they must adjust to the conditions imposed by the aims of the parties. How to achieve this, and over what length of time, remain questions which show that the Chilean peasantry is still not ready for a total integration into a system which requires it to undergo a revolution-

[46] These and other points which restate the Unidad Popular's programme, were the object of an agreement between the MIR, the Provincial Peasant Council and the Unidad Popular Political Committee of the province of Linares, as part of the election platform of the Unidad Popular's candidate in the by-election for a provincial deputy. The declaration, signed by representatives of all the parties in the coalition government except the radicals, was strongly denounced by the Communist Party's National Executive, which branded it as the product of the 'extreme left'. See 'Esta gran humanidad ha echado a andar' in *Punto Final*, Year VI, no. 4 (4 January 1972), pp. 2–5.

ary cultural change. Even should the peasant sector become a major force in the political life of the country, its role in the political processes will thus tend to be limited by the conditions imposed by the system and its political institutions.

Should the peasantry succeed in 'changing its mentality', it will become a factor of great importance for the transition. If it does not, however, it will in all likelihood contribute to strengthening the present system. This is in fact very probable since none of the measures adopted in the agrarian reform imply a decline in the actual living conditions of the peasantry, but on the contrary contribute to its improvement.

To sum up, agrarian reform must continue, since in spite of the changes which it has introduced into the system, various problems remain, which go beyond the problem of peasant participation. These problems include the under-occupation of the agricultural population and the fate of the small landowners. Reform Centres and co-operatives are, respectively, part of the solution, but there is no doubt that in the short term, agrarian reform will have to broaden its approach. An overall policy is required which will go further than just establishing new systems of land exploitation. There will have to be a radical change in the activities of the active rural population. Most of it is, at present, engaged in cultivating the land. It will have to be diverted to industrial work or to the provision of services within the agricultural sector. This broader policy will strengthen the integration of the Chilean peasantry into the process of transformation of the country, going further than simple political integration.

9 Chile, France and Italy: A Discussion

IS MITTERAND ANOTHER ALLENDE? WOULD BERLINGUER, ONCE IN power, observe the constitutional rules of the game as carefully as the Chilean communists? Is the Chilean road to power likely to provide a model for the accession to power of Communist Parties in other countries, notably France and Italy, where these parties command a sizeable electoral following, and where they could, as in France, since 27 June 1972, form part of an electoral, and subsequently of a governmental, coalition with the socialist parties and other left-wing parties or wings of parties? Such questions are bound to occur.

It will have been noticed from the present collection of essays by Chilean political scientists and politicians, that the Chileans themselves do not indulge in such prognostications. On the contrary, President Allende's maxim that 'Our revolution is not for export' seems to represent the majority opinion in Chile. It is in Latin Europe, rather than in Latin America that the evolution of the Chilean experiment is watched with mixed hopes and fears. Extrapolations from the Chilean experience are used as arguments for and against the prospects of the French and Italian left; hopes are raised and dangers evoked. Some would like to see the con-solidation of revolution à la Allende; others are more concerned with the ends of revolution than with the means. It is note-worthy that the European Communist Parties, which are associated with the CPSU, and which have in common a new search for respectability, seem to be the most anxious that the Allende government should keep to the constitutional means of achieving its revolutionary ends. They are concerned lest revolutionary zeal, and the application of Leninist-Stalinist methods which this would entail, should jeopardize *their* reputation and *their* popularity with *their* electorates.

The object of the following pages is not to assess the mutual relevance, and even less the interrelated inspirations, of the developments in Chile, France and Italy, but, more directly, to see how comparable these apparently similar situations are in essence. This brief comparative exercise is based on the factual documentation contained in the studies published in this volume, and on a discussion, held with this purpose in mind, at the University of Manchester in March 1972.[1] We are concerned here primarily with an analysis of the global strategy of Communist Parties since the 20th Congress of the CPSU, and its interpretation by the Communist Parties of Chile, France and Italy, in their different historical, economic and social backgrounds. There are obvious risks of arbitrariness and indeed artificiality in such an approach. But it can be justified by the fact that in the three countries concerned, the Communist Parties are the prime movers of, or the inspiration behind, the policy of creating the unity of the left. And moreover they are the strongest and most efficient political organization in the actual Chilean coalition and in any hypothetical French and Italian coalitions.

PLURALIST CONSTITUTIONALISM

The first, permanent, comparable feature, common to the political backgrounds of all three states is the viability of their pluralistic-constitutional systems. The political institutions of Chile have proved both lasting and resilient.[2] Not only do they compare well with those of France, but when it comes to longevity and stability, they have a better record over the last half century than those of Italy, where they were submerged by the interlude of the fascist dictatorship. Moreover, in all three countries, the functioning of representative institutions is affected by some characteristics common to Latin political culture.

One is the acceptance of some degree of paternalism – even in

---

[1] The participants were: Dr J. Biehl, the Catholic University of Santiago; Dr Martin Clark, University of Edinburgh; Professor S. E. Finer, University of Manchester; Professor G. Ionescu, University of Manchester; Mr D. Kavanagh, University of Manchester; Dr K. Medhurst, University of Manchester; Professor Landsberger, University of North Carolina; Dr I. de Madariaga, University of London; Dr S. White, University of Glasgow. The writers of these notes, G. Ionescu and I. de Madariaga, would like to express their gratitude to the participants in this conference, which helped to clarify many of the issues of comparability – while at the same time making it clear that the opinions expressed here do not represent the views of the conference as a whole.

[2] See in particular the article by H. Bicheno, pp. 351–88.

France. This however is a trend which is no longer so easy to distinguish from the objective institutional evolution towards a presidential regime, both in Chile and in France, and which might possibly take root again in Italy, now that thirty years have elapsed since the disappearance both of the dynasty and of the dictator. Linked to this trend is the tendency to *personalismo* in party politics, drawing on an emotional attachment to a charismatic leader, by whose name his followers are subsequently identified. Of these two trends, that towards a presidential type of regime gives more food for thought. For, by introducing an institutional stabilizer into a precariously balanced system, it can be said to represent an institutional correction, calculated to counter the specific Latin trait of individualism and volatility in political and electoral behaviour. It is a guarantee both against anarchistic atomization and against *partitocrazia*, and its corollary of political instability. But it also provides guarantees, by ensuring that the system works, against the recourse to dictatorship on the grounds of the ungovernability of Latin peoples.

On the other hand, in terms of the comparative projection of the Chilean experience to some form of left coalition in Italy or France, a presidential regime might prove to be the key to that continuity required by the transition to socialism. In a revolutionary view, it is an historical undertaking which should not be interrupted by the changes, or moods of the electorate. A reflection by Maurice Duverger gives the measure of his concern. 'The Chilean example', he writes, 'shows that a president elected by universal suffrage is better suited than an omnipotent assembly to achieve the construction of democratic socialism. In a purely parliamentary regime, Mr Allende's experiment would have failed long ago. Moreover the prerogatives of the president in the French political system, the fact that he is the real head of the government, can ensure the equilibrium in a left-wing coalition.'[3] The relevance of the presidential regime for the construction of socialism has evidently not escaped the attention of the French Communist Party, which in its new programme[4] has proposed to extend the presidential mandate from five to seven years. The extent to which President Allende has been able to make use of presidential powers to push through his reforms to 'the limits of legality' have been strikingly illustrated by J. Garcés in this

[3] *Le Monde*, 19 March 1972.
[4] Parti communiste français, *Programme pour un gouvernement démocratique d'action populaire*, Editions Sociales, Paris, 1971.

volume.[5] At the same time he has been able to avoid until now a head on clash with the Christian Democrats, and hence with parliament, because the Christian Democrats have also willed it so. But should the Christian Democrat line harden, or should the president find his presidential powers insufficient for the next stages in the enactment of the revolution in Chile, Allende will be faced with a foreseeable conflict between the constitutional *means* and the revolutionary *ends* of his government.

In so far as the personality of a president, in a presidential regime, is of greater importance in the Latin political background than for instance in West Germany, Switzerland or Austria, one may be justified in thinking that negotiations for left-wing coalitions will prove most difficult on the issue of leadership. Already the French and Italian parties, which for reasons analysed at greater length below, believe themselves to be the strongest partner in any possible coalition, seem to resent the 'charisma' of some socialist personalities, as for instance of Mitterand in France.

CATHOLICISM

All three countries are (nominally) predominantly Roman Catholic, and in all three the Church has exerted a powerful influence on the political attitudes of great numbers of the population. Particularly in Italy the Church exerts a direct influence on political developments by the involvement of the priesthood in the political activities of the Christian Democratic Party. In France, the Christian Democratic Party, the MRP has now lost ground and has been partly absorbed by the Centre Party of Lecanuet. Though there may be occasional flare-ups, on educational matters, when the old hostility between catholics and anti-clericals comes to the fore, the political interests of right-wing catholics seem now to coincide with the nationalist conservatism of the Gaullists. The left-wing catholics are engaged in an active dialogue with the communists and the socialists, but this has not the cardinal importance for the future political evolution of the country which it has in Chile and in Italy.

In these two countries, Christian Democracy is the principal target of the left-wing parties and of the Communist Parties in particular. But there is a striking difference between their situa-

[5] J. Garcés, 'Chile 1971: A Revolutionary Government within a Welfare State', pp. 281–304.

tions. Firstly, the Chilean party was split in the elections of 1970. Only this circumstance, and the further guarantees given by Allende to the Christian Democrats before his election as a minority president, made possible the electoral victory of the Unidad Popular, and his own personal success. From this point of view the Chilean experiment provides important indications for other countries. The Italian Christian Democrats were deeply divided over the issue of a referendum on the Divorce Bill in 1972. But a split has been avoided, because the elections took place in May, the referendum was postponed, and the party was thus still united at the polls. The results of the May elections show that both the Christian Democrats and the Communist Party have maintained their dominant positions almost unchanged. Insofar as a *Grosse Koalition* between these two parties remains inconceivable, the Christian Democrats will have to govern in precarious coalitions with other parties. But the Italian Communist Party has shown itself fully aware that a new start in Italian politics can only be made after the Christian Democrats have been defeated in elections, and have turned their attention to the 'switching' of the centre of Christian Democracy.

From this point of view especially, the *vía Chilena* might be a precedent of some significance in Italian politics. It might provide a salutary warning against a split which would open the way to the creation of a coalition of the united left. But it might also lead to the external manifestation of the deep division within the Church itself, on the problems and prospects of moral, political and socio-economic modernization, which might lead the Church to tear asunder and even sacrifice its previous political spearhead.

The Church in Chile was among the first to support programmes of agrarian reform, without which the Unidad Popular would have been unable to embark on its vaster, perhaps more coherent and surely more drastic restructuration of the country. Dr R. Tomic's hopes of winning back to Christian Democratic reformism the support it requires failed to make headway among left-wing voters in industrial constituencies and among revolutionary peasant groups, though as L. Quiros Varela indicates, many among the peasantry may still regard the Christian Democrats as the party most responsive to specific peasant demands and to the preservation of the traditional peasant mentality and way of life.[6] Like the Chilean Socialist Party, the left wing of the Christian

[6] L. Quiros-Varela, 'Agrarian Reform and Political Processes', in *Chileans' Chile*, McGibbon and Kee, forthcoming.

Democrats may well find it more profitable to move to new positions from which it could criticize as obsolete the centralistic, bureaucratic, *étatist* tendencies of the orthodox Communist Party. Like the principles of populism, the principles of Christian social justice might be more easily harmonized with the sweeping theories of participation by means of decentralized self-administration and self-management. That the Christian Democrats are moving in this direction is evident from the project for constitutional reform which they put forward in October 1971.[7] Such theories are anathema to the Soviet type Communist Parties.

THE POSITION OF THE ARMED FORCES

Of the three countries, only Italy is a fully fledged member of a defence organization which includes the United States. France's position within NATO is hedged with reservations and conditions. It is frequently argued that this formed an indirect link between Gaullists and communists, which had repercussions on domestic problems. Chile belongs geographically to the American hemisphere; like all other Latin American states, with the exception of Cuba, while asserting its national sovereignty, it maintains a traditional professional collaboration with the armed forces of the United States. In all three countries however, the left, sometimes in unison with the right or the extreme right, consider one of their principal aims to be the emancipation of their countries from unsolicited American tutelage.

In the case of the left, and especially in Chile and in Italy, severance of the military link with the USA is seen as a means of depriving right-wing forces of what is assumed to be the indispensable support of US military power. In Italy, the Communist Party has argued that without NATO, and hence of the danger that the NATO powers, and particularly the USA, might 'assist' the government if in danger, the internal political balance would be quite different. Even in France, where the divorce imposed by de Gaulle between NATO and the French armed forces, and where the strategy of 'tous les azimuts', based on its own *force de frappe* gives to them an exclusive national character, the Communist Party frowns upon the *rapprochement* operated by Pompidou with Britain. Such a *rapprochement* implies a more favourable approach to NATO, and the communists see in it a

[7] H. Zemelman, 'Political Opposition to the Government of Allende', pp. 328–50.

further move away from the USSR. This was one of the con-
tributory factors to their demand for a resounding 'No' in the
referendum on the admission of Britain and the other powers to
the Common Market on 23 April 1972.

President Allende has taken no steps to disrupt the collaboration
between the Chilean armed forces and those of the United States.
In 1971, he personnally asked the United States government for a
loan of five million dollars to equip the Chilean armed forces, over
and above the regular assistance provided for in previous agree-
ments. He has personally seen to it that the 'Unitas' joint
manoeuvres of the US and Chilean fleets should take place in
October 1971 for the first time in many years without violent anti-
American demonstrations and clashes. Moreover the Panama
agreement, whereby Chilean officers are given training in modern
warfare (and allegedly in anti-guerrilla tactics and in ideological
matters) at the special US training base in Panama continues to be
observed. The traditions of the Chilean armed forces[8] may explain
the Chilean government's toleration of a relationship unacceptable
to left-wing parties in either France or Italy.

In all three countries, as in all pluralistic-constitutional states,
the armed forces are not only the organ for the defence of the
state against its external enemies, but also the final resort of the
government in the event of national disorder or disintegration.
How the armed forces of the three countries would react in such a
case, whether they would obey the orders of *whatever* government
was in power remains a moot question. The armed forces might in
certain circumstances themselves disintegrate under the pressure
of divisive events, though their links with other western armed
forces, and especially those of the United States, might help to
preserve their *esprit de corps*.

The *vía Chilena* does not provide a clear model of what a
revolutionary government could and should do with regard to the
armed forces. The extreme left in Chile has made the point that as
long as the government does not completely control the armed
forces, as long as, to paraphrase Mao, the 'party does not control
the gun', the future of revolution, or even of reform remains
precarious. President Allende has however preferred to profess his
confidence in the armed forces. They have, it is true, an almost
unbroken record of loyalty to the constitution since 1891. Their
public and national spirit is on record, and in any case in Allende's
view, a popular government should not be afraid of the armed

[8] See J. Garcés, pp. 284 ff., above.

forces, which are only 'the people in uniform'. The 'Tacnazo affair' of September 1970, which might have led to a rallying of discontented officers around a potential leader of a coup like General Viaux misfired after the assassination of General Schneider, Commander-in-Chief of the army, probably by right-wing elements. This confirmed the support of most officers to loyalist generals. President Allende has himself constantly maintained friendly contacts with the armed forces – he may indeed be said to devote considerable attention to cultivating their goodwill. Steps have been taken to improve pay and equipment. Senior officers in posts of responsibility have been invited, and have accepted, to participate in the administration of the nationalized economy, particularly in fields of importance to the supply of the armed forces (some 35 giant enterprises). In February 1971, the armed forces were asked to participate in plans for regional development.[9]

Judging by Joan Garcés's article one can assume that President Allende's intention is to 'neutralize' the armed forces by stressing the legality of his regime and to recruit cadres closer to his concept of the people in uniform. But there has been no drastic purge of the officer corps, which is basically middle class in composition, and the gap between officers and other ranks is as great as before. If anything, the armed forces' independence and self-confidence can only have increased, particularly in view of their new role in the economy. While their composition remains unchanged, they may be expected to act in a time of national emergency according to their collective conscience or *esprit de corps*.

ECONOMIC OR POLITICAL PRIMACY?

The problems and prospects of the Chilean economy under a revolutionary government underline only too clearly the fundamental dissimilarity between Chile on the one hand and France and Italy on the other. For all intents and purposes the Chilean economy is still a dependent economy, and the problem of a revolutionary government is how to achieve economic emancipation, through rapid development and industrialization, without falling even more under the control of the 'imperialist' providers

[9] But a shrewd observer has noted that the army's co-operation has been invited precisely in those regions where tension between armed landowners and aggressive peasants might lead to serious trouble. See A. Labrousse, *L'expérience chilienne*, Paris, Seuil, 1972.

of technical and financial capital; and how to achieve such a development at a time of increasing expectations, how to bring about, in the words of Garcés,[10] socialism in prosperity.

The concept of *dependencia* is present in all minds – especially now that the penetration of the country by foreign capital, through the multi-national corporations, is subtler, more intensive, more ubiquitous and irresistible than before. The nationalization of foreign owned industries, notably the great copper industry, has committed the government to the payment of compensation of over 700 million dollars, and it is known that the US government is pressing for payment to be made as soon as possible. On the other hand the development plans for industry require heavy investment of funds which are simply not available.

There is here a vicious circle, and unlike in Italy or in France, it can only be broken if the political solutions are given priority over the economic ones. In the words of Oswaldo Sunkal, 'This implies, in the first place, taking away the control of the state from the social groups which are more closely associated with the development strategy of dependent state capitalism. Having taken over the control of the state the large section of the middle class faces three essential development tasks: in the first place, this means transforming the agrarian structure, which is the fundamental root of inequality, marginalization and stagnation; secondly, using the primary export sector, which represents an under-developed country's most important source of capital accumulation, to support the expansion of heavy and consumer industries; and finally the re-organization of the industrial sector.'[11]

The fact is however that this transfer of power from some groups to other groups in society has not yet been effected in Chile, though it forms part of the programme of Unidad Popular.[12] It is true that the agrarian reform has radically altered the structure in the countryside – though agricultural productivity has not as yet noticeably increased; and that the new economic plans provide for a drastic reorientation of both export and domestic production. But the economic revolution has run aground thanks to the

[10] J. Garcés, *op. cit.*

[11] Oswaldo Sunkal, 'Big business and "dependencia"', *Foreign Affairs*, April 1972.

[12] The opposition voted a law in Congress on 19 February 1972 which severely limited the power of the president to nationalize industry by executive action alone. See also H. Zemelman, *op. cit.*, p. 348.

political stalemate now facing the regime. The argument put forward by the splinter pro-Chinese Revolutionary Communist Party, that 'to build socialism it is not enough that the means of production should be in the hands of the state; what is needed is first that the state should be in the hands of the proletariat' is not so far from the conclusion reached by the ex-Minister of the Economy, Pedro Vuskovic. But the recent crisis which led to his resignation proves that the coalition which maintains Allende in power does not believe that the conditions for increasing the political pressure on the economy are yet present in Chile. The 'second network of power', which should in theory be created when the 'mobilized working classes themselves' form their own organs of 'government of the people', and which should supersede the network of power of the old state, has simply failed to materialize. This may be explained in part by the innate strength of the institutions of the old state, which still function as legitimate organs of the present state, and are still used satisfactorily by different groups and sectors. As long as parliament, the Supreme Court, the Contraloría General, and freedom of the press and information continue, it is difficult to visualize another 'network of power' gradually, and by consensus, taking over the state. In part also, the new network may have failed to emerge because of contradictions within the different layers of the working class, some of which oppose, while others favour this kind of mobilization and the liquidation of the organs of the old state.

THE ATTITUDES OF THE COMMUNIST PARTIES

The primacy of the political solution takes us straight to the crucial issue of the attitude of the three Communist Parties concerned. Common to them all is their stated willingness to participate loyally and consistently in an electoral coalition, and subsequently in a governmental coalition, observing the rules of the pluralistic-constitutional systems in the three states. Without this willingness, indeed without the determination of the Chilean Communist Party to propose and to follow these policies, the left-wing coalition could not have come into being, and it will collapse whenever the communists should decide to withdraw from it. The same is true, bearing in mind specific connotations, of France and Italy, where the two Communist Parties would be the keystones in any eventual coalition.

Yet, once this is said, one sees immediately that the common denominator, the willingness of the Communist Parties to form left-wing coalitions, is *induced* into the situation, and not *produced* entirely by factors common to all three countries. For individual and common reasons the three parties in the three states have decided to propose and pursue a policy of left-wing coalition. But each or any of them might reverse this decision, and the induced comparative factor would thus disappear.

Since the 20th Congress of the CPSU in 1960, when it was officially stated that 'socialist revolution by peaceful means' should no longer be regarded as something exceptional, but as the 'most probable' form of transition from capitalism to socialism, there has been a major reorientation in the theory and practice of Communist Parties associated with the CPSU. The 1960 theses were formulated even more explicitly in the Party Programme of 1961, which was adopted at the 22nd Congress of the CPSU in 1962, when the breach with China was a *fait accompli*. They are worth quoting from here since they provide a useful guide for the identification of the various stages in which Chile, France and Italy now are, and they can be compared with the statements made by the parties in these countries. Thus, on peaceful transition to socialism:

> Revolutions are quite feasible without war. The great objectives of the working class can be realized without world war. Today the conditions for these are more favourable than ever. The working class and its vanguard – the Marxist-Leninist parties – seek to accomplish the socialist revolution by *peaceful means*... The working class, supported by the majority of the people and firmly repelling opportunist elements incapable of renouncing the policy of compromise with the capitalists and landlords, can defeat the reactionary anti-popular forces, with a solid majority in parliament, transform it from a tool serving the class interests of the bourgeoisie into an instrument serving the working people, launch a broad mass struggle outside parliament, smash the resistance of the reactionary forces and provide the necessary conditions for a peaceful socialist revolution. (Italics in the text.)

This must be linked with the strong recommendation to ally with other working-class parties:

> The Communist Parties favour cooperation with the Social Democratic Parties not only in the struggle for peace, for better

living conditions, for the working people and for the prevention and extension of their democratic rights and freedom, but also in the struggle to win power and build a socialist society.

However, the 'peacefulness' of the transition is qualified in two other statements. First, 'Where the exploiting classes resort to violence against the people, the probability of *non-peaceful transition to socialism* should be borne in mind'; that is to say, should the capitalists use violence to resist, so will the people. Secondly, there is a reminder that the actual revolution itself can only be effected by the dictatorship of the proletariat: 'But whatever the form in which the transition from capitalism to socialism is effected, that transition can come about only through revolution. However varied the forms of a new people's state power in the period of socialist construction, their essence will be the same – *dictatorship of the proletariat*, which represents genuine democracy, democracy for the working people.' (Italics in the text.)

In terms of the comparative analysis pursued here it is useful to remember the elements of the strategy of those Communist Parties whose policy is coordinated by the CPSU: these are a preference, wherever possible, for the advent to power to take place by peaceful means, through the electoral, parliamentary and governmental success of the alliance of working-class parties; and the assertion of the indispensability of the dictatorship of the proletariat as the actual perpetrator of the revolution, which, moreover represents a further stage in the transformation of society and its political institutions, or at least of their definitions and roles.

If one were to compare the situation in France, Italy and Chile, in terms of the above programme, then is it evident that in France and Italy, the coalition has still to be negotiated, whereas in Chile a coalition of the working-class and left-wing parties, the Unidad Popular, has come to power by electoral means, and is in charge of the government with the initial assistance of the Christian Democrats. To this extent, the Chilean experiment might be regarded as a model, i.e. insofar as the Communist Party, in alliance with other parties, has accomplished the first of the stages outlined in the programme of the CPSU, namely the transition to a socialist government by peaceful means. But the second thesis of the programme has not been fulfilled: there is no dictatorship of the proletariat, hence the revolution itself has not yet been successfully achieved. The reforms or 'concrete tasks' carried out by the Allende government do not as yet amount to the crossing of the revolutionary Rubicon.

How have the Communist Parties of the three countries concerned themselves interpreted the directives of the Party Programme of the CPSU in 1961? According to Luis Corvalán, the General Secretary of the Chilean Communist Party, 'We declare ourselves for a popular government – formed by several parties, vast, strong, revolutionary, efficient, which gives democratic stability to the country, which develops the social and economic progress and gives the people its full freedom ... The people's power which we create and the revolution which we ought to achieve are anti-imperialist and anti-oligarchic, and have as their goal, socialism ... The path towards socialism goes through the anti-imperialist and anti-oligarchic transformations ... The passage from the anti-imperialist and anti-oligarchic revolution might be very rapid, and constitutes a continuous, unique process, as was for instance the case in Cuba. For this very reason, the emphasis must be laid on the concrete tasks which correspond to this historical stage.'[13]

From the above quotation, it can be noted that although the Chilean Communist Party speaks of two distinct revolutions (corresponding to the two phases laid down in the programme of the CPSU) the transformation of the first into the second is conceived as a unique, continuous process, according to whether the 'concrete tasks', which is the operative concept in this interpretation, have, or have not, been carried out.

According to Georges Marchais, the deputy secretary general of the French Communist Party, introducing the Programme for a Democratic Government of Popular Union, 'The task will be the work of a democratic government drawn from the working classes and backed by them, of a government of popular union in which our party will have the place which it deserves. We do not claim any monopoly, or hegemony. We are ready to open at any moment discussions with the other democratic parties and groups with a view to arriving at a true common programme for the political struggle and for government. It is known that we attach a special importance to the understanding between our party and the Socialist Party.[14] In the understanding reached on 27 June the Communist Party accepted most of the socialist proposals,

---

[13] Luis Corvalàn, *Camino de victoria*, Horizonte, Santiago, 1971.

notably respect for parliamentary rules. But the Communist Party programme, which provided the blueprint for the policies of a government of popular union within the framework of the French parliamentary regime (with some modifications, e.g. the lengthening of the president's mandate to seven years) alludes to the transitional purpose of such a government. Thus: 'The fulfilment of this programme will establish a new regime of economic and political democracy *opening the way to socialism*' (our italics): or 'From the very start of the legislature, the policy of nationalization must go beyond a minimum threshhold. The progression will afterwards be necessary'[15] and 'We want to create the political conditions for the transition to socialism, i.e. the conditions of a movement of the majority of our people to socialism.'[16]

In Italy, the electoral programme of the Communist Party provides a clearer and more dialectical description of the 'Italian way to socialism' and of its 'democratic turning point'. It draws a distinction between the old Popular Front which had 'its historical function' and the new unity of the left which 'acknowledged from the very beginning the diversity of tendencies which exist in the working-class movement which is democratically advanced and therefore acknowledges the autonomy of each of these tendencies. But, the newly elected secretary general, Berlinguer, explained: 'The plurality of forces and of common actions leads first to convergence and then to unitary commitments on the great problems which belong to the realm where the hegemony of the working class in society asserts itself.' The democratic 'turning point' goes through three stages: the unity of the left; the switching of the centre of Christian Democracy, and the use of the new structures of participation. The first requirement is to defeat official Christian Democracy at the polls, while absorbing into the new unity of the left 'the most advanced elements of Christian Democracy'. In such conditions, a coalition government of popular union could rule within the present constitutional institutions of Italy, by strengthening parliament, and by using state powers to the full in the pursuit of an economic policy directed towards changing the structures and giving to the regions (the 'fifteen Italies') their full autonomy. This system would in turn be superseded by the new forms of participation and of

[14] Parti communiste français, *Programme pour un gouvernement démocratique d'union populaire, Le Monde,* 13 October 1971.

[15] *Programme,* p. 149 and p. 155.

[16] 'What is Popular Union' in *Nouvelle Critique,* March 1972.

workers' control, the 'basic democracy', which alone will give a
general vision of the class and social problems against all corporate
and sectional limitations.[17]

THE OLD AND THE NEW LEFT

The similarities between the attitudes of these three Communist
Parties, revealed even in this summary examination of their
doctrinal statements, must have some common causes. One cause
is their common adoption of the general strategy of revolutionary
movements as formulated by the CPSU after consultation with all
the Communist Parties willing to continue this collaboration. This
does not mean that these parties are following the orders of
Moscow. Indeed there are grounds for the belief that most
Western European parties have tried to influence Moscow to
adopt the policy of peaceful transition. Nor does the general
approval of a common policy mean that it is to be uniformly
applied. There are considerable differences of emphasis between
each of the three parties, and between them and the CPSU. But
co-ordination is the law of the Communist Parties, and constant
consultation with the CPSU leads not only to further bilateral
exchanges, but to the formulation of the world strategy acknowledged by individual parties. The CPSU has always striven to
secure obedience to the party line in Latin America as well as in
Western Europe with two objects in mind: the one, internal, to
enlarge the influence of each party within its own country. The
second, external, to ensure that the USSR should not be engaged
now in a third world war; with this in mind it has tried to detach,
by popular demand, as many countries as possible from the
Western alliances and from the US orbit. This has entailed
acceptance of the policy of peaceful transition and of broadening
the popular base in all classes of the societies concerned, and
especially within the working class. It has been easier for the
CPSU to achieve its aims in this respect in Europe than in Latin
America; the Chilean Party for instance has preferred, perhaps for
tactical reasons, to define its approach not as 'peaceful' but as 'non
armed' (*vía no-armada*).

A second common explanation for the attitude of the three
Communist Parties is that orthodox parties at the national level
and the CPSU at the world level have been challenged by the
aggressive revolutionary strategy of the Chinese party, based on

[17] *Unità*, 19 March 1972.

armed insurrection with a view to opening military fronts wherever possible. This has led to war in SE Asia, to the activity of guerrilleros, both urban and rural, and to the emergence of revolutionary groups in Western Europe. The revolutionary appeal and, especially until the dramatic defeat of Che Guevara in Bolivia, the occasional spectacular successes of the new revolutionaries have contrasted strikingly with the slow reflexes of the *embourgeoisé* Communist Parties. All traditional Communist Parties are by now openly fighting 'Chinese or Trotskiyst adventurism'. In France, the principal enemy of the Communist Party is now seen to be the *gauchistes*, especially since the May 1968 events, which are regarded by the party as having played into the hands of the Gaullists and the reactionary forces.[18]

In Chile, the Communist Party within the government has had to contend with the Communist Revolutionary Party (its own pro-Chinese dissidents), the Movement of the Revolutionary Left (MIR), and other smaller groups. In Italy too, the Communist Party is threatened by the outflanking movements of the left, but it does not show such an uncompromising hostility as does the French Communist Party towards the left groups or the militant students. But both in Italy and in France there is a further danger for the Communist Parties, namely that the Socialist Parties which they used to regard as opportunistic and obsolete are taking a more left-wing stand and outbidding them in revolutionary fervour. This has of course already occurred in the case of the Chilean Socialist Party. And in France, the new programme of the French Socialist Party, under Mitterand, went much further than the agreement of 27 June in advocating participation and workers' control. The same applies to the Nenni socialists in Italy. Finally, and this applies more particularly to Chile and Italy, where the principal targets of the Communist Parties are the Christian Democrats, there is the danger that the left wing of the Christian Democrats may operate an ideological and political *rapprochement* with the anti-communist left.

The emergence of the extreme anti-communist left leads on to

---

[18] 'These are not an adventurist Leftism, and a "serious", "political" leftism; leftism is in any case adventurism with political justifications without any consistency which produce the most unlikely and most dangerous methods. To those who light fires and afterwards ask us to put them out when things go badly, we reply "No! We don't play this game!" . . . The leftist agitation and its provocation can only favour the game of the reaction.' H. Krasucki, Secretary of the CGT, member of the political bureau of the French Communist Party, in *Le Monde*, 23 March 1972.

the question of the basic relationship between the working class
and the working-class parties in the three countries. There are at
least two different political causes behind the outbreak of 'leftism'
and exalted revolutionary activity. One is the success of the
military activity of the Chinese, North Korean, Cuban, North
Vietnamese Marxist-Leninist revolutionaries. The other is the
radicalization of intellectual revolutionaries in the West, at the
sight of the *embourgeoisement* of the urban working classes as they
are drawn into the consumer society. In their view, the revolutionary ardour of the working class would die out, if new, incendiary
tactics were not used to rekindle it. The relaxation of the class
struggle of the working class in the West coincides with the
relaxation of the USSR's commitment to violent revolutionary
means, in New Left political analysis. What this analysis leaves out
of account, however, is that the Communist Parties might be
primarily concerned with the danger of losing their traditional
link, directly, or through the trade unions, with the modern
working class, should they preach violence. Even if they wished
to push the workers into revolutionary action, they could not be
sure of the response. Their strategy of peaceful transition to
socialism is at least in part the reflection of a cool assessment of the
working class, entrenched in its newly conquered positions in
the industrial-technological society. It is significant that the new
programme of the French Communist Party proclaims as its aim
'Towards a *better* life', not 'towards a *good* life'. It is significant too
that in Chile, a country which shows marked contrasts in economic
development, the Communist Party draws its strength from the
industrial regions, notably perhaps among the 'aristocracy' of
the miners. The cleavage between them, and the clientele of the
revolutionaries, the lumpen-proletariat of the towns and the
countryside is economically, socially and ideologically virtually
unbridgeable. Finally it is significant that the Italian Communist
Party is especially successful in its new capacity of entrepreneur and
administrator, for instance in Emilia-Romagna, an advanced
area, where the efficient communist local administration might
well prove their best certificate for admission to governmental
responsibility. One of the main concerns of modern Communist
Parties is not to lose touch with and be separated from workers
in industrial and post industrial societies. Hence the new image
which they now project, of efficient, technocratic management.[19]

[19] An image reflected in the very modern, functional building of the
French Communist Party in Paris.

The image of the party as the party of responsibility and competence in industrial technological societies is replacing the old image of violent, revolutionary, destructiveness, which has been borrowed with enthusiasm by the new left.

Above all however the danger for the modern Communist Parties lies in the possible coming together of the left revolutionaries, the socialists, and possibly the Christian Democrats, and the really militant workers on the crucial issue of workers' control in industry, and workers' management. These are the slogans which arouse response in the working class. Ever since Lenin first suppressed the Workers' Opposition in the Soviet Union, the most successful, recurrent opposition to Communist Parties in power has arisen when workers have claimed the right to manage 'their' enterprises, and have questioned the right of the party or the state (with the exception of Yugoslavia, where self-management is, at least in theory, the official doctrine). With the concentration of industry, the growth of corporations and the accelerated technical and political education of the top levels of the working class, the workers have shown an increasing interest in their right to participate in management. The strikes at Renault in France (a public corporation) or at Fiat in Italy (a private one) are increasingly provoked by problems of management and participation in decision-making. In Chile too, in the select industries, like mining, the workers show greater interest in industrial problems than in political or ideological ones. These developments in the West, coupled with the re-emergence in socialist countries of workers' councils whenever there is a break in the dictatorship of the party, underline the depth and actuality of the problem.

For parties whose recipe for power is still 'democratic centralism', the control of all industrial production by the state, *qua* employer, and the party, *qua* manager, the continuation of the old anarcho-syndicalist demand for workers' control into the modern 'technostructure' presents questions which they may not yet be ready to answer. The argument of the left revolutionaries is that the revolution can be effected at once by handing over the nationalized industries and the land to the workers, without the intermediary of the centralistic state and party. The argument of the rejuvenated socialists and Christian Democrats is that modern industrial production demands a broad participation in management and that state control in any case breeds reactionary government. One reason why Communist Parties may want to come to power now, even in coalition governments, may well be their fear that the clamour for workers' self-management may spread too far, and reduce them to the role of Cassandras, abandoned and unheard by the new left and the new right in the modern working class.

SOME COMPARATIVE CONCLUSIONS

The Chilean experiment does not as yet provide the answer to the question whether Marxist economic and social restructurations of a society can be achieved within the framework of a pluralistic-constitutional system. In one sense, however, the Chilean experiment does not really pose the problem fully. We still do not know whether given a majority in parliament, congress, chamber of deputies, a Communist Party could construct socialism by constitutional means. Allende has not got this majority, his government is still on this side of the revolution and has to face its revolutionary 'moment of truth'. Its future must be decided on the political plane, while economic reform slows down. The choice seems to lie between the Jacobin call to 'save the revolution, threatened by external and internal enemies', the prelude to Leninism and the dictatorship of the proletariat; or a constitutional acceptance of the limitations on the power of the government. Alternatively some improvised compromise solution might be found. The Chilean political genius has already produced original political formulae for the first phase of its revolution. It may do so again.

Two institutions are worth dwelling on in this context. One is the presidency. Many of the authors in this volume have stressed its importance. Should any redefinition of its role take place, should the constitutional rules of the game be modified, it might still prove to be the trump card. Such an evolution might have some relevance to the French situation, where the role of the president is constitutionally parallel to that of parliament. But the French parliamentary opposition by no means accepts this situation and the Socialist Party is unlikely to change its policy on this issue without the certainty that in a coalition the president would be a socialist. The question of the presidency is less relevant for Italy, where the constitution does not provide for such an institutional *deus ex machina*.

The second institution which may have a key role to play in Chile is the army. Will it have been won over to the objects of the Chilean revolution to the extent of forgetting its traditional role of

guardian of the constitution? How will it act should the constitution be violated, however gently? Only time will tell, but one
can state with a certain amount of confidence that even should the
Chilean armed forces opt for revolution, it is most unlikely that
the French and the Italian would do so.

Index

Vicuña Fuentes, C., note 23, 103
Vignola, General, note 83, 116, 118
VPS, 127
Vuskovic, Pedro, 185

War of the Pacific, 11, 114
Western Europe, 143, 144, 190, 191

West Germany, 179
White, S., note 1, 177
Workers' Opposition, 193

Zamorano, Antonio, 57
Zañartú, Carlos, note 55, 110
Zujovic, Perez, 34, 92; note 2, 97; note 3, 98